This collection of essays is a fitting tribute to the remarkable legacy of Elizabeth Baxter. It offers profound reflections on the integration of theology, healing, and human flourishing, rooted in the unique community of Holy Rood House. The contributors draw on diverse perspectives to celebrate Elizabeth's pioneering work, making this a deeply enriching read for those invested in theology, pastoral care, and holistic healing. It is an inspiring resource for anyone seeking to connect faith with compassionate care.

John Swinton
Professor in Practical Theology and Pastoral Care,
University of Aberdeen, Scotland, UK

—

This book is a fitting tribute to Elizabeth Baxter's energy, compassion and courage and testament to her continuing legacy. The essays capture something of her vision for Holy Rood House in campaigning for greater inclusion in the church, fostering spirituality for human flourishing and promoting the creative arts in the service of health and healing. Above all, these essays are testament to Holy Rood as a place of generous, Christ-centred hospitality.

Elaine Graham FBA
Professor Emerita of Practical Theology at the University
of Chester and a former Trustee of Holy Rood House

Theology and Human Flourishing

Essays in Honour of Elizabeth Baxter

EDITED BY

— HELEN L. LEATHARD —

Sacristy
Press

Sacristy Press
PO Box 612, Durham, DH1 9HT

www.sacristy.co.uk

First published in 2024 by Sacristy Press, Durham

Texts from *Holy Rood House Community Prayers*, and other Holy
Rood House publications, which appear in various chapters,
are reproduced by kind permission of Elizabeth Baxter.

Hymns in Chapter 3 that have been published in *A Rainbow to
Heaven* by June Boyce-Tillman are copyright Stainer & Bell, and are
reproduced by kind permission of Stainer & Bell Ltd., 23 Gruneisen
Road, London N3 1LS, www.stainer.co.uk; 6 March 2024, 22.24.

Scripture quotations, unless otherwise stated, are from the New Revised
Standard Version Bible: Anglicized Edition, copyright © 1989, 1995
National Council of the Churches of Christ in the United States of
America. Used by permission. All rights reserved worldwide.

Every reasonable effort has been made to trace the copyright holders
of material reproduced in this book, but if any have been inadvertently
overlooked the publisher would be glad to hear from them.

Sacristy Limited, registered in England & Wales, number 7565667

British Library Cataloguing-in-Publication Data
A catalogue record for the book is available from the British Library

ISBN 978-1-78959-364-8

To the Reverend Elizabeth Baxter, MPhil

A tribute, in recognition of her inspirational vision and leadership as Executive Director of Holy Rood House Centre for Health and Pastoral Care and Centre for the Study of Theology and Health 1993–2024

Contents

Editor's Preface

In 1993, Elizabeth and Stanley Baxter were appointed to Holy Rood House to serve as residential leaders, developing a Christian "Centre for Health and Pastoral Care" in the former convent. At an early stage, they recognized the need for their practice to be informed securely by theology and theory, and how desirable it was that the learning they gained through their practice would inform the theory of relevant disciplines. "The Centre for the Study of Theology and Health" was established in 2000, with an extensive library and regular summer schools, Hildegard lecture weekends and other instructive events for staff and the wider community. Emergent wisdom was disseminated through diverse means, including *Wounds that Heal* (London: SPCK, 2007, edited by their son, Jonathan Baxter, who was Coordinator of the Centre 2003–6) and "Proceedings" of the Centre published regularly in *Chrism*, the Journal of the Guild of St Raphael, from 2009; and most recently through the Holy Rood House YouTube channel. Following the death of her beloved Stanley in 2016, Elizabeth continued as sole Executive Director, and highlighted "ecology of health" as a priority of the Community among other developments.

Details of developments and activities in abundance will emerge from the pages of this book, but first it is important to mention a significant mark of recognition of Elizabeth's achievements. In 2018, Elizabeth received The Langton Award for Community Service, one of the Lambeth Awards, presented by the Archbishop of Canterbury at Lambeth Palace. The award was for "developing the counselling, healing and inclusion of those marginalized by the church and for theological study of feminist theology, sexual identity and of related abuse, using this to provide the church with improved understanding and inclusive liturgies".

All good things come to an end, however, and during 2023 Elizabeth resolved to step down from her role as Executive Director of Holy Rood House. Consequent on that decision, in October 2023, during a visit, I was approached somewhat conspiratorially with a proposition that led to the production of this book. It had been announced that, in May 2024, Elizabeth Baxter would be stepping down after 31 years' leadership of that unique place. Discrete consultations had revealed strong support for the idea of producing a book of essays as a tribute to Elizabeth and her work at Holy Rood House; and they needed an editor. Would I take on that role? The request was conveyed by Richard Bradshaw, Clerk to the Trustees, and Elaine Wisdom, Art Therapist, good friend of Elizabeth and member of the Holy Rood House Community for many years. Richard would "drive" the project, recruiting published authors from among the House's Consultants and Trustees as contributors, and dealing with other administrative aspects. How could I refuse such an honour? Excited and not a little daunted at the prospect, I agreed, and the project was endorsed by the Trustee Board. By mid-December, we were in a position for me to write to those recruited by Richard, with some editorial guidelines and the challenge of a close deadline. The target was to make this a surprise tribute to Elizabeth, with a presentation of the typescript at an event in May 2024 to mark her stepping down, and an announcement, at that time, of a launch event for the published version in October.

By late January 2024, the flow of inspired and inspirational essays commenced, the wide diversity reflecting Elizabeth's career, the variety of provision at Holy Rood House and the theoretical and theological underpinnings of that provision. How could they be arranged in a sequence that would best inform readers who are unfamiliar with this unique manifestation of "church"? In my mind's eye, I began to imagine them as parts of an evergreen flowering shrub, with shoots, flowers, fruits and foliage above ground, and roots drawing nourishment from the fertile earth beneath: the interaction of theory and practice resembling the circulation of fluids and nutrients through the xylem and phloem, and Elizabeth's inspirational leadership at the centre, "the heartwood", embodying the vision and orchestrating the whole complex process. And so, we start with what is visible to guests, along with some historical context; move on to an "Interlude" of creative writings (fruit of the Holy Rood spirit), drafted by guests during residential stays or Garden Quiet Days; and then delve into examples of the theological and theoretical work that informs and nourishes the ethos, hospitality, worship and therapeutic offerings of Holy Rood House. This division is, admittedly, imprecise. As with any vibrant organism or organization there is intertwining, entanglement and integration of the constituent elements, a bit like the "Ivy Tree" evoked poetically in the "Interlude". And so it is with Elizabeth and Holy Rood House—its community, guests, activities, grounds and buildings. The emergent essays are as varied as their authors; each contributing in their personal, God-given style, from their distinctive wisdom and from their passion for the extraordinary phenomenon that is Holy Rood House under Elizabeth's leadership.

An insightful introduction is provided by John Pritchard in Chapter 1: "Tomorrow's church: Haunted by hope". Based on his extensive episcopal experience, Bishop John locates Holy Rood House within the context of the wider (declining) church and illustrates how it represents a beacon of hope, revealing how a Christian community can and should reveal God's love of the world. Having located the ministry of Holy Rood House in the context of the wider church, we turn to locate it in the historical context of Elizabeth's passionate pursuit of justice, exemplified by the campaign for the ordination of women as priests in the Church of England. This comes through in Chapter 2, "Yes to women priests", with Wendy Wilby's exhilarating evocation of some of the activities and events that led to Elizabeth being one of the first of those, very early in her time at Holy Rood House.

These background pieces lead us on to illuminate something of the experience of being at Holy Rood House. June Boyce-Tillman has befriended Elizabeth since before her move to Holy Rood House, and has stayed at the house as tutor, performer and guest for many years. In Chapter 3, "Birthing, belonging and becoming", she provides a sense of the atmosphere at community residential events and reveals inspirational themes that inform her hymnody, many examples of which are embedded within her essay. A complementary experience of being a guest at the house is conveyed by Jenny Kartupelis in Chapter 4, "Creating place and space". As a trustee, Jenny was given access to the "bedroom books" to provide a review of and reflection on comments offered by guests over many years; her distillation of these provides fascinating insights into diverse benefits of spending time at Holy Rood House.

Feminist liturgy is another type of writing to emerge from Holy Rood House at Elizabeth's instigation, and we are blessed with two essays that explicate this in different ways. In Chapter 5, "The beating heart of Holy Rood House and what happens there", Nicola Slee considers the diversity of factors that make liturgy in the chapel "thoughtful, inclusive, creative and engaging" in a setting that is "welcoming, energizing, healing and relevant [to personal lives and world events]". This theme is extended in Chapter 6, "Celebrating the audacious Elizabeth Baxter", where Alison Jasper references meetings of "Vashti's Voices" and supporting literature to reveal the wonders achieved down the ages by "disobedient women"; extolling Elizabeth as one of that inspirational group of faithful women.

Wholesome, life-enhancing prayer and worship, facilitated by Elizabeth's feminist liturgy, is one of many ways in which the life of Holy Rood House engenders human flourishing; and in Chapter 7, "Theology and human flourishing: another conversion?", Elizabeth's son Jonathan Baxter illustrates how her creative liturgy leads to concerns about wider aspects of God's creation, embodied and nurtured in an ecologically rich environment. These concerns are manifest in the easy access that has been created between the chapel and the wildlife-friendly garden, with its current cultivation of organic produce and the potential for permaculture as the next innovation. The importance of these ecological considerations is highlighted by many of the short pieces of creative writing that constitute the "Interlude", all of which are evocative products of time spent at Holy Rood House.

After the "Interlude", we move on to essays that are not so much descriptive of experiences of being at Holy Rood House, although elements of that are included, but examples of the theological and theoretical work that undergirds the outward appearances. The first of these is my own endeavour at feminist scriptural interpretation in Chapter 8, "Radical Apostolic Women". This raises the profile of the woman who engaged with Jesus at Jacob's well and of Mary Magdalene, leading to advocacy of Elizabeth as a worthy successor, in our own generation, to those commonly underestimated women.

Staying with the feminist theology theme in Chapter 9, Jane Craske's "Storytelling while walking: Feminist theologies and healing" narrates her long association with Holy Rood House from the perspective of being a Methodist minister, highlighting the ecumenical inclusivity of the place. After noting that 2024 marks the fiftieth anniversary of women's presbyteral ministry in the Methodist Church, she provides a review of 30 years of feminism and feminist theologies and relates these to the inclusive and health-enhancing ethos of Holy Rood House. Extending the accolade of wholesome inclusivity in this healing place, in Chapter 10, "Holy Rood House and 'Living in Love and Faith'", Christina Beardsley provides a critical analysis of the Church of England's eponymous project and contrasts that convoluted process with the truly Christlike embrace of the graced embodiment of all who seek shelter and nurture in that brave and safe space.

Linking that theme of compassionate care for people in need or distress with the desire to engender hope for a brighter future, we find in David Gee's Chapter 11, "The little that becomes enough", a deep reflection on "hope as character, community and culture". He relates the bookending of Mark's Gospel, from the call to "Follow me" into an uncertain future to the sending of disciples to spread the good news of the resurrection, to the experience of entering Holy Rood House for the first time and later emergence, having found something to help in life's onward path. Then, David Jasper's Chapter 12, "Theological humanism and human flourishing", takes us on a learning journey through models of human flourishing to an understanding that human flourishing emerges in "a community that does not separate the human from the divine". Holy Rood House is such a place—a community that respects the integrity of human life and provides a garden for the soul. Part of that garden for the soul is the Art (Therapy) Room, where many find a gateway to healing. In Chapter 13, Art Therapist Elaine Wisdom provides "A reflection on the creative arts as a healing process", in which she elucidates many ways in which "making marks" and other creative activities to which the approach is spiritual rather than cognitive, access and release health-impairing psychological factors that lie beyond the reach of intellectual approaches.

Lingering in the intermingling areas of psychology, spirituality and theology, which inform much of the therapeutic work of Holy Rood House, we have essays on psychology meeting theology, spiritual darkness and accompaniment, and spirituality and mental health. In Chapter 14, "When psychology meets theology", David McDonald provides informed accounts of his ruminations on diverse outcomes of his original meeting with Stanley and Elizabeth Baxter in 1994, and their continuing shared engagement with a range of topics of mutual interest, that saw him recruited as consultant, trustee and eventually Chair of Trustees of Holy Rood House.

Spiritual darkness is a soul-eroding experience that needs sustained spiritual accompaniment and guidance alongside psychotherapeutic approaches to healing. In Chapter 15, Andrew De Smet embraces a synthesis of practical and theoretical approaches to "Spiritual darkness and spiritual accompaniment" in an essay that is based on a study day he delivered for spiritual accompaniers. He distinguishes cogently between "spiritual greyness" and "spiritual darkness" and offers differentiated ways of guiding people through distinct degrees of those experiences. "Spirituality and mental health" are of considerable interest in clinical and pastoral care, and diverse perspectives on these sometimes related but distinct subjects are explored thoroughly by David Ibrahim and Christopher C. H. Cook in Chapter 16, concluding that it is important not to view religion or spirituality as either entirely beneficial or entirely harmful to mental health, but to take a respectful and curious approach to individuals who are suffering.

The wheel comes full circle, and we return to pastoral care and what it means to be "church", this time engaging with theoretical and theological scholarship. For Jan Berry, the disruption of personal contact caused by the Covid-19 pandemic lockdowns ignited concerns about its impact on the practice of embodied expressions of faith and, in Chapter 17, she provides a cogent analysis of "Embodied theology in an age of Zoom". Then, in the "grand finale" that is Chapter 18, Paul Avis (Elizabeth's brother) explicates how we are "Called to go deeper in pastoral care". This essay intertwines and synergizes with many of the earlier essays, and explores connections and parallels between the priestly, pastoral work of the church and the work of various therapists.

As a whole, the essays provided by our inspired contributors paint a glorious word picture of the nature and ministry of Holy Rood House as it has developed under the leadership of Elizabeth, together with Stanley for many of those 31 years. The production of this book was instigated as a tribute to Elizabeth's guidance and management of this sacred enterprise, but such is the quality of its content that it has potential to serve as inspirational guide to all who are passionate about "Theology and Human Flourishing".

Helen L. Leathard
Lent 2024

Acknowledgements

First and foremost, thanks are due to the Revd Richard Bradshaw, Secretary to the Trustees of Holy Rood House, for consulting with various supporters of Holy Rood House, initiating and "driving" (his word) this project: recruiting contributors and editor, negotiating with Sacristy Press and, with Elaine Wisdom, organizing the artwork for the book cover. Thanks, too, to Carolyn Williamson, Community Programme Manager, for her discrete support of these endeavours; and to Elaine Wisdom for permission to use her "CrossPeace" on the book cover and facilitating photography of it.

Thanks to all contributors for their wonderful evocations of so many different facets of Elizabeth's vision and its implementation at Holy Rood House, and for their patience in dealing with me as a novice editor of a multi-author book. Likewise, to Natalie Watson and colleagues at Sacristy Press for their courteous support of this endeavour.

Cover artwork: CrossPeace

Elaine Wisdom

The genesis of CrossPeace, which hangs in the chapel at Holy Rood House, evolved from two roots: my distress at the then government's decision to join America in the invasion of Iraq and a pilgrimage the Holy Rood community made to the many medieval crosses on the North York Moors during Lent of that year. I took the image of the cross as a Christian symbol for peace. The crosses were originally placed in medieval times to guide travellers across the moors. Iraq in medieval times was part of a rich Eastern empire ruled by a Caliphate, and far in advance of the West in medicine and science. There was a link for me in what was happening in these two cultures of East and West in both medieval and our own times.

The image is a composite of all the crosses visited, but I forgot to include Whitby's cross so put in the figure of Hilda of Whitby, seen more as an absence than a solid figure. CrossPeace is made up of four separate parts representing North, South, East and West. The four pieces symbolize the brokenness of our world in terms of its political, religious, capitalist and militaristic structures, which contribute so much to the ecological crisis we are now experiencing. It is made of simple materials and uses layers of paint and collage, which can be imagined as the layers of time through the centuries passed, like archaeological layers.

The paper used is from the art room at Holy Rood painted with poster paint, which is used by guests working in the art room because it is a water-based medium and easy to use. It is an opaque medium unlike the transparency of watercolour. We are not a transparent world. Poster paint can be changed with water (which has its own associations) and can be painted over. So, there is a transformational element to the medium.

It can also be worked into with simple tools: toothbrushes, old combs, sticks, old credit cards—all items to hand in our culture and usually binned as rubbish when their life is perceived as over. And fingers. The oldest and most elemental of tools, used by children on steamed-up windows, our earliest ancestors in their cave art, and Jesus, who wrote in the sand with his finger when defending the woman taken in adultery. Making marks with our fingers connects us in an embodied way with the creative healing process and is a metaphor for the marks life makes on us and the marks we make on life.

The colours used are based on the revelation that the earth seen from the moon is a blue, green and white sphere; and our world is full of colour all around us. The trails of white weaving through are an attempt to express divine energy manifest and moving through our world, creating and re-creating through time. An expression of hope that somehow, through listening to each other and working together, peace will prevail.

Contributors

Paul Avis is an honorary assistant priest in the Church of England, serving in the Diocese of Exeter, and a brother to Elizabeth Baxter. He was in parish ministry for 23 years before becoming General Secretary of the Council for Christian Unity. He is currently an honorary professor in the University of Edinburgh School of Divinity. Paul is Editor-in-Chief of the peer-reviewed journal *Ecclesiology* and Editor of the monograph series *Anglican-Episcopal Theology and History* (both published by Brill). He has also edited *The Oxford Handbook of Ecclesiology*. Paul's recent publications include *Jesus and the Church: The Foundation of the Church in the New Testament and Modern Theology* (2021), *Reconciling Theology* (2022), *Theology and the Enlightenment: A Critical Enquiry into Enlightenment Theology and its Reception* (2022), and *Revelation and the Word of God* (2024). He is a long-serving consultant to Holy Rood House.

Jonathan Baxter is an artist, peer-educator and curator. He is the second son to Elizabeth Baxter. Jonathan was formerly the Coordinator of the Centre for the Study of Theology and Health (2003–6), where he developed the Centre's "ecology of health" framework. Jonathan also edited, and contributed to, the Centre's first publication, *Wounds that Heal: Theology, Imagination and Health* (2007). Jonathan currently works as an embedded artist in residence at St Mary's Episcopal Cathedral, Edinburgh, and as an artist in residence for Art Walk Projects (UK). Both projects address the climate and ecological crisis through practical interventions, peer-led programmes and exhibitions.

Christina Beardsley is a Church of England priest and a Visiting Scholar at Sarum College. Tina has been a parish priest, a healthcare chaplain and a lecturer in healthcare chaplaincy. She was the first transgender trustee of Changing Attitude, England (2007–14) and continues to work for the full inclusion of LGBTI+ people in the Church of England. She is the author of *Unutterable Love: the Passionate Life and Preaching of F. W. Robertson* (2009), and has co-edited/authored a trilogy of books about trans people and the church: *This is my Body: Hearing the Theology of Transgender Christians* (2016); *Transfaith: A Transgender Pastoral Resource* (2018); and *Trans Affirming Churches: How to Celebrate Gender-variant People and their Loved Ones* (2020). Now retired, she assists in London parishes, north and south of the Thames, and continues to write and research.

Jan Berry is a feminist theologian and writer, offering a ministry of spiritual accompaniment, and leading quiet days and retreats. She is a retired minister of the United Reformed Church, who was involved in theological education for 20 years at Luther King Centre in Manchester; and also served for three years as the half-time Director of the Centre for the Study of Theology and Health at Holy Rood House, Thirsk. She writes liturgies, poetry and hymns and has published a collection of her own hymns, prayers and poems in her book *Naming God*. Much of her writing has been included in various anthologies produced by the Iona Community. She is also one of the editors (along with Andrew Pratt) of *Hymns of Hope and Healing* (published by Stainer & Bell) which was the result of the Hymns for Healing Project at Holy Rood House.

June Boyce-Tillman is an international performer, composer, hymn writer and keynote speaker. She is an Emerita Professor of Applied Music at Winchester University UK, and an Extra-ordinary Professor at North West University, South Africa. Her large-scale works for cathedrals involve professional musicians, community choirs, people with disabilities and school children. She is editing the series on Music and Spirituality for Peter Lang which includes her autobiography, *Freedom Song*. She founded MSW—Music, Spirituality and Wellbeing—an international network sharing expertise and experience in this area. She is an Anglican priest serving All Saints, Tooting.

Christopher C. H. Cook is Emeritus Professor in the Institute for Medical Humanities at Durham University, Honorary Chaplain for Tees, Esk and Wear Valleys NHS Foundation Trust, and a consultant to Holy

Rood House. From 1997 to 2003, he was Professor of the Psychiatry of Alcohol Misuse at the University of Kent. He was ordained as an Anglican priest in 2001. Chris was Professor of Spirituality, Theology & Health in the Department of Theology and Religion, and Director of the Centre for Spirituality, Theology & Health, at Durham University from 2012–22. He has twice been Chair of the Spirituality & Psychiatry Special Interest Group at the Royal College of Psychiatrists and was Co-Chair of the Section on Religion & Spirituality at the World Psychiatric Association from 2022–3. His books include *Hearing Voices, Demonic and Divine* (2018), *Christians Hearing Voices* (2020), and (as lead editor) *Spirituality and Psychiatry*, second edition (2023).

Jane Craske is a Methodist minister and theological educator. She has served in Methodist Circuit appointments in London, Manchester, Leeds and Lowestoft, and also as a tutor in theological education in Manchester and in her current appointment as Director of Methodist Formation at the Queen's Foundation in Birmingham. She has research interests in feminist approaches to doctrine and in Methodist studies. Her most recent publication was *Doing Theology in the Tradition of the Wesleys* (2020).

Andrew De Smet is an Anglican priest, counsellor/psychotherapist, spiritual accompanier, trainer and mediator based in East Yorkshire. Until April 2024, he was Pastoral Care Adviser in the Diocese of York. As a priest he has ministered in urban, small town and rural parishes and run a retreat centre. He has published articles on the relationship between spiritual direction and counselling, as well as its role in matters such as forgiveness and bullying. Andrew facilitates a supervision group for spiritual directors and chaplains at Holy Rood House and is one of their consultants. He also enjoys painting icons and landscapes, sketching and being in the countryside.

David Gee is an activist and writer, and a consultant with Holy Rood House. His latest book is *Hope's Work: Facing the Future in an Age of Crises* (2022). He lives in Oxford on a narrowboat, *Promise*.

David Ibrahim is a psychiatry trainee in the second year of training at Northamptonshire NHS Foundation Trust. He is a trainee representative on the executive committee of the Spirituality and Psychiatry Special Interest Group of the Royal College of Psychiatrists. He has a long-standing interest in the intersection of spirituality and mental health that started from his practice in Egypt in the field of addiction psychiatry and outpatient clinics prior to his move to the UK. David has given lectures on the topic of spirituality and mental health to the World Council of Churches Ecumenical Youth Group in 2022 and the Emerging Peacemakers Forum, second edition, in Geneva in 2023.

David is a graduate from the Emerging Peacemakers Forum that was held in Cambridge in collaboration with Rose Castle Foundation and the Muslim Council of Elders as a representative of the Coptic Orthodox Church. This has helped grow his interest in interfaith and intercultural dialogue and the effect of different faiths on mental health.

Alison Jasper was a teacher of Religious Education in a variety of English secondary schools before she received her PhD from Glasgow University for a thesis on feminist biblical hermeneutics and took up an academic position teaching Religion in the Faculty of Arts and Humanities at Stirling University. Before her retirement in 2019, she was instrumental in establishing a master's level programme in gender studies to which she contributed for a number of years as lecturer and tutor. She has published widely on topics relating to feminist biblical hermeneutics, feminist theology and feminist theory. Since retiring she has been an honorary research fellow in the Faculty of Social Sciences at the University of Stirling and has continued participating in research, writing and some teaching at master's level.

As a member of the Scottish Episcopal Church, she has served on both its Doctrine and its Liturgy Committees. In 2021 she headed up a small group that organized an online conference on gender and liturgy, *Responding to the Sacred: Conversations between Liturgy and Gender*. In 2023, the team organized a second online conference under the title of *Responding to the Sacred: Inclusive Liturgies, Porous Walls*. She is hoping to organize a follow-up event. She has visited Holy Rood House and Hilda House on many occasions, acting as a theological consultant, and, in 2022, participated in the annual Summer School, giving an address entitled, "A theology of hope for partial survival and flourishing in a damaged world".

David Jasper is Emeritus Professor at the University of Glasgow, where he was for many years Professor of Theology and Literature. He has also taught in universities in China, Australia and the USA. He holds degrees from the universities of Cambridge, Oxford, Durham and Uppsala. He has been an Anglican priest for almost 50 years. For most of that time, he has been licensed within the Scottish Episcopal Church and has served in a number of charges in south Glasgow during his years of teaching at the University. He was Canon Theologian of St Mary's Cathedral, Glasgow from 2017–23. He is a Fellow of the Royal Society of Arts and a Fellow of the Royal Society of Edinburgh. His recent books include *Heaven in Ordinary: Poetry and Religion in a Secular Age* (2018) and (with Jeremy Smith) *Reinventing Medieval Liturgy in Victorian England* (2023).

Jenny Kartupelis started her career in public relations, establishing two consultancies in Cambridge, where she was involved the growth of the 'Silicon Fen' area, working with some of the leading technology businesses and their support services. In 1998 she was invited by faith leaders to help set up a regional multifaith body and for her work as its director, she was made an MBE. She is also a Director of the company Faith in Society Ltd., which advises on co-operative work between faith groups, and with public sector bodies.

Since 2014, Jenny has given much of her time to researching and writing on the care of older people, being given access to visit and interview in a wide variety of charitable, private and Local Authority care settings. Her work has resulted in two published books (2018 and 2021) about the theory and practice of relational care, a concept which she has developed over the last ten years. Her work in this respect has been the subject of an Open University research project into the conditions that promote its benefits, the findings of which were launched in 2023. Jenny is a Visiting Fellow at The Open University and is now working with its academic team to promote the value and implementation of relational care across the sector through consultation, publicity and policy engagement.

Jenny lives in the Peak District with her husband Trevor, with whom she enjoys walking and travelling; and her labradoodle Joy, who shares her enthusiasm for open water swimming.

Helen L. Leathard is Professor Emerita of Healing Science and Pharmacology at the University of Cumbria, Honorary Fellow of the British Pharmacological Society, and Honorary Associate Priest with Permission to Officiate in Blackburn Diocese. She has been involved with Holy Rood House for more than 25 years, originally as a consultant to the Centre for the Study of Theology and Health and then more generally. After researching and teaching in London medical schools, she moved back to her northern roots, for family reasons, in 1992. At St Martin's College, Lancaster, she taught biomedical sciences to nurses and other healthcare professionals, and evolved her research interests to explore holistic health and Christian spiritual healing, supported by taking an MA in Theology and synergizing with her nascent Anglican Reader Ministry. Also, as Director of the Graduate School, she led a generic PhD programme (under the auspices of Lancaster University) as the college prepared for university status. As a long-standing member of the Council of the Guild of St Raphael, she edited their journal, *Chrism,* from 2009 to 2015, developing their publishing collaboration with Holy Rood House. She helped steer the reuniting of that Guild with the Guild of Health, serving as a trustee until 2020.

David McDonald qualified as a medical practitioner in 1969 and has worked as a consultant psychiatrist for over 40 years in adult forensic and child and adolescent mental health services, and as an analytic and systemic psychotherapist for individuals, groups and families. He has also been involved in training and advising clergy and pastoral teams in mental health disorders relevant to the healing and deliverance ministries of the church. He was a co-author of *Deliverance* (ed. M Perry, 1996), and a member of the House of Bishops' Working Party publishing the book *A Time to Heal* (2000). His clinical work, embracing a wide diversity of individuals and cultures, led him to study for an MA degree in Theology and Interreligious Dialogue in 2004. He is currently Chair of Trustees to the Centre for Health and Pastoral Care at Holy Rood House, and a trustee to the Guild of Health and St Raphael.

John Pritchard is a retired Bishop of Oxford and author of many books on prayer, apologetics and the Christian journey. He previously served as Bishop of Jarrow, Archdeacon of Canterbury, and Warden of Cranmer Hall, Durham, after enjoying parish ministry in Birmingham and Taunton. He is married with two daughters and five grandchildren and is a theological adviser to Holy Rood House.

Nicola Slee is Professorial Research Fellow at the Queen's Foundation for Ecumenical Theological Education, Professor of Feminist Practical Theology at Vrije Universiteit, Amsterdam, Visiting Professor at the University of Chester and a Visiting Scholar at Sarum College. She has published widely over four decades in the fields of feminist theology and liturgy, practical theology, poetry and spirituality, including *Praying Like a Woman* (2004), *Fragments for Fractured Times: What Feminist Practical Theology Brings to the Table* (2020) and *Abba Amma: Improvisations on the Lord's Prayer* (2021). She is an experienced leader of retreats, writing workshops and creative events, enjoying working collaboratively with others (including a number of those associated with Holy Rood House). She is also a spiritual accompanist, as well as an experienced supervisor and examiner of doctoral research, who has worked internationally as well as widely in the UK. She is honoured to be a Patron of Holy Rood House, as well as a Vice-President of Women and the Church (WATCH).

Wendy Wilby was ordained deacon in 1990, followed, in 1994, by ordination to priesthood, to which she had felt called for well over 30 years. After a number of diverse parish ministries and chaplaincies, Wendy was the first woman Canon Residentiary to come into the Bristol Cathedral Chapter in 2007. There she served as Precentor, thus employing both her musical gifts and skills, developed at the University of Oxford and the Royal College of Music, and her passion and expertise for liturgy. In addition, she also took over the role of Dean of Women's Ministry for Bristol Diocese in June 2011, eventually becoming Chair of the National Association of Diocesan Advisers in Women's Ministry. NADAWM aims to be a resource to the Church of England, advising and supporting the National Church, Diocesan Senior Staff and women in ministry on a range of issues. The organization aims to make the Church of England a place where women can flourish in their calling. Wendy has served as a trustee of Holy Rood House, including as Vice-Chair, for several years.

Elaine Wisdom holds BA Hons. Fine Art; Post Grad. Dip. Art Psychotherapy; Dip. Social Studies; and Dip. Pastoral Theology. She has a mixed denominational background, having been baptized into the Methodist Church, confirmed in the Church of England, and joined the Roman Catholic Church in her mid-twenties. She spent some years in a Roman Catholic religious order specializing in the education of girls, during which she completed several theological courses in Dublin and Heythrop College in London. She joined the community at Holy Rood as a residential member in 1996, retraining in Art Therapy while setting up the Creative Arts space at Juliet House (then Thorpe House). She now lives on the edge of the North York Moors and coast and continues her association with Holy Rood as a volunteer since retiring from her art therapy role in 2018. She also now serves as a consultant to Holy Rood House.

Tomorrow's church: Haunted by hope

John Pritchard

"Houston, we have a problem." Those famous words spoken from the command module of Apollo 13 in 1970 have an echo in the experience of many organizations, one of which is the church in the UK.

The problem

"The problem" is demonstrated in a number of ways. One is in the inexorable decline in Sunday morning attendance, accelerated by the Covid lockdowns, which in many cases have led to a 20–25 per cent reduction. Another piece of evidence is the way the church generally, and the Church of England in particular, is mostly ignored by the media and seen as fair game in a way that other faiths do not experience. Public figures seem to line up to define themselves by their lack of belief. A third obvious sign of a significant problem is the furore over same sex relationships, viewed by the general public (if at all) with bemusement, as churches tie themselves in knots over an issue that society passed by long ago. It looks as if the church is so far behind the curve as to be completely irrelevant and belonging to a different time altogether.

The public view of churches has been badly damaged by the revelations constantly spilling out into the open of their failure to deal responsibly with the abuse of children over decades. Horrendous cases of institutional blindness and cover-up have afflicted Anglican and Catholic churches and given the media yet more opportunity for understandable outrage. Those failures have been compounded in the Church of England by very lumpy progress towards proper independent oversight of safeguarding.

Further criticism has been rife over a perceived downplaying of the centrality of the parish in church polity amidst a plethora of tactics seen as centralizing, top-down moves towards a command-and-control model inconsistent with the traditional dispersed authority of the Church of England. A worthwhile attempt to give some coherent leadership to the national church has instead run into protests that the laity, who pay the piper, are being sidelined, and their voice lost in a more prime-ministerial style of governance, with a cabinet of bishops and a shadowy set of special advisers.

The churches' response to "the problem" has been tentative, but the overall picture has been of a church in this country obsessed with its own life, fighting itself in a dark corner of the room and ignored by the rest of the room's occupants. As Bishop David Jenkins of Durham once said, "Too much absorption in church affairs is a damaging thing, and total absorption in church affairs is devastating."[1]

"The problem", outlined above in several of its guises, is not of course the whole picture. In every part of the country, there are churches that are flourishing. In particular, Black churches are often growing fast, helped by a steady influx of Christians from other lands. The same is true of churches set up for Christians from Southeast Asia. Roman Catholic churches have often benefitted from arrivals from Eastern Europe. Moreover, there are churches that are well integrated into their communities and serving them in practical ways through food banks, debt advice, homeless shelters, breakfast and homework clubs, and emergency relief through thousands of small Christian charities. These churches are often at the heart of their communities and belie the rumours of the church's demise.

The edge

It is, however, the perception of the church as a cranky institution out of touch with a rapidly changing society that has probably kept Elizabeth Baxter on the edge of the church at Holy Rood House. She has appeared

---

[1]   David Jenkins, *The Calling of a Cuckoo* (London: Continuum, 2002), p. 148.

to both love the church and distrust it, recognizing the necessity of a body of belief and practice bound by authority, but at the same time not wanting to be drawn into its political machinations and religious games. Holy Rood House has its place firmly in the wider church but properly placed on the edge. Indeed, the most productive place for a progressive Christian is on the *inside edge of the outside*, a place of affirmation and critique, where the believer can offer left-field insight to the institution but also slip over the border if necessary. Clergy and laity are called to be "loyal rebels", loyal to the church where they are sacramentally fed and institutionally nurtured while at the same time being free, and indeed called, to challenge the status quo. With its broad healing mandate combined with a significant theological arm, Holy Rood House is a properly restless, thought-provoking part of the church, on the edge.

Christians believe that the Kingdom or reign of God is unstoppable. God's ultimate purposes of peace and justice in a new world drawn together in Christ will inevitably be fulfilled because God is God. The mighty river pouring through history will finally arrive at the healing and restoration of all things, the new creation where love and its social expression, justice, are completely vindicated and pervade everything. That is not in doubt. What is in doubt, however, is what part, if any, the churches will play in this divine consummation. They all say they are trying to cooperate on God's great project of the Kingdom, to prepare the ground for it, or at least to help with the architect's drawings, but sometimes it seems that the best thing they could do is get out of the way and let God get on with it, because our tinkering with the plans is counterproductive.

If we're honest, we know that there's a deep rhythm running through all reality that's best described as death and resurrection. It runs through nature. It's seen in countless organizations, families and individual life stories. It runs through novels and films and our own consciousness. It's the way life works. So maybe it's the way that our church, or at least many of our churches, have to go. Can we embrace death, not knowing for certain if, how and when resurrection will occur, but trusting the One who knows the way out of a grave? This may be the scary calling of the church and of churches in the next generation: to let go, to move into palliative care, and be healed in death. If we believe in a God of resurrection, why not? When Jesus handed over his life in Gethsemane, he had no guarantee that the achievements of his ministry embodying the reign of God would not be wiped out and forgotten. He only had his love and knowledge of God, his Father. He could only trust.

Can we? Jesus challenged his friends not to hold on to their lives, because they would lose them, but rather to lose their lives for the sake of the reign of God, for then they would find them, filled out and beautiful. The hard moment for all of us is to give our lives away, to trust that God will use that *kenosis* and maybe—but without guarantee—give back a hundredfold in resurrection. That's a big enough step for a local church deciding its time and witness is spent, and handing itself over for God to do as God wants. It's an even bigger step for a denomination to embrace that option at a higher level: not to disappear but to be radically changed in vision, strategy, staffing and financing; in style, tone and voice.

Church as movement and community

If the church were to take this direction, it would first of all require a reimagining of itself. The American writer Brian McLaren asks the question, "What would it mean for Christians to rediscover their faith not as a problematic system of beliefs, but as a just and generous way of life, rooted in contemplation and expressed in compassion? Could Christians migrate from defining their faith as a system of beliefs to expressing it as a loving way of life?"[2] This is a return to Christianity not as an institution with commands, prohibitions, creeds and doctrines, but as a movement of people touched by the reality of God at the heart of their lives. Jesus's purpose was to proclaim, express, inhabit and demonstrate the reign of God. He invited his followers to live in the radical upside-downness of the Kingdom and outlined in his teaching how everything could be done in a different way, not emanating from obedience to laws and doctrines but from the Spirit-filled reality of a new relationship with God.

---

[2]   Brian McLaren, *The Great Spiritual Migration* (Danvers, MA: Convergent, 2016), p. 2.

McLaren was surely right when he wrote, "Jesus never announced to his disciples 'Hey folks, we're going to start a new, centralized institutional religion and name it after me.' Instead, he played the role of a non-violent leader and launched his movement with the classic words of movement, 'follow me . . . .'"[3]

What happens with a movement is that communities begin to form around and within the movement, but they resist the temptations and false securities of institutional life. They remain fluid, flexible, responsive to the needs and changes of the times. It's to such communities that we may be drawn as we envisage tomorrow's church. Brother Sam of the Franciscans wrote, "I sense that both the renewal of the church and society will come through the re-emerging of forms of Christian community that are homes of generous hospitality, places of challenging reconciliation, and centres of attentiveness to the living God."[4] In this, he was writing in the wake of another prophetic voice, that of philosopher Alasdair MacIntyre, who famously wrote, "What matters at this stage is the construction of local forms of community within which civility and intellectual and moral life can be sustained through the dark ages which are already upon us . . . This time, however, the barbarians are not waiting beyond the frontiers. They have already been among us quite some time . . . We are waiting not for Godot but for another doubtless very different St Benedict."[5] If you've spotted him, would you let the Archbishop of Canterbury know?

Such communities of faith, however, have to realize that community really only happens fully when we're doing something else. Victor Turner in his book *The Ritual Process* draws a distinction between community and *communitas*.[6] Community focusses on the inner life and security of existing relationships where people know and care for one another. *Communitas*, on the other hand, focusses on tasks outside the group,

---

[3] Brian McLaren, "Three Christianities", *Oneing: Journal for the Centre for Action and Contemplation, Albuquerque* 7:2 (2019), p. 72.

[4] Brother Sam S.S.F., *The Bible in Transmission* (The Bible Society, Spring 1998).

[5] Alasdair MacIntyre, *After Virtue* (London: Duckworth, 1981), p. 263.

[6] Victor Turner, *The Ritual Process* (Chicago, IL: The Aldine Press, 1969).

so that building community isn't an end in itself but a by-product of other intentional activities. It's when the church is serving the wider community that the special belonging-together of *communitas* emerges by happy accident. Many readers will know how energized and cohesive people are when putting on a theatrical performance or singing in a choral society or taking part in a sports team or working for a charity event. Churches will only become mature communities when they focus outside themselves. One question to ask is, "How is this church a blessing to the wider community?"

Reimagining the church's values

When an organization is worried about its performance it tends to examine its structures and see what needs to be changed. However, it would usually do better to look first at its values and then make sure that its structures are aligned to its best values, rather than the other way round. We need to make sure that the loom on which we're going to weave new cloth is fit for purpose. Without that, nothing will work. So what are the values that the church needs to have in place, whatever the denomination? What follows are only one person's suggestions but they're the fruit of many decades of participant observation of the life of the church and its churches.

Welcome

The experience at the church door is usually indicative of the quality of overall welcome the church offers. Jesus welcomed everyone into his friendship and his community of followers without any entrance qualifications. Whereas the priests in the Temple were concerned about people's purification through making animal sacrifices, and the Pharisees looked at people's seriousness about the Law, and the Essenes needed people to live ascetically cut off from society, Jesus welcomed all and sundry, especially if they had been rejected elsewhere or found themselves on the margins of society. He demonstrated in his whole attitude to those he met that God's compassion extended to them, and God's desire was that they flourish.

So it is that our church, as a movement of God-inspired people, has to welcome everyone, regardless of age, race, sexuality, belief or motivation. Everyone has to be embraced as a child of God, imprinted with the image of God, whether they fit the conventional Christian picture or not. Human beings are made of dust, but we are "dust that dreams". Add a little water to the dust and we become mud, and we come to church much muddier than we let on. However, the church needs to welcome all of us because we are made "little lower than the angels" (Psalm 8). Sunday by Sunday we come to church as the walking wounded, bearing the scars of the week, and we need to find that there are no entry requirements, no exams in righteousness or self-righteousness. Instead, we are welcomed home. It's a value you see in operation at Holy Rood House every day.

God-centredness

God has to be the supreme obsession of the church, or what's the church for? God is the burning fire of the Christian movement, the joy-giving companion whose presence is all-pervasive but as light as a lover's touch. God is as St Augustine saw God, the circle whose centre is everywhere and whose circumference is nowhere. If a church has this core value, it won't be concerned that its members have all sorts of understandings and imaginings of who God is; it will just want God to be seen as the divine presence in all things: one who is infinite in reach but could also be met in the coffee queue. In this kind of church, people will know that they have been made from love, and for love, and that it's only in love that we discover who we really are and what we're for. All this might sound obvious, but it's intriguing how rarely Christians talk about God outside set contexts such as worship and discussion groups. God is more than that; God is everything the church is about.

Life

John V. Taylor was a poet, a prophet, a theologian, and Bishop of Winchester. In his addresses to the University Mission in Oxford in 1986, he said this: "It has long been my conviction that God is not hugely concerned as to whether we are religious or not. What matters to God, and matters supremely, is whether we are alive or not. If your religion brings you more fully to life, God will be in it; but if your religion inhibits your capacity for life or makes you run away from it, you may be sure God is against it, just as Jesus was."[7] Jesus himself said that he had come that we might have life and have it abundantly (John 10:10). God's Spirit of life is always struggling with our dull, cautious spirits to bring us fully to life.

The creed says that God is "the Lord, the Giver of Life". The central gift of God, then, is aliveness, in contrast to the deadness that lies over the land and often lies over our own lives. There needs to be that sense in our churches, that just below the surface "life" is bubbling away and might erupt at any time in worship, in celebration of each other, in acts of uncommon generosity, in loving prayer and acts of compassion and forgiveness. The church needs to be a source of life in a huge diversity of forms and, in its commitment to healing, wholeness, justice, peace and the integrity of creation, Holy Rood House is part of that groundswell of life that the Christian movement is called to embody. "Life" doesn't necessarily entail the absence of struggle, as those who volunteer at Holy Rood House know only too well. Indeed, struggle might be a defining mark of people involved in a movement towards life. But that should always be the direction of a church haunted by hope.

Love

It might seem obvious, therefore, that one characteristic of a church that is authentically alive will be the love that, at some level or other, flows through its every action. The problem is that the word "love" is its own

---

7   John V. Taylor, *A Matter of Life and Death* (London: SCM Press, 1986), p. 18.

worst enemy. It can mean everything and nothing. It can easily sound fluffy, so much sentimentality and pink mist. But that's not the love that Jesus demonstrated. The reign of God meant living the love of God and of neighbour in every situation. It also meant loving our enemies (hard), loving ourselves (often even harder), and loving creation, which Jesus spoke of all the time in his conversation, teaching and parables. Love has a social and political expression too—in peace and justice. Love is infinitely compassionate because it's the nature of God, but it also has a steel core.

The range of that understanding of love as a central value of the church and its churches was well articulated by Bishop Michael Curry, Presiding Bishop of the Episcopal Church of the USA, at a royal wedding in 2018. He said, "Imagine a world where love is the way. Imagine our homes and families where love is the way. Imagine our neighbourhoods and communities where love is the way. Imagine governments and nations where love is the way. Imagine business and commerce where love is the way. Imagine this tired old world where love is the way. When love is the way, then no child will go to bed hungry in this world ever again. When love is the way, justice will roll down like a mighty stream and righteousness like an ever-flowing brook. When love is the way, poverty will become history. When love is the way, the earth will be a sanctuary . . . "8

This is the wide-ranging potential of the love that Jesus demonstrated, love that's the ever-present, ever-active source and sustenance of all reality, and not just a well-meaning personal benevolence. A restaurant without food isn't a restaurant; a bank without money isn't a bank; so too, a church without love isn't a church. This is a core value for the church because it's the very nature of God.

---

8   Bishop Michael Curry, sermon preached at the wedding of Prince Harry and Meghan Markle, 19 May 2018.

Learning

A learning church is on the move. I once listened to an African bishop who had been consecrated when he was 30. Now over 60 and hugely respected, he said he'd come to the conference to learn how to be a bishop. Such humility is immensely attractive and not always evident in politics, business or the church. If a church thinks it has arrived, it's probably in the process of dying, because growth is the only sign of life. A learning church is open, eager, humble, ready to be shaped into a community of God's growing people.

Elizabeth Baxter has consistently emphasized that Holy Rood House also sponsors the Centre for the Study of Theology and Health. The Centre is committed to holding together theology and therapy and has encouraged research and reflection in partnership with medical, social, educational and religious communities. Through seminars, conferences, research days and workshops the learning has gone on, launched by Archbishop Rowan Williams, with him as Patron and the Archbishop of York or another York diocesan bishop as Visitor, the whole sustained by the continuing interplay of research and praxis. This is what is meant by a learning church.

Participation and engagement

These values ensure that a church is well rooted in its own life but essentially orientated towards the wider community in which it's set. There was a town in Nebraska that until recently had only one resident, and she was the town's registered mayor, clerk, treasurer, librarian and licensee. She collected taxes from herself, granted her own alcohol licence and repaired the town's roads. She said, "Someday this town will be just memories. But I like it here."

There are some churches with similar characteristics, or at least where they centralize all important functions on the vicar or the churchwarden or some powerful figure who no one will defy. However, that "do-it-all-yourself", command and control model is dying quickly. They will soon be "just memories"; but in the meantime, many "like it here" and, by extension, "like it the way it is". In an effective church, nearly everyone participates and is involved in some way in the functioning of the Body of Christ at the level they want, because leadership is dispersed throughout the church's life and gifts are to be found everywhere.

This dispersed participation is there to serve the wider community. Archbishop William Temple spoke of the local church as being the only organization that exists for those who are not its members. A telling question for a church council would be, "If we weren't here, would the wider community notice?" It's an interesting exercise to look at the council agenda and see how much of it is concerned with rearranging our own furniture and how much with serving the community. How that service is offered outside the church has to be discerned locally, but the task inevitably has to be undertaken or the church is just another organization for those who like that sort of thing.

Quality

Nick Page writes, "We built an entire system based on persuading people to come into a big old building, sit down and listen. It stopped working sometime in the 1950s."[9] People are used to high quality in the presentations they receive, whether that be at work conferences, at the movies, on television and in streamed programmes, or at concerts and leisure events generally. They are less happy with unidirectional, non-participating, second-rate offerings in conditions of cold, discomfort and isolation. Cathedrals buck the trend of course because they are usually able to offer inspiring architecture, evocative history, and high-quality music, preaching and ecclesiastical theatre. Local churches won't be able to offer what cathedrals do but they need to offer as high a quality as they can with the resources they have. That means those who lead services thinking imaginatively about each act of worship as unique and a privileged opportunity to enable worshippers to encounter God. The heating matters too!

---

[9] Nick Page, *Church Invisible* (Grand Rapids, MI: Zondervan, 2004), p. 122.

Seriousness

Philip Larkin, though an atheist, wrote of the church as a "serious house on serious earth".[10] Indeed it is, because it deals in things of the highest, ultimate importance. It's also a place where serious matters can be tackled in the context of the largest understandings of Reality. Here is a place where the trivialities of contemporary culture are relativized, and we stand before the God who loved the world so much that he sent his only son. This doesn't mean being solemn (see next value), but it does mean that there is a place where we are permitted to spread our minds and hearts over large matters of life and death, pain and suffering, major ethical and social issues, and the uncertainty of a fragile future. We can go beyond the echo chambers and instant prejudices of social media or the shallowness of three-minute interviews. In the movement we call church, depth must not be sacrificed to relevance, nor must church life and worship be reduced to entertainment. We have to look beyond binary arguments and easy-to-fix answers, and instead admit the possibility of paradox, of not-knowing, of mystery. Churches, therefore, need to be places of realism, thoughtfulness, enquiry and doubt, as well as centres of life-giving spirituality. In a society facing crises with the climate, poverty, inequality, extremism, violence, the proper use of science and a host of other problems, it's important to have places like Holy Rood House that encourage serious thinking about how to "heal creation" personally, politically, ecologically and spiritually.

Playfulness and joy

This is not to argue for churches that are superficial and childish, and where serious exploration of faith and life are buried in a welter of bouncy castles and family fun days. But we need to acknowledge and celebrate the goodness of God and the fullness of our humanity. Jesus said that if we were to enter the Kingdom of God we would have to become like

---

10   Philip Larkin, from the poem "Church Going", in *The Less Deceived* (Faber & Faber, 2012 [first published 1954]).

little children (Mark 10:15). Our inner child often feels it has to behave in church, to keep quiet and listen. It's surely a better approach to see church as a place where our rich humanity is given generous space and encouragement, and maybe allowed to turn occasional cartwheels. One wise bishop used to tell his clergy that the two things they should concentrate on in ministry were prayer and parties. It's a good menu.

Right brain

Iain McGilchrist's influential book *The Master and His Emissary* explores the different functions of the left and right hemispheres of the brain.[11] The left is more literal, good for analysis, rational thinking, and planning. The right brain is creative, intuitive, and uses metaphor, irony, and humour. Western society has increasingly chosen the way of left-brain thinking which has made possible huge advances in science and technology, and in medicine and engineering, but it has dangerously paid less attention to the potential of the right brain. Social media platforms are commercially designed to dispense with empathy, nuance, metaphor and allegory. Discourse is therefore impoverished and channelled along prefabricated lines, to our serious detriment. When we transfer that analysis to church life, we can see how important it is to value both halves of the brain, and therefore to release our imagination from its captivity to doctrine and convention. Many Christians are exploring silence, symbols, sacraments, and story, and using poetry and art to enrich their spiritual journeying. There's common ground here with many secular seekers, dissatisfied with dry materialism but unable to relate to the church's stale diet. We need a spiritual palette that sweeps across the entire sky.

---

[11]   Iain McGilchrist, *The Master and his Emissary* (New Haven, CT: Yale University Press, 2019).

Conclusion

I have tried here to reimagine the church's self-understanding as a movement that generates community and has to take seriously the death-and-resurrection paradigm embedded in reality. I've also tried to reimagine the values that could underlie a healthier version of the church's life. We cannot, however, be naïve about the need for structural renewal alongside these deeper moves of the heart in the church. From an Anglican perspective, it's clear that the paradigm of a single church with a vicar and a cluster of souls to look after has long gone. But the wonderful buildings remain, mute witnesses to a fast-disappearing way of grace and truth, maintained heroically by battalions of elderly people running out of energy.

How we respond structurally to the challenge is another piece of work, but unless the loom is sound, the cloth weaved on it will be disappointing. We have to get the fundamentals right. And one of those fundamentals is the church as a movement that values the "little ships" that scoot around exploring, nudging and questioning accepted modes of operation. Holy Rood House is one of those edgy little ships, committed to the enterprise of the reign of God but wanting to live with vulnerability and experimentation. Unless the wider church can grasp the importance of communities such as Holy Rood House, there is little hope for the church as a monolithic institution.

We have to trust that the church will not retreat but rather step forward to a more diverse, humbler, and more creative future—haunted by hope.

2

Yes to women priests

Wendy Wilby

Let me say that it is only proper for us not to discriminate between sexes, but with one heart and one mind bear witness to Christ. "For all of you who were baptized into Christ have clothed yourselves with Christ. There is neither Jew nor Greek, slave nor free, male nor female, for you are all one in Christ Jesus." If we stand steadfast in our faith, and both male and female cooperate in bringing heaven on earth, decisive victory is certain through the power of the Holy Spirit.

Florence Li Tim-Oi, from her memoir Raindrops of my Life[1]

St Martin-in-the-Fields, London, has held quite a celebration today. You see, today happens to be 25 January 2024, and it has to be a most suitable day to start to write this essay in honour of my good friend, the Revd Elizabeth Baxter, priest of the Church of England. So why that celebration in London today? On 25 January 1944, Florence Li Tim-Oi was ordained priest by Bishop R. O. Hall in China. She was the very first woman ordained in the Anglican Communion. Bishop Hall bravely wrote to his friends and explained this radical action and his conviction that what he had done was God's will. So, here we are 80 years later, and we are all giving thanks for the Revd Florence Li Tim-Oi, and, as an added bonus, the Eucharist today in St Martin-in-the-Fields was presided over by Bishop Hall's granddaughter—the Revd Frances Shoesmith. Florence

---

[1] Florence Li Tim-Oi, *Raindrops of my Life* (Hong Kong: Anglican Book Store, 1996).

Li Tim-Oi's story, her priestly ministry and service, has certainly given huge inspiration to so many women and men, including, of course, our very own Elizabeth Baxter.

The idea of women priests actually began to be discussed in the 1920s and indeed probably a long time before that! But it was only in 1975 that the Church of England General Synod passed a motion stating it had "no fundamental objections" to the ordination of women to the priesthood. However, a motion to remove legal barriers to the ordination of women was defeated in the House of Clergy at the General Synod meeting on 8 November 1978. So, now where were we? Feelings were running high, and the church had a veritable battle on its hands.

On 21 November in the same year, attendees of a meeting chaired by Dame Betty Ridley decided to set up a national movement to work for the ordination of women. So, the early days of what became the Movement for the Ordination of Women (MOW) began. Entering the scene were very many talented, idealistic women and men, lovers of justice and truth, prepared to work hard for just one aim—an inclusive priesthood in the Church of England.

Incidentally, the archive of the Movement for the Ordination of Women has now been fully catalogued and is available for consultation in the Women's Library, now held at the London School of Economics. The archive covers the entire years of MOW's work—from 1979–94—and contains publications (including *Catalyst* and *Uppity*), correspondence, financial and other records and photos, and publicity materials. It will be a great resource for researchers and others who are interested in the place and progress of women within the Christian churches—in this case the Church of England.

Well, let's return to 1978 as the campaign got going, and proceed to switch on a bright spotlight over West Yorkshire in 1980. Enter stage right a young woman called Elizabeth Baxter working with Stanley, her energetic, radical and courageous husband. Stanley had recently become a priest in the Church of England, following a spell in the Lutheran ministry. These two "spirit-filled" individuals were already hard at work, driven by their love for and dedication to God. Their new initiatives and projects built up their congregations whilst, at the same time, they brought up four lively children—a full-time task in itself!

I just want to interrupt the MOW flow at this point with a typical story about Stanley, shared with me recently by a former bishop's chaplain. Stanley was an uncompromising, outspoken man, full of personal integrity. "Bishop or no bishop", he was certainly not going to perjure himself during any service which licensed him to a parish or benefice. With a full congregation, the bishop turned to the registrar, John Balmforth (a tall and imposing man dressed in full legal wig), and asked him to please read the licence and direct Stanley through the oaths. This is a standard legal obligation for any priest leading a church and we've all heard it thousands of times. The priest was asked to say:

> *The Oath of Allegiance*
> I, *N*, do swear that I will be faithful and bear true allegiance to her Majesty, Queen Elizabeth the Second, her heirs and Successors, according to Law; so help me God.

> *The Oath of Canonical Obedience, facing the bishop*
> I, *N*, do swear by almighty God that I will pay true and canonical obedience to the Lord Bishop of Ripon and his Successors in all things lawful and honest; so help me God.

At each point, following the oath, Stanley added his own words, which were "and as far as my conscience doth allow". After the first oath (with this unique addition), there was silence. No one knew quite what to do next—this sort of thing did not happen—so, unable to think of anything else to do, the registrar proceeded to the next oath, and it all happened again: "and as far as my conscience doth allow". The bishop's chaplain said to me that he was terribly impressed. After all, many of us have wanted to say that!

It was in 1982 that this intrepid pair came to live and work at St Margaret of Antioch, Leeds, which was soon joined by All Hallows Church. This latter church became an alternative haven for many students from the university with social consciences, and was fertile ground for countless vocations to the priesthood.

By this time, I had already come across Elizabeth. I had been licensed as a Reader in 1980, full of enthusiasm myself, and found myself blown away by her capacity to present a vision of the Kingdom which very much tuned in to mine. As she described the beloved people of her church, I remember her saying that you knew you were in St Margaret's parish on Cardigan Road when all the leafy green trees stopped. Indeed, there was hardly a living tree or shrub in the parish at all. Into this desert sprang up a number of "green shoots", including an unusual urban farm complete with livestock and a new group that formed one of the northern branches of the Movement for the Ordination of Women. I was just ready for this! I had felt a calling to the priesthood since I was 12 years old. My passion for justice and equality at 31 was equalled only by Elizabeth's, whose strength of personality, at 31 also, gathered an endless diverse company of people around her. She was now perfecting the art of giving people tasks, whilst I, as treasurer, collected the subscriptions. During this fertile period of campaigning, Elizabeth became a deaconess in 1984 and then was ordained a deacon in 1987. She was one of the first women to enter the threefold order of ministry in the Church of England.

The next few years in MOW were fuelled by that heady combination of a uniting common purpose alongside a thirst to learn and develop. Elizabeth loves theology. There's nothing she likes more than "talking about God" with others, and so she encouraged us to think theologically. Following her lead, we all began to explore what it meant to conceive of God as female, or, at least, to envisage a God who embraced female attributes as well as traditional male qualities. It utterly changed the way we approached worship and liturgy and prayer; and many acts of worship, of an inclusive nature, were produced by like-minded people. Some of these were published, and they sit on my bookshelves even now, so influential were they for me. For so many women and men, this fresh approach was life-giving and liberating.

In London, a group of women and men founded the St Hilda Community. In order to show that they believed in the priestly orders of women, they would openly invite women ordained abroad to celebrate communion for them, and they would advertise such liturgies in the church press. Quite soon, they discovered that there was an American woman, ordained into the Episcopal Church in 1978, called Suzanne Fageol, studying in London, and she was prepared to act permanently as the Community's priest. As you can imagine, it wasn't long before she came into conflict with the Church of England, highlighting the continuing differences within the church over the ordination of women. Elizabeth, of course, in true fashion, introduced us all to Suzanne. She came up to Leeds and shared her experiences. We lapped it up, felt that we were "ahead of the game", that we had a prophetic message to share, that there was work to be done; and if a "teensy weensy" bit of persecution came our way, then it was par for the course! I remember well attending a meeting of the General Synod in York University when a number of us (organized by Elizabeth, of course) were standing outside the debating hall as the delegates entered. We weren't noisy or disruptive, though we no doubt handed out pieces of improving literature to those unsuspecting church men and women. However, some of the traditionalist priests walked between us all, kept their heads bowed down and made the sign of the cross as they passed with stony leaden faces. This was certainly a new experience for me! I wasn't sure whether they were absolving us because of our defiant actions or protecting themselves from these malevolent women.

Elizabeth relished it all as, figuratively speaking, she led us up to the gates of the creaking church and hammered alongside us on the door, asking for us to be let in to share our gifts and contribute towards a whole priesthood. To do this we went to speak to PCCs, contributed to debates, trawled through membership lists of diocesan committees and boards to check that there was female representation. We held fundraisers, auctions and parties and went on trips.

Somehow or other Elizabeth had got our Ripon branch invited to a trip to Westminster Abbey to contribute to a "pro-women priest" service. It was always such a privilege to be invited into these ancient places of worship, which for centuries had pointed to Christ, and to feel at last that we were accepted for who we were. I suspect that the Minor Canon of the Abbey, one Paul Ferguson, had something to do with all this. He has been a constant friend of Elizabeth's and the women's cause (and now Holy Rood House) for decades, currently acting as the episcopal visitor to Holy Rood House, since he was made the Bishop of Whitby.

Those campaigning days weren't all terribly serious and earnest. There was much fun to be had in the group. One such moment happened in Ripon Cathedral on the eve of an ordination to the priesthood—an all-male one of course. The Dean, the Very Revd Christopher Campling, had always been a great supporter of the cause, and he graciously allowed the movement to take over the cathedral for an all-night vigil every year at the Petertide ordinations. In the morning of the ordination, badges and bookmarks were given out to the worshippers and guests. They all had on them the words "Pray for all called to be priests". Elizabeth and Christopher always seemed to hit it off, and she seemed to have no trouble encouraging him to allow his cathedral to be used as a public witness for our cause. Of course, now that I've worked for many years in cathedrals, I realize just what a gift that was to us, poised as the building would have been to welcome hundreds of guests for the big service the next day. The vergers would not have easily tolerated stray crisp packets scattered around or chairs moved randomly to various chapels. It certainly wasn't like that with us, of course. We cleared up everything and left it as we found it. We couldn't risk losing Dean Christopher's goodwill!

That particular year, on the hour, every hour, through the wee small hours, we would have a short liturgy and pray together for justice, and then depart to our sleeping bags to try to sleep. I had set up my sleeping bag and pillow by the nave organ console and, bleary-eyed, made my way back after the hourly prayers at 1 a.m. to try to shut my eyes. The lighting was very dim, and I squeezed into my makeshift bed with great relief, only to feel something drop on my head from a great height. To my horror I instinctively felt for it; it moved and then rapidly flew away. This little black bat was as astonished as I was! I let out a blood-curdling scream and so woke up all the other campaigners. How we laughed and laughed and laughed!

Elizabeth had an attitude of zero-tolerance towards anyone who was prepared to undermine and abuse women, and especially towards those who had been called to licensed ministry in church. She always worked towards raising our awareness, and brought to us what she considered unjust or treacherous behaviour. Sadly, it is human nature, I suppose, but we soon became sensitized to the fact that a goodly number of male priests could be extremely friendly and supposedly supportive to us individually, whilst speaking negatively towards us behind our backs. Indeed, some would actively vote against the ordination of women to the priesthood if they thought that they wouldn't be found out. I'm sorry to say that trust in each other reduced hugely in those days. Even worse than that, of course, were those who, in their benign geniality, weren't prepared to lift a finger for the truth, but were only prepared to sit on the fence. Elizabeth had got their measure, and we soon got their measure too!

I can remember a number of anti-women's ordination demonstrations during this time. One such protest occurred in Ripon on 9 April 1994, following the momentous and successful vote in General Synod on 11 November 1992, and soon after the first ordinations of women to the priesthood in Bristol Cathedral on 12 March 1994. A priest was slowly driving a car round and round the cathedral just as the congregation was arriving. In my memory, he was towing what can only be described as a trailer that would normally carry double glazing. Instead of glass panels, there were two enormous hoardings in their place. The posters on the hoardings read: "The party after the murder. Today a bishopess joins in the 'fun' in Ripon Cathedral as the priestesses and their friends celebrate the killing of the Church of England."

Elizabeth wasn't having any of this nonsense, of course. That day in Ripon, the service happened to begin in the little garden over the road on the north side of the cathedral. Many of the women, especially those who were waiting to be ordained priest, and those who had been ordained priest already, were gathered there, whilst the men who had been involved in the campaign stood outside the cathedral doors. Peri Aston, an inspirational dancer, had been invited to lead the procession with her rainbow kite on the end of a long pole. She whirled this above our heads as we gathered to hear the Gospel reading of Mary Magdalene in the garden, read simultaneously in the cathedral to the waiting congregation, by Bishop Stanley Booth-Clibborn.

Then, like a bad penny, around the corner came the van with its offensive hoardings. With a huge whirl of her rainbow kite, Peri stepped across in front of him, barring his way, and all the women walked across the road with heads held high. The men opened the cathedral doors wide, and the procession of women went in with Peri dancing up the aisle whirling and swirling the rainbow kite over the heads of those already seated.

Here is Elizabeth's description about the involvement of the Rt Revd Penny Jamieson, Bishop of Dunedin in New Zealand. Penny had been asked to preach:

> It was marvellous that Penny was willing to be involved. I still have the letter from the Bishop of Ripon, David Young, who was one hundred per-cent supportive. Nevertheless, he had to explain that Penny would be unable to wear her mitre for the occasion! When it came to it, all the bishops processed without their mitres in solidarity, with the exception of David Young, who made it very clear that as the Bishop of the Diocese he was personally welcoming and supporting her. Indeed, he followed this up with his superb after dinner talk back at the College that evening.

We are now 30 years on from that spectacular and inspiring Thanksgiving Eucharist called "... a new order has already begun ...".[2] We are all much older, and hopefully much wiser. Today, female priests make up well over 30 per cent of all stipendiary clergy, and 31 of our 108 serving bishops are women, although only five are in charge of a diocese (these figures are from 2022 and keep changing rapidly). It was such a momentous day when, in January 2015, Libby Lane was consecrated the first woman bishop in the Church of England. So now, women serve as parish priests and bishops, as archdeacons and rural deans, cathedral deans and cathedral canons. They are to be found in all walks of chaplaincy and theological education. Many of the pioneers in the movement have sadly died, including a number of those we fondly call the '94 priests. I was told a good few years ago that the '94 priests had a bit of a reputation for being difficult and outspoken. I was, I suppose, rather upset to hear that, but I shouldn't have been, and Elizabeth would certainly say we are most definitely not challenging enough! She has led us through so much and we are indebted to her for all she has given us.

To finish this essay in honour of Elizabeth's contribution, let her tell us in her own words what she believes has happened over 25 years in

---

2   "... a new order has already begun ..." Liturgy for A Thanksgiving Eucharist for the Vote on 11 November 1992 (constructed by Elizabeth Baxter) MOW.

her reflection on the 1994 service of Thanksgiving at Ripon Cathedral in the WATCH journal *Women and the Church*:

> Looking back at this most amazing and challenging time, I find myself committed to a new wave of consciousness raising, as it seems there has been a sliding back in our alertness to the challenges we faced then, which we still face today in the Church. There seems to be little commitment to the empowerment and liberation found through inclusive language and a celebration of embodiment. As I reflect on the last quarter of a century of my own priesthood, and as I experience the Church today, I long for the mutuality of holding the pastoral and prophetic together, so the wonder of being Easter people can inspire mission that leads to the flourishing of the many ways of being human within a world that also groans for liberation.[3]

---

[3]   WATCH journal, *Women and the Church*, 1 July 2019.

Birthing, belonging and becoming:
A tribute to Elizabeth Baxter

June Boyce-Tillman

My first encounter with Elizabeth and Stanley was while they were still at St Margaret and All Hallows, Leeds. It was a performance of *Singing the Mystery—Hildegard of Bingen*. This was a dramatic time for me because my fingers were recovering from third-degree burns following an accident involving electrocution. I realized then that they were a special pair of people in a distinctive church context that they had created with vision and enthusiasm. In 1995, I was invited to continue my link with them at the Holy Rood House Centre for the Study of Theology and Health. They became my very dear friends; they made me a consultant to the house and have given me many times of rest and acceptance. They have played an important part in my own development.

My initial ideas on music and health were tested here: I had the chance to blend more orthodox ideas with some of those I had encountered in the New Age, which I had researched in order to write *Constructing Musical Healing: The Wounds that Sing.*[1] This drew heavily on the bank of developing feminist theology that Elizabeth and I were sharing. This hymn, which encompasses the thinking that underpins that book, became a favourite at Holy Rood:[2]

---

[1] June Boyce-Tillman, *Constructing Musical Healing: The Wounds that Sing* (London: Jessica Kingsley Publishers, 2000).

[2] June Boyce-Tillman, *A Rainbow to Heaven—Hymns, Songs and Chants* (London: Stainer & Bell, 2006), pp. 32–3; to be sung to the tune Abbots Leigh.

God of justice, wind the circle,
Making all the cosmos one,
Show us in millennial visions,
How on earth Your Will is done;
Help us see the mercy flowing
From the wounding of Christ's side;
Heal us with compassion spreading
As a purifying tide.

God of dreams and intuition,
Inspiration from the night,
Temper reason's rigid systems
With the leap of faith's insight.
God of passion, fill our knowing
With Divine authority,
And a sense of mystery leading
To a right humility.

God of faith's heroic journey,
May Your Truth direct our way;
Guide our footsteps, give us courage
In the challenge of each day.
God of Wisdom's spinning spiral,
Soothe us with your gentle charms,
Weave our lives into the pattern
Of Christ's all-embracing arms.

God of order, God of chaos,
In love's creativity
Move the mountains of tradition
Stifling earth's fertility.
Break the barriers, guide the learning,
Bind the wounds and heal the pain,
Bring to birth our human yearning,
Integrate the world again.

Many of my one-woman performances have been trialled at Holy Rood House with advice and encouragement from Elizabeth. Many hymns that form the basis of this chapter were inspired and written there and encompass much of the theology that Elizabeth loves.

I have led two memorable Easter retreats. Memories of the "Skirt of Christ" Easter retreat are still encouraging me—making the wonderful patchwork together and then cutting it up and sitting in the chapel looking at the broken pieces accompanied by Tavener's music; hiding the pieces around the garden with Elizabeth; searching the garden for the hidden pieces and then sewing them together; dancing with the Risen Christ at dawn; and the dwelling in the pitched tent of Christ.

The community recognizes the interconnectedness of all things and builds on the continuity of the churches' healing ministry from the home of healing founded by Bishop Morris Maddocks at Spennithorne, Wensleydale. It is an exploration in community to learn what it means to be wounded healers.[3] At Holy Rood House, I found Jesus/Sophia the Wisdom of God, present at the crossroads of our lives (Proverbs 8:1–2).[4] This chapter will explore three of the themes that Elizabeth has explored in her ministry there and how these fit in the wider developments within the church's theology.

Birthing

Elizabeth, with Stanley, birthed the Holy Rood community; and motherhood is central to Elizabeth's management of Holy Rood House. This, combined with maternal images of the divine, explored tehomic theology, which underpinned my last presentation, entitled *Hidden Wisdom*, that celebrated Elizabeth's achievements at Holy Rood House. Elizabeth has always been deeply committed to feminist theology, particularly the work of the Revd Carter Heyward. A maternal view of

---

[3]   Henri J. Nouwen, *The Wounded Healer* (London: Darton, Longman & Todd, 1979).

[4]   Carter Heyward, *Touching our Strength: The Erotic as Power and the Love of God* (San Francisco: Harper & Row, 1989), p. 33.

the Divine includes the notion of birthing. Catherine Keller explores tehomic theology, which is based on the Hebrew word *tehom*, usually translated as "ocean, deep, abyss" (Genesis 1:1–2).[5]

A tehomic theology envisions "the Deep" as a fluid, indeterminate, germinating compilation of potentiality that generates itself and everything else infinitely, with no clear beginning or end. A tehomic theology also envisions God as the maternal "fluid bottomless potentiality" and "womb of self-organizing complexity" that erupts and then differentiates, and not as the paternally derived image of the traditional Jewish, Christian and Muslim visions of God.[6]

Keller sees God as continually interdependent with us and therefore not fixed and closed, because of the Divine continual entanglement with and within the material universe.

There is an emergent sense of becoming from the deep, through a continual interdependent multiplicity of difference—"all in all" and, as such, relational through and through, requiring our participation.[7]

Keller draws on the process philosophers, such as Alfred North Whitehead[8] and Hannah Arendt,[9] in developing the idea of God continually birthing creation, from which emerges a theology of flourishing. This was developed by Grace Jantzen, who had such an influence on feminist theology in the late twentieth century and longed for:

---

5   Catherine Keller, *The Face of the Deep: A Theology of Becoming* (London: Routledge, 2003).

6   <https://metanexus.net/review-catherine-kellers-face-deep-theology-becoming/>, accessed 2 April 2024.

7   Catherine Keller, *Political Theology of the Earth: Our Planetary Emergency and the Struggle for a New Public* (New York: Columbia University Press, 2018).

8   Alfred North Whitehead, *Process and Reality: An Essay in Cosmology, Gifford Lectures Delivered in the University of Edinburgh during the Session 1927–1928* (New York: Macmillan Press, 1929).

9   Hannah Arendt, *The Human Condition* (Chicago, IL: University of Chicago Press, 1958).

a new religious symbolic focused on natality and flourishing rather than on death, a symbolic which will lovingly enable natals, women and men, to become subjects, and the earth on which we live to bloom, to be "faithful to the process of the divine which passes through" us and through the earth itself.[10]

Elizabeth's favourite theologian, Carter Heyward, develops this into a new Christology:

These ideas have started a radical shift in Christology. Jesus can now become a model of human flourishing rather than a male saviour rescuing damsels in distress, by means of a messy and an inevitable death. He becomes an insightful teacher, a person of humour and compassion.[11]

Beatrice Bruteau draws together the themes of *Theotokos*—God-bearer— with the ecological movement and notions of ecstasy, drawing on Romans 8:

Birth is bringing what is inside out. I am saying that the whole natural order, the cosmogenesis, is a cosmogestation. It is growing as an embryo grows, organizing itself, and progressing from stage to stage . . . This is the ecstasy of the Earth, reaching out of itself, well beyond itself. There is another saying from the Talmud that I like: "Who has Wisdom? The one who sees the unborn?" Our effort is to "see the unborn" in the *Theotokos* and help bring it to birth.[12]

This thinking embraces rather than resists darkness, making it a necessary part of life, a discussion that Elizabeth and I have had often:

---

[10] Grace M. Jantzen, *Becoming Divine: Towards a Feminist Philosophy of Religion* (Manchester: Manchester University Press, 1998).

[11] Heyward, *Touching our Strength*, no page number.

[12] Beatrice Bruteau, *God's Ecstasy: The Creation of a Self-creating World* (New York: Crossroad Publishing, 1997).

It was dark in the dawn of time
When the waters of chaos seethed,
Darkness was brooding across the abyss
As the Spirit she gently breathed.
Slowly she hovered across swelling waves
Till the world from the chaos emerged
Then the rest in the dark was transfigured with light
As the Spirit worked out her plan.

It is dark in the moistened earth
Where the seed for a season lies,
Buried down deep like a dry pregnant husk
Till the earth is pushed aside.
Nurtured by warmth, it has waited alone
Till the time to spring up has come.
Then the rest in the dark was transfigured with light
As the Spirit works out her plan.

It is dark in the sheltering womb
Where the baby for nine months lies
Curved like a moon near a warm woman's heart
Till the waters roll aside.
Waters of life kept the child safe inside
Gently folded, enclosed in love.
Then the rest in the dark is transfigured with light
As the Spirit works out her plan.

It is dark in the heart's deep cells
Where the Spirit of Wisdom lies.
Firm are the strong rooms and bars of the mind
Till the barriers are rolled aside.
Yet the idea in the dark has been formed
Till the time for release should come
Then the rest in the dark is transfigured with light
As the Spirit works out her plan.[13]

---

[13] Boyce-Tillman, *A Rainbow to Heaven*, pp. 42–3.

The image of a birthing God was always present in Elizabeth's ministry at Holy Rood House, and led to radical theological questioning, such as the workshop with Jackie Scully and Rachel Mann on the theology of IVF (*in vitro* fertilization). During that workshop, I wrote a hymn, a radical rework of birthing after *Away in a manger*:

> Away in a manger, no crib for a bed,
> Where embryo blossoms can lay a sweet head;
> We wondering parents are standing nearby
> And even the starlight is stuttering "Why?"

> Such yearning, such longing, such resting in hope!
> We ponder our dreaming and how we might cope;
> A fat child, a thin child, a child with no arms?
> Can we stand securely and keep them from harm?

> The DNA glitters and dazzles our minds;
> O God of amazement, are you cruel or kind?
> Please answer our questions and make the way clear;
> Create in our baby someone to hold dear.[14]

Behind Elizabeth's thinking on birthing is her understanding of process theology. Process theology enabled me to invent a new word as in this hymn written for Holy Rood House, which is often sung in the beautiful chapel with the wonderful glass doors remembering Stanley. Elizabeth and I think that God as verb—a-godding—makes more sense than as a noun:

> CHORUS: And we'll all go a-godding
> To bring the world to birth.

> 1. New life is calling;
> Help set it free.
> And we'll all go a-godding
> With a song of liberty.

---

[14] June Boyce-Tillman (4 July 2018, unpublished).

CHORUS

2. Hunger is calling,
Find food to share;
And we'll all go a-godding
To give out abundant care.
CHORUS

3. Hopelessness calling,
Lonely and drear;
And we'll all go a-godding
In warm friendship drawing near.
CHORUS

4. Warfare is calling.
When will it cease?
And we'll all go a-godding,
In our arms, the flowers of peace.
CHORUS

5. Justice is calling
Scales in her hand;
And we'll all go a-godding;
In her strength we'll take a stand.
CHORUS

6. Wisdom is calling;
Search out her ways;
And we'll all go a-godding,
To the ending of our days.
CHORUS.[15]

---

[15]   Boyce-Tillman, *A Rainbow to Heaven*, p. 97.

Belonging

Community is an important theme in Elizabeth's thinking. This is most clearly expressed in her considered and consecrated hospitality, welcoming all who come through the doors of Holy Rood House:

> Hospitality lies at the heart of all we are and do ... Holy Rood House is a charity with a gentle Christian ethos, providing safer space for those of us who are finding life unsafe ... *Space—for the possibility of seeing things from a different perspective.*[16]

Central to Elizabeth's theology and to life at Holy Rood House is the Eucharist, which she continually reworks to make sure everyone belongs. The Eucharist focusses the unity/diversity of God, humanity, and the wider world, the full burgeoning of the Body of Christ:

> Creative freedom is co-creative, always in relation to someone or something. Individuals with creative freedom are embodied and engaged in a web of relationships. Creative freedom makes new relationships and makes existing relationships new.[17]

We have the same dance of oneness and diversity in us, and our creativity is based in this—a reworking of the traditional doctrine of the Trinity. Elizabeth has always held tightly on to a belonging within the wider church while reworking its theology. Early in her ministry, one group that she embraced fully and with loving welcome was the LGBTQIAA+ community. Traumatized groups, particularly survivors of sexual abuse, were also warmly welcomed in work such as that undertaken with Barbara Glasson.[18]

---

16   Holy Rood House publicity leaflet.

17   Carol P. Christ, *She Who Changes: Re-imagining the Divine in the World* (New York: Palgrave/Macmillan, 2003).

18   Barbara Glasson, *A Spirituality of Survival: Enabling a Response to Trauma and Abuse* (London and New York: Continuum, 2009).

Elizabeth's embracing of creativity as a way of belonging and healing has been demonstrated in her encouragement and initiation of many creative activities as part of the Holy Rood activities. Painting, weaving, dancing, drama, musicking—all have formed a significant part of the ministry of healing, alongside counselling and therapy, which are open to the wider local community as well as residents and visitors.

In the idea of belonging, inclusive language has played a very significant part in Elizabeth's liturgical theology. All her work, including the powerful liturgies she has crafted for Holy Rood House, is expressed using inclusive language. In this context, she and I had many discussions about the word "Lord". She found its male gender unacceptable in the pursuit of unqualified inclusive language. However, I preferred a translation of Lord as "loaf-giver", which seemed an appropriate description of God. When Hexthorpe Manor was opened, she asked me for a special hymn, and I saw a chance to redeem the word as I do in the first line here. The hymn encompasses all the belongings that Elizabeth embraces—spiritual, emotional and practical. It was sung at the opening event in which I led a group of singing/dancing young people in a sort of conga round the garden, in a gathering that included the huge diversity of participants that Elizabeth loves:

Loaf provider, wine fermenter,
Set the table for our feast,
Plump the cushions, make a welcome
For the greatest and the least;
We would tap your flowing Wisdom
And the richness of your peace.

Here we gather, here we draw on
Your warm hospitality;
May we gently face our problems
In your creativity,
Knowing that your arms are holding
Our diverse community.

Guard our visions, shield our dreaming
In the darkness of your womb;
Float them gently on your waters,
Nurture them and give them room,
So that when they come to birthing
They will touch earth's deepest wounds.[19]

Many people who come to Holy Rood House feel isolated from the church and from society in general, as they write in the books in the various rooms:

Thank you for being here for me—a place of safety full of God's peace and love.
I came . . . I stayed . . . I am not alone.

In a state of belonging, people have been able to share stories that could not be shared more widely. These are often of abuse of various kinds—spiritual, sexual, emotional. Elizabeth has been regularly associated with ways of healing trauma of various kinds. In the sitting room, the sharing of stories is part of many sessions—informal and formal. This sharing on the nature of abuse (as happened during a New Year House Party, 31 December 2012–1 January 2013) is reflected in the final verse of this hymn:

1. When we see love contorted and embattled
Amidst the trash and rubble of our world,
Entwined with guilt, unmerited and twisted,
Our hearts cry out, obscenities are hurled.
Creator God, will you respond with kindness,
Or are your ears stopped and your tight lips curled?

---

[19] Boyce-Tillman, *A Rainbow to Heaven*, p. 45; to the tune usually used for "Christ is made the sure foundation" (Westminster Abbey).

2. When sweet endearment leads to monstrous violence,
    And hopes are dashed and gentle trust is bruised,
    And power misused and weaknesses exploited,
    And youth's naïveté hurt and accused,
    Deep God of Love, are You within our struggling?
    Can you be found in actions of abuse?

3. We long to hope that good at last will triumph,
    And flowers grow from out the gaping wounds;
    Can resurrection joy transfigure darkness
    And shape harsh crying into beauty's tunes?
    Redeeming pow'r flow out from Jesus' story,
    Infuse our terror, find in us a room.

4. Protect us from a premature forgiveness,
    From preachers' words that reinforce the pain,
    From glib dogmatic institution statements
    That crush bright anger's liberating flame;
    So when in time the kairos moment beckons
    We will find trust in humankind regained.

5. In telling stories, listening and acceptance;
    May we perceive the action of Your grace;
    Your living shows love's Crucifixion strangeness,
    How contradictions dwell in time and space;
    Great God of question, paradox and myst'ry,
    Your Being holds us in this sacred place.[20]

For me, never has belonging been clearer than at the New Year gatherings which I have attended for over ten years. New Year is always an exciting time, and I have written several songs and hymns to celebrate it. First was this New Year song written in 1996; it has been sung regularly ever since,

---

[20]   Jan Berry and Andrew Pratt, *Hymns of Hope and Healing: Words and Music to Refresh the Church's Ministry of Healing* (London: Stainer & Bell, 2017). To the tune Finlandia—"Be still my soul".

with a wonderful stamping dance on the word "celebrate". Like many of
my pieces, it uses the four elements as seminal images for the theology:

> Come, sparkling water in celebration of a New Year
> To cleanse our deep wounds and purify our lives.
> Wash away, wash away
> All that prevents us reaching full maturity.
> Celebrate, celebrate sacred endings and beginnings.
>
> Come, fertile good earth in celebration of a New Year
> To keep us grounded in God's security.
> Form our roots, form our roots
> That we can firmly stand in all adversity.
> Celebrate, celebrate sacred endings and beginnings.
>
> Come, flowing pure air in celebration of a New Year
> To fill our bodies with consecrated health.
> Set us free, set us free,
> That we may breathe the airy Spirit's pow'r.
> Celebrate, celebrate sacred endings and beginnings.
>
> Come, shining candles in celebration of a New Year
> To burn our cold hearts and make them warm with love
> Pierce our eyes, pierce our eyes
> That we may see anew the wonders of God's world.
> Celebrate, celebrate sacred endings and beginnings.[21]

I remember dancing to this in a circle at the Millennium, high up on the
hill at a monastery, and listening to the bells in the valley.

When I was younger and fitter, on New Year's Eve we all went by
minibus to Ripon Cathedral and then down the cobbled streets to the
square, where the mayor leaned out of the town hall to offer a blessing
for the New Year while the Hornblower blew the horn. This represented
how Elizabeth always wanted to keep a foot within the wider church

---

[21] Boyce-Tillman, *A Rainbow to Heaven*, p. 106.

which she so wanted to reform. What became clear was the poverty of material, especially hymns, for the Watchnight New Year service in the cathedral. We all often critiqued it, even when one year Alice in Wonderland appeared in a blue dress. Although the cathedral never saw fit to use it, this hymn has been sung regularly at Holy Rood House:

Hymn for time of change

1. Sing high, sing low, swing free, let go,
   God of the turning round,
   In times of change may we discern
   The true angelic sound.
   For there are songs of gentler power,
   That warfare needs to hear.
   These nurturing sounds will bring us strength,
   And make the peace song clear.

2. Sing high, sing low, swing free, let go,
   God of the circling sphere,
   In looking back, may we discern
   The times you have been near.
   We face the joy, we touch the pain
   And give you thanks for both;
   We weave the two as glistening strands
   Within our travelling coat.

3. Sing high, sing low, swing free, let go,
   God of the open road,
   In moving on, may we discern
   The contents of our load;
   Help us to sift, help us to lose
   All we no longer need,
   That we may leap and dance and sing
   At Your God-chosen speed.[22]

---

22   Boyce-Tillman, *A Rainbow to Heaven*, p. 61.

When I became less fit and the cobbled streets of Ripon became an accident waiting to happen, I stayed home with others who also felt vulnerable. We used a wonderful hymn by Doug Constable, that seemed to express the sort of people who came to Holy Rood House:

1. In the Church of the Unlikely God's saints may be found;
   They are words in Love's story resounding around.
     Each person is anointed to glorify Love's Lord;
   And the people least expected now light the way forward,
       Way forward, way forward,
   And the people least expected now light the way forward.

2. In the Church of the Unlikely the last become first,
   And the silenced find their voices; fear's bubble gets burst;
     Each person is appointed to magnify Love's Lord;
   And the people least respected are brightness outpoured,
       outpoured, outpoured,
   And the people least respected are brightness outpoured.

3. In the Church of the Unlikely live fools for Christ's sake;
   They are noisy, they are nosey; fear's bondage they break.
     Each person fitly-jointed to tumble for Love's Lord;
   And the people least projected to heights are now soared,
       now soared, now soared,
   And the people least projected to heights are now soared.

4. In the Church of the Unlikely the Sp'rit is not quenched;
   Charismatic, and ecstatic, by Love folk get drenched.
     Each person is acquainted with Jesus and Love's Lord;
   And the people least accepted sit right at heav'n's board,
       heav'n's board, heav'n's board
   And the people least accepted sit right at heav'n's board.

5. In the Church of the Unlikely the Trinity's all;
One for all, and all for each one, and upward the call.
Each person integrated, embodying Love's Lord:
Mother-Father, Son-and-Daughter, in Spirit's accord,
accord, accord,
Mother-Father, Son-and-Daughter, in Spirit's accord.[23]

In the years when the weather was really bad—snow falling on the wonderful landscape of Yorkshire—everyone joined us, as we moved through the house celebrating earth, air, fire and water and making a new start. The liturgy was really created by everyone, and included pieces chosen by participants such as:

Waiting Time by Jan Younger

I'm here once again
Returned to the sacred space and I wait.
Suspended: betwixt and between.
Not fully arrived from whence I came.
Nor very sure of what lies ahead.
Like a butterfly inside a cocoon waiting
To complete the transformation
Of this long-forgotten creature
Hidden in the dark.[24]

When we were all together, I adapted a wassailing song for the wonderful community. Here are a few verses:

---

[23] Doug Constable, *Strength and Tenderness: Hymns, Songs, Poems* (Cambria Books, 2021).

[24] Jan Younger, *Seeking the Hidden Way: A Poetry Collection* (Thirsk: Holy Rood House Publications, 2013).

CHORUS: Wassail! wassail! all over the town,
Our bread it is white and our ale it is brown;
Our bowl it is made of the white maple tree;
With the wassailing bowl, we'll drink unto thee.

So here is to Stanley and to his right cheek
Pray God send our master a good piece of beef
And a good piece of beef that may we all see
With the wassailing bowl, we'll drink unto thee.

Here's to Elizabeth, and to her right eye,
Pray God send our mistress a good Christmas pie;
A good Christmas pie as e'er I did see,
With my wassailing bowl we'll drink unto thee.

Then here's to Elaine in the lily-white smock,
Who tripped to the door and slipped back the lock;
Who tripped to the door and pulled back the pin
For to let these jolly wassailers in.

Be here any flowers? I suppose there be some;
Sure they will not stay put when Elsie has come.
Sing hey O, Elsie! Come put water in,
And you fair maid will let us all in.

So here's to this house, and all gathered here,
Pray God send all in her a happy new year:
A happy new year as e'er they did see,
With my wassailing bowl we drink to all thee.[25]

The other part of the gatherings at New Year where I really felt I belonged was the evenings when we played games and offered poetry and songs of our own choosing. These always reminded me of my childhood gatherings where I felt I really belonged with my grandparents. Beautiful

---

[25]   June Boyce-Tillman (unpublished).

poems emerged in these gatherings, often being created during the gathering itself, such as Ruth Sillar's poem, of which this is the first verse:

New Leaf

Today is the first day of my new book.
I've written the date
and underlined it
in red felt-tip
with a ruler
I'm going to be different
with this book.

There were also communally sung offerings which included Stanley singing *Silver Threads among the Gold* or *Come into the Garden, Maud*. The song sheets became more modern over the years, but I cherish the old memories of my own childhood within the old and fading sheets, from which I often played on the old upright piano. Stanley always offered *Macavity* from T. S. Eliot's *Old Possum's Book of Practical Cats*. Elizabeth and, later, Carolyn made sure we were all plied with drinks of various kinds and treats, while Elaine Wisdom trimmed and tended all the candles. The game initiated by Pat, called *The Fattest Robin*, generated much mock rivalry and general laughter. The repeated nature of each year reminded me of older days when such gatherings were more commonplace, now often replaced by karaoke. The song I sang, *The Cat came back*, happened every year by popular request. It dates from Harry Miller in 1893 with various additions over the years, and starts:

Old Mister Johnson had troubles of his own
He had a yellow cat which wouldn't leave its home;
He tried and he tried to give the cat away,
He gave it to a man going far, far away.
But the cat came back the very next day,
The cat came back, we thought he was a goner
But the cat came back; it just couldn't stay away.

It is a wonderful resurrection song, for the cat is still there at the end after numerous attempts to get rid of it, including a hurricane and a range of bombs.

Justice has always been central to Elizabeth's theology, starting with the ordination of women but widening out into many marginalized groups. Belonging for Elizabeth includes justice for all the world, and the beautiful prayers for peace at midday, with the table covered by a map of the world, are close to her heart. She loves this hymn, written for another gathering, for which it was rejected; however, like so many rejected people, it found a place in Holy Rood House's liturgy.[26]

1. Compassion flows and warms our hearts
Calls upon us to free the earth.
The barriers fall; divisions end;
And everyone can claim their worth.
The poor can speak, the fearful stand,
The dispossessed can claim the hills,
And justice reigns and peace prevails
Reshaped through God's transforming skills.

2. And all shall teach the common good,
See that all life is interlinked;
The fertile soil will yield for all
Life-giving food, reviving drink.
Respect for God, Creative Love,
Will honour humans, trees and rocks,
Build universities of hope
Where Wisdom's power is unlocked.

3. And so we make our kinship here
Echo the one that reigns in heav'n,
Where each is valued in God's love
And to that mercy says Amen.
The convicts leap, the outcasts dance,

---

[26]   June Boyce-Tillman (October 2009, unpublished). To the tune Jerusalem.

The trapped throw off addiction's chains.
All sing in Christ the freedom song
Created from our joys and pains.

In Elizabeth's own writing, her longing for justice is beautifully expressed in *Call to Prayer*:

We hear the call to prayer from the mosques
The peal of bells from the bell towers

We see Sabbath candles lit
In basement flats
And the proud houses of the suburbs

We smell the fragrant temple air
Listening to guitars on street corners

We hear the cries from baby lungs
And the flicker of recognition
In the voice of the old

We sense the sounds of love in the night air
And the contented gulps of a child at the breast

Longing for home
We are accompanied by flutes in subways
Calling us to act for justice
When the muffled cries of the hurt and the wounded lie still
With the silence of the abused
Lying in the shadows

We look to the open secrets of God
To disturb and unrest the secrets of oppression

Through all the danger and chaos
Be present . . .
Be for us the risk we must take
For love
And
For living.[27]

Elizabeth initiated beautiful art displays in Juliet House (then called Thorpe House) regularly. They inspired theological thinking and devotion. I remember clearly the Guild of Health conference on 5 April 2014, with the Gethsemane Garments of Peter Privett of the Westhill Endowment. Bishop John Pritchard inspired us with the notion of inhabiting the world through observing or even wearing the beautiful garments; this inspired the hymn that follows, but it also represents Elizabeth's desire that we are aware of and empathetic with the pain of the world in general:

1. I inhabit the birth, the birth of the world,
   Of all that is coming to be.

2. I inhabit the pain, the pain of the world,
   The land is laid waste with that pain.

3. I inhabit the tears, the tears of the world,
   My eyes flow with grief for our world.

4. I inhabit the hope, the hope in our world,
   The shoots of new life in our world.

5. I inhabit the joy, the joy of the world,
   A blessing restored for our world.[28]

---

27   Elizabeth Baxter, *Holy Rood House Community Prayer* (Thirsk: Holy Rood House Publications, 2017), p. 23.

28   June Boyce-Tillman (2014, unpublished).

Becoming

Elizabeth embraced the healing ministry of the church following Holy Rood House's predecessors, both Spennithorne House and the Sisters of the Holy Rood, who had lived in Holy Rood House. So, through her ministry, the House has become a place of becoming. The church has not been a safe space for many groups of people whose stories have not been told. At the heart of Christian faith is the therapeutic journey of the Crucifixion/Resurrection story. At Holy Rood House, this is interpreted not as a set of doctrines creating guilt and fear but rather as a journey of hope and liberation. Through Elizabeth's vision, the community reflects the way Jesus accompanied people on their journeys, and his own need for a therapeutic community, the home of Mary, Martha and Lazarus at Bethany, where he felt welcomed and even enjoyed foot massage! The notebooks in every room tell the stories of transformation.

Elizabeth has always been thirsty for knowledge and new ideas. She has always been on her own journey, and as part of that she set up the Centre for the Study of Theology and Health, with its rich library and its publications, such as *Wounds that Heal*,[29] that have explored new theological/spiritual developments:

> We are living through one of the most significant religious paradigm shifts, since the Protestant Reformation in the sixteenth century . . . The different worlds of spirituality that are emerging are not simply due to young people ditching formal religion or the archaic formulas of doctrinal creeds—both of which are real— but more so, the new religious consciousness reflects a new type of person emerging in evolution. To put this metaphorically: we are not rearranging the furniture in the same house; rather, the house is being demolished and a new one is being constructed.[30]

---

[29] Jonathan Baxter (ed.), *Wounds that Heal: Theology, Imagination and Health* (London: SPCK, 2007).

[30] <https://christogenesis.org/religion-in-transition-living-between-the-worlds-of-god/>, accessed 2 April 2024.

Holy Rood House has been an important part of Elizabeth's own journey. She has developed her poetry and her photography skills in relation to the Holy Rood Community (as well as undertaking endless fundraising). As a leader, she models the journeying for all who visit. Elizabeth is a person who, in my opinion, will never have arrived, will always be moving on. For Stanley's seventieth birthday, I wrote a song, of which this is the opening, but it could have been written for Elizabeth as well:

> CHORUS: Moving on, moving on, we must keep on moving on,
> For the Spirit is calling us on
> We must walk the God walk; we must talk the God talk;
> For our God keeps on travelling on.
>
> We must pack in the sack that we carry on our back,
> (As we keep on travelling on)
> All the things we will need to keep up with God's speed
> For the Spirit keeps calling us on.[31]

Many of the participants in Holy Rood House are on a journey:

> This is the first place where I have felt safe enough to feel unsafe.
>
> My time here has definitely been an adventure and the start of a new stage of my journey.

Holy Rood House is a place where many embark on profound life changes and these endings need to be turned into new beginnings as in the New Year song above. It is a place of pilgrimage—a hospitable inn in a life journey.

Spending time in places without the daily routines, distractions and comforts allows for the possibility of inner struggles to emerge and be resolved. In the language of psychotherapy, we might say that spending time in the outer wilderness enables an exploration of the inner wilderness, the unconscious.[32]

---

[31]   Boyce-Tillman, *A Rainbow to Heaven*, p. 138.

[32]   N. Totton, *Wild Therapy: Undomesticating Inner and Outer Worlds* (Monmouth: PCCS Books, 2011).

Elizabeth's embracing of the garden has facilitated many of these journeys. This involved a rethinking of God:

> We are asking whether one way to remythologize the Gospel for our time might not be through the metaphor of the world as God's "body" rather than as the king's "realm". . . . When the world is viewed as God's body, that body includes more than just Christians and more than just human beings.[33]

The garden now includes a labyrinth; but I remember building one with string and ribbons as part of a session on Music and Healing. People danced it, walked it slowly, sang it and so on. Even the teenage son of one of the cooks crept out surreptitiously to try it. It is a wonderful meditative tool and transforms a small space into a long walk.

Elizabeth's vision for Holy Rood House is now deeply imbued with ecological awareness, and in the purchase of Holy Rood House she insisted that the garden should be a necessary part of the deal. From the twentieth century she has followed ecotheologians, among them the former patron of the house, Professor Mary Grey, who comments:

> People feel accepted as they are in all the pain, brokenness and fragmentation, in their vulnerability and fragility. It is also very striking in the poems people wrote here, that it is the link with the earth, nature and with the place itself that is the healing experience. They write about birdsong "the joy of the blackbird's song" . . . the snowdrops, starlings and clear autumn skies.[34]

The birthing explored in the first section of this chapter is also caught up in the becoming:

---

[33] Sallie McFague, *Models of God: Theology for an Ecological, Nuclear Age* (Minneapolis, MN: Fortress Press, 1987), pp. 61–71.

[34] Elizabeth Baxter, *Poetry and Art from Holy Rood House: A Celebration of 25 Years 1993–2018* (Thirsk: Holy Rood House Publications, 2018).

The entire universe is a continual process of emergence, in which nothing is certain or fixed, but is always becoming itself through its intra-action with everything else.[35]

In this becoming, belonging and creativity are central to theology. To be "non-binary, decentralized, unknowing . . . is to reject utterly the false dichotomies that produce violence as the direct consequence of inequality".[36] This means embracing paradoxical ways of knowing:

CHORUS: Come, healing power, that fills the cosmic space,
  Reveal in greening growth your lively grace.

1. You curled with joy within a woman's womb,
Wandered dark deserts, opened wide a tomb.
CHORUS

2. Birthed in a darkness shafted by love's light,
Like clouds at midday, moonshine in the night.
CHORUS

3. Born in a war, you call us to forgive;
So reconciled, we lovingly can live.
CHORUS

4. Healer of woundings, perfuming our lives
With Wisdom's saging, quieten our cries.
CHORUS

5. Flow through our bodies, activate our minds,
Lead us through forests, sharing bread and wine.
CHORUS.[37]

---

[35]   James Bridle, *Ways of Being: Animals, Plants, Machines: The Search for a Planetary Intelligence* (London: Penguin Random House, 2022).

[36]   Bridle, *Ways of Being*, p. 213.

[37]   June Boyce-Tillman (July–Sept 2017, unpublished). To the tune Crucifer by Sydney Nicholson; usually used for "Lift high the cross".

Many of my hymns have followed Elizabeth's vision, as the pilgrimage of our planet turns ecologically:

> Sing a song of whirling worms,
> Deep within a mud-soaked soil,
> Wellspring of our verdancy,
> Processing with endless toil.
>
> Tell your stories, crawling ones,
> Circling round the roots and rocks;
> As you green the land above
> Hidden Wisdom is unlocked.
>
> Ancient healing cavern pools,
> Underworld of dust and dark,
> Turn detritus into gold—
> Substance of the bear and lark.
>
> In the tunnelling of God's grace
> We are rooted deep in earth,
> Smear us with your dirt and grit
> For in darkening God gives birth.[38]

Summary

We all hope that Holy Rood House will carry on developing thanks to Elizabeth's vision. I tried to encapsulate this in a hymn I wrote for the anniversary of Holy Rood House. A summary of the atmosphere Elizabeth has created is in verse 3. It is sung to Stanley's favourite hymn tune, *Great is Thy Faithfulness*:

---

[38] June Boyce-Tillman (May 2021, unpublished). To the tune Aberystwyth by Joseph Parry; usually used for "Jesu, Lover of my soul".

Times for returning and times for a journey,
Times to look forward and times to look back;
Reshape our mem'ries, support our forgiving,
Urge our unloading and help us repack.

CHORUS:
Great is Thy faithfulness! Great is Thy faithfulness!
Morning and evening new mercies we see.
All we have needed Thy hand hath provided;
Loving community guides us to Thee.

We are rejoicing and we are lamenting,
Dancing together and sharing our tears.
Walks on the hillside and sleep for refreshment
Bring joyful wonder and soothing for fears.
CHORUS

Place for renewal, rethinking, reworking,
Where faith seeks justice and fairness for all;
Warm hospitality, joy in belonging
Can set us free from what holds us in thrall.
CHORUS.[39]

One of Elizabeth's favourite phrases is "worshipping at the shrine of St
Mattress", as a metaphor for staying in bed rather than attending what
was going on—so line 3 of verse 2 could be: "Walks on the hillside and
sleep with St Mattress", which would enable us all to reflect on the joy
that Elizabeth brought to her ministry at Holy Rood House.

---

[39]   June Boyce-Tillman (30 December 2016, unpublished). To the tune
       Faithfulness, by William Marion Runyan, 1923.

4

Creating place and space: A reflection on the unique offering of Holy Rood House and the pioneering role of Elizabeth Baxter

Jenny Kartupelis

Whether healing from trauma, living with the challenges of a mental or physical health problem, or simply seeking a path forward in life, guests of Holy Rood House have, for the last 30 years, been offered an environment that enables them to draw deep upon themselves and their own, untapped resources to find a way forward into the light of hope. This does not just happen by chance but as the result of the theological and practical insights of a steadfast leader able to bring a varied community with her and support the individual talents of each person.

Insights of those visiting Holy Rood House

This short essay focusses on the practical achievements of Elizabeth (with her husband, Stanley, for many years) in forging the unique environment of Holy Rood House, and draws primarily on the testaments of its guests and those of community members. For those not familiar with Holy Rood House, each guest room has a small visitor book, in which those staying can record thoughts on their visit and how (if at all) it has changed them. These "bedroom books" often contain the inmost and very personal contemplations of guests, generally recording only a first or no name, so they are in effect anonymous.

In 2021, I was given the privilege of access to these, in total covering many years from the early days of the establishment—that is, from 1993 onwards—with the purpose of writing a report that could reflect how guests see the interaction between their personal journey and their experience of a visit. Their thoughts provide a powerful way to help us to understand how a very effective healing environment can be shaped by a community that is held together over a long period of time under the aegis of the right person. The "voices" of the guests were complemented by five in-depth interviews with staff and volunteers. Illustrative examples of their words also appear here in quotation marks.

What helps people to find their strength?

Many guests arrive feeling "broken". A significant number of them may also feel "unsafe" in their everyday lives: unable to risk being or expressing who they are, threatened by attacks on their character, or even physically threatened. Their lives may be turbulent and insecure in various ways.

Whatever guests bring to Holy Rood House with them—pain, loss, rejection—is actively received into the community, a process that happens gradually as guests, staff and volunteers talk, eat and pray together. There is also an implicit challenge: acceptance cannot equate to total inclusiveness because, while the Holy Rood House community may not exclude anyone, its acceptance of some people will lead to others excluding themselves. In this respect, Holy Rood House models Christ's advocacy for the marginalized regardless of alienating the opinion of "conventional" voices.

It also provides the security of acceptance. Safety and security are closely related but are not the same thing. One is about being protected from harm, while the other is more about feeling free to act as one wishes without any harms arising. Security can also mean being known and knowing others and is closely related to acceptance and belonging. Holy Rood House provides people with the security they need to move forward and make their own changes, rather than being the disempowered subjects of change.

Creativity runs through all aspects of the Holy Rood House process of liberating guests to reimagine their strength. The opportunity to create art, crafts, music and writing is empowering in itself; some guests may also value what they have created, while for others that is almost irrelevant in comparison to the transformative process. Many referred in the bedroom books to finding new ways and paths on their journey, and also used beautifully creative phrases to describe their experience: "My creativity emerged like a butterfly" or "I can pray through art".

Elizabeth has led Holy Rood House through many challenging times—not least the Covid-19 pandemic—and has helped the community to respond to change, yet at the same time has maintained a sense of constancy that will take it forward far into the future. For guests, this is the place where they can come and find what they expect and need. A place where there are no new losses to face.

"Peace" is the single most commonly occurring word in the bedroom books. The desperate need for peace on the part of those who come to Holy Rood House is palpable in their writings. It seems to be both a good in itself and also a precursor to healing. People need to be away from the turbulence and trauma of their lives to experience the calm and reflection in which healing is rooted. At Holy Rood House, they are guided gently towards finding their own inner resources to heal and be restored.

Building a place of healing

Elizabeth's commitment has always been to envision a place and space where people can find their own healing by re-creating their lives and individual powers: a therapeutic community. The development of Holy Rood House has, therefore, been an ongoing and delicate balance between supporting guests and setting them free to be part of their world again. This is not a simple trajectory: many people will return again and again, sometimes to renew their belief (in themselves, the presence of God, the wisdom of Sophia) and sometimes because Holy Rood House has quite simply become their spiritual home, possibly for the rest of their lives.

Guests say that they feel "held", "enfolded", "embraced" and validated in their choices: "Holy Rood is like a big hug". The enfolding is embodied through therapies, counselling and meals that nourish with delicious food: "Each meal was a thoughtful and inclusive experience." It is a carefully envisioned physical and emotional environment.

Holy Rood House has neither the monkish austerity nor the exclusive sybaritic vibe that the word "retreat" may conjure up. Laughter can often be heard in the communal lounges and dining room; the art room provides all that is needed for experimenting with paints and crafts; guests and community alike may coax lovely music from the piano in the main lounge. Interestingly, "laughter" is another of the most commonly occurring words in the bedroom books: "Thank you for giving me the space to laugh."

Complementing the companionship available, the guest rooms—each individual and reminiscent of the home that some will have lost along the way—are totally private: "It feels like this room was made for me—I feel so protected"; "This room is a stable place of quiet". Together with the two chapels, there is the choice of spaces for reflection and reconstruction of lives that feel broken or on the edge.

The room arrangement and interior design of Holy Rood House speaks of choice and is a vital part of the overarching atmosphere of acceptance. Each guest can be as sociable or otherwise as they wish. The house provides an apparently effortless but actually very carefully managed blend of joy, companionship, solitude and privacy. By leading in the creation of such a distinctive place over many years, Elizabeth has both pioneered and given the world an important model of healing.

Spiritual life: Everyone matters

Holy Rood House (which is actually two buildings, the other being Juliet House, as well as a garden for contemplation) is a purposeful community of staff and volunteers (to say nothing of the animals, including Thomas's "Tortoise therapy"!). Whether they live there or very nearby, it is their home. They give of their time, experience and themselves, while Elizabeth has maintained the vital balance between the blessings of giving and receiving. Guests and community are equally important, without an obvious "them" and "us", yet with the privacy of the community being subtly upheld.

Guests feel accepted into the family of Holy Rood House, saying: "I arrived as a stranger but leave as part of the family" and "I was told today I was like family—thank you". Yet at the same time, members of the residential community feel protected and supported by each other, and by the spiritual life nurtured by the community's leader.

Some guests may not be faith adherents, while others may be wrestling with aspects of their religion. The prayer life of the community holds them whether or not they are physically present. For some, this is vitally important, perhaps the most important part of their relationship with Holy Rood House, and the Christian services in the chapel give a structure to their lives. For others, it is a background theme, in which they are not actively engaged, but may sense it as part of the "enfolding": "The generosity of spirit permeates this place".

"Home" is a state of being as well as a physical space, and opening one's home to others is always a risky as well as a rewarding business. To provide a community and family to each other and to guests who may be demanding and very needy represents a cost to the staff and volunteers, but also a source of fulfilment. The Holy Rood House model is one that could inform the development of any setting where there is the possibility of people being asked to give too much, or guests simply to be the recipients of care; it recognizes that where care is a "one way" flow, there can be a loss rather than a restoration of autonomy.

Other writers in this book are reflecting on the lived theology of Elizabeth; suffice it to say here that without the gentle Christian ethos she has encouraged and lived, Holy Rood House could not offer the transformation that it does.

> If I was a runner bean, you'd have been able to see me growing.
> I leave today with hope, where there was none before.

5

The beating heart of Holy Rood House and what happens there: Elizabeth Baxter's pioneering leadership of worship

Nicola Slee

"The more one becomes a feminist, the more difficult it becomes to go to church." So said Rosemary Radford Ruether in 1983, in her groundbreaking *Sexism and God-Talk*.[1] I reiterated this conviction in my 2003 introduction to feminist theology, *Faith and Feminism*, some 20 years later.[2] I wish I could say this is no longer the case in 2024, four decades after Ruether's original statement. Alas, I cannot. I think it's fair to say (though I haven't done any systematic research to test it out) that the majority of churches of all mainstream denominations in the UK show little, if any, knowledge of feminist theology or feminist liturgy; or, if they do, it is often superficial and/or contradicted by their theologies. The liturgies, sermons, prayers, hymns and images we meet in many churches shout aloud the ongoing dominance of patriarchal ways of thinking, worshipping, praying and behaving. The liturgical commission of the Church of England remains lukewarm and cautious about taking on board feminist insights in its revisions of liturgy, doubtless through a concern not to alienate sections of the church which uphold patriarchal theologies. What I call "the hegemony of the he" is still enormously

---

[1] Rosemary Radford Ruether, *Sexism and God-Talk: Towards a Feminist Theology* (London: SCM Press, 1983), pp. 193–4.

[2] Nicola Slee, *Faith and Feminism: An Introduction to Christian Feminist Theology* (London: Darton, Longman & Todd, 2003), p. 83.

powerful. There are exceptions, and I am enormously grateful to belong to a parish church and a theological education institution that are such alternative spaces.[3] I might well have left the church had I not been able to find alternative spaces to support, nurture and uphold my own feminist convictions, my lesbian identity and my intellectual curiosity. Holy Rood House is, of course, one such space, and Elizabeth Baxter is the person, above all, who has shaped and led it over the decades that she has been Director.

What I want to do in this short space is therefore to laud and celebrate the fact that, whenever I come to Holy Rood House, I know that I will not experience the kind of patriarchal language, actions or theologies that I routinely experience in many churches. Elizabeth has been absolutely resolute and consistent in her commitment to feminist prayer and feminist liturgy, as well as feminist theology, over the decades that she has been Director of Holy Rood House. I, and the hundreds of other people who come to Holy Rood House, know that when we walk into the chapel, we will experience thoughtful, inclusive, creative and engaging liturgy that is welcoming, energizing, healing and relevant to our own lives and what is going on in our world. We don't have to hold our breath or steel ourselves to cope with dominating leadership, excluding theologies or out-of-touch liturgy. We are welcomed into a space that is always carefully prepared, with attention to colour, symbols that resonate and a simplicity and unclutteredness which speak to our souls. We know we are safe here, and that we are free to come and go as we please. We can relax and be who we are and experience a communal sharing that is liberating and healing.

At the same time, we know that we will be challenged and encouraged to consider our faith, our lives and our society critically and politically, with a strong justice orientation. This is liturgy for transformation, at an individual, a social and a cosmic level. When liturgy enacts truth about who we are and what we may become, as well as truth about the state of the world in which we live and how we may act positively in the world, it *is* itself an act of transformative justice. As Janet Walton puts it, "Feminist liturgy seeks to engage imagination, resist discrimination,

---

3   All Saints parish church, Kings Heath, Birmingham and the Queen's Foundation for Ecumenical Theological Education, Birmingham, respectively.

summon wonder, receive blessing and strengthen hope. It intends to enact redeemed, free and empowered relationships."[4] This could serve as a good summary of the kind of worship Holy Rood House aspires towards and embodies.

Many people at Holy Rood House help to create such beautiful, liberating, justice-oriented liturgy, and many people lead worship here, but Elizabeth has led the way and opened the door for many, one amongst a not large number of pioneering feminist liturgists in the UK. I want to mention some of the features of the liturgy that Elizabeth, with others, creates and that we experience at Holy Rood House.

First of all, Elizabeth knows that liturgy is created out of many different elements, not only, or even primarily, language. She recognizes the different discourses within liturgy that Marjorie Procter-Smith draws attention to, in her primer of feminist liturgy, *In Her Own Rite*: "the verbal language of prayer, of song, of acclamation, of creed; the kinaesthetic language of gesture, of posture, of movement; and the visual language of art, icon and space".[5] Procter-Smith does not refer to aural discourse which would include music and other sounds beyond spoken words, but this is another important dimension of liturgy. I want to consider each of these discourses and the way in which, at Holy Rood House, we experience them as emancipatory, in a range of ways.

If we think of the space in which worship is conducted at Holy Rood House, the chapel expresses an open, oval area in which worshippers gather on the level (no one is elevated above anyone else), in the round and face to face.[6] There is no "front" or "back", and all are equal in the gathered space. The energy and the power flow around the circle, and leadership is facilitative rather than calling attention to itself. The chapel opens out to the gardens, so that there is a porous boundary between

---

[4]   Janet R. Walton, *Feminist Liturgy: A Matter of Justice* (Collegeville, MN: Liturgical Press, 2000).

[5]   Marjorie Procter-Smith, *In Her Own Rite: Constructing Feminist Liturgical Tradition* (Nashville: Abingdon Press, 1990), p. 62.

[6]   For more on this, see my essay "Riting the Body: Making and Reclaiming Liturgical Space", in *Fragments for Fractured Times: What Feminist Practical Theology Brings to the Table* (London: SCM Press, 2020), pp. 60–78.

"inside" and "outside", the natural world and the constructed, human world. Sometimes liturgies take place outside in the gardens or move from chapel to garden or vice versa (and there is a whole section of garden prayers in the Community Prayer Book[7]). Whether inside or outside, we are in touch with the sustaining earth and the dynamic flow and flavour of each season. The solid earth upholds us, growing plants absorb toxic elements and cleanse the air, birds and other creatures join in the human worship, and we know ourselves to be one with all created matter. There are also prayers for other parts of the community in the Community Prayer Book: the conference room, library, kitchen, counselling room, resource room/office, arts studio, children's room and living space,[8] emphasizing that each space is prayed in and inhabited by the Spirit.

The chapel space itself is ordered and adorned with symbols and objects that have been carefully chosen to enhance what the space itself proclaims. The eucharistic table is always present, reminding worshippers of the way in which we are fed and nourished by God, even when the worship is not eucharistic. Colours of the different liturgical seasons mark the changing rhythm and foci of the liturgical year. Sculptures celebrating the human form, particularly the female form, speak of the sacredness of flesh and the embodied nature of our lives. Candles and flowers, water, symbols and images from the Bible and from human experience "speak" to worshippers at a profound level, beyond the operation of the conscious mind. There are no imposing, dominating symbols of cross or crucifix, which valorise violence and Jesus's shedding of blood while ignoring the life-giving blood of women and the life orientation of feminist worship. At the same time, the cross of Jesus is honoured in cross prayers around a cross.[9]

Within this beautiful, deeply prayed-in space, worshippers are free to come and go as they please, to stand, sit or kneel and to participate as actively or passively as they wish. There is no coercion. There is an

---

[7]   Elizabeth Baxter, *Holy Rood House Community Prayer* (Thirsk: Holy Rood House Publications, 2017) pp. 59–67.

[8]   *Holy Rood House Community Prayer*, pp. 48–9.

[9]   *Holy Rood House Community Prayer*, pp. 34, 41.

invitation to join in printed words of prayers or hymns and songs, but there is an acceptance that individuals may approach or withdraw in their own time and space. There is a deep awareness, embedded into every aspect of life at Holy Rood House, that many who come have been deeply hurt by the dominating and excluding hierarchies and theologies of the church, as well as by coercive violence in the home or by bullying and discrimination in the workplace, by various forms of deprivation and poverty, or simply by the overwhelming pace and relentless demands of contemporary life. Hence, every care is taken to create an environment that is safe, warm, nurturing and healing. The chapel is not the only place where this is experienced, but it is the beating heart of the house, and what happens here ripples into the rest of what goes on in meeting rooms, therapeutic spaces, the art room and the dining room. It is all of a piece, and all speaks of the sheltering, healing love of God. There is a recognition that, unless and until worshippers feel safe, included and met in a genuine, authentic manner, they will not be capable of responding to the challenges of faith—challenges which are explored in much of the educational work of Holy Rood House and often brought into worship through readings, prayers, visual images and in other ways.

Profound attention is paid to the way that bodies move and speak, and the way that bodies carry the wounds and scars of their histories. Touch is offered gently and never coercively, with an awareness that touch may be traumatic for some. Worship offers an opportunity to experience closeness and togetherness without coercion, and it is always possible to leave. Worshippers are not commanded to kneel for confession or bow their heads for a blessing, as often happens in churches. There is a freedom for bodies to sit, stand, move and gesture as they will. Circle dances which join worshippers in a circle, touching lightly and moving in simple, repeated patterns to a range of music from different cultures and contexts, is one expression of the unity with freedom that we experience in this healing place. Body prayers by Jan Berry[10] and breath prayers[11] are another expression of the beauty and fragility of the body and a

---

[10]   *Holy Rood House Community Prayer*, p. 27.
[11]   *Holy Rood House Community Prayer*, p. 58.

recognition that the body has a deep need to pray. Christian prayer is never disembodied.

Times and seasons are marked, celebrated and reflected upon in ways that chime in with the church's liturgical year, but the community also recognizes times and seasons that the church has not always honoured or recognized. Liminal spaces of the day—morning and evening—are marked with attention to their significance within the rhythm of the week, each morning welcomed as an opportunity for fresh adventure and discovery and each evening as an opportunity to let go "the anxieties of the day" and "the fears of the night", preparing gently for sleep.[12] The liturgies speak, too, of the worshippers' reality, whether tearful, prayerful, hopeful, joyful, playful, mindful, restful or peaceful.[13] Saints are honoured,[14] including female saints such as Julian of Norwich.[15] Ordinary (extraordinary?) human friendship is also honoured, and God recognized as "Holy Befriender", "Holy Mentor" and "Holy Advocate".[16] There are, of course, many prayers for healing, since healing is so central to the work of Holy Rood House; but also prayers for ministry and commissioning, prayers of blessing for a community or home, pastoral services of baptism, the blessing of relationships, the death of a loved one, including an unborn child, the scattering of ashes and our own passing. Animals, birds and plants as well as humans are honoured in prayers and liturgies.[17] There are prayers for water and stories around the well.[18] In all these liturgies, traditional and biblical images are placed next to new and emerging images and names, so that "treasures old and new" (Matthew 13:52) comingle and mix, and each illuminates the other.

I have come to verbal discourse—the use of words, texts, hymns and formal liturgies—last, not because it is not important, but because it is embedded within the other discourses of space, visual language and

---

12   *Holy Rood House Community Prayer*, p. 180.

13   *Holy Rood House Community Prayer*, p. 24.

14   *Holy Rood House Community Prayer*, pp. 147–52.

15   *Holy Rood House Community Prayer*, p. 123.

16   *Holy Rood House Community Prayer*, p. 157.

17   *Holy Rood House Community Prayer*, pp. 20–1.

18   *Holy Rood House Community Prayer*, p. 6.

imagery, and bodily comportment and movement. Much attention, in the literature of feminist theology and liturgy, has focussed on language, and of course this is crucial, but there is a danger of ignoring the other discourses which often work at a deeper, subliminal level. The way we speak about God and human beings, as well as creation; the kinds of language we use in confession, creed, thanksgiving and eucharist; the words we sing in hymns or listen to in choral pieces, are all absolutely vital in creating the kinds of theologies and awareness that are either liberating or oppressive, healing or wounding, empowering or demeaning. Elizabeth has led the way in crafting language that is creative, healing, inspiring and freeing, as is evident in the Community Prayer Book.

The liturgies in the community's prayer book are deeply embedded in the trinitarian theology that is at the heart of Christianity but expressed in such a way as to expand and evolve our awareness of the nature and names of God, Jesus and Spirit. God is named as the God of grace,[19] the source of life,[20] the one who calls into community;[21] gentle one who befriends us,[22] God of creation, generosity, love, passion, wisdom and peace,[23] as well as Lover.[24] God is the God of silence, word and becoming.[25] Explicitly feminine terms for God abound: God our midwife, life giver, the birther of life, and so on.[26] But even when names and images for God are not overtly feminine, they are always inclusive and often suggest women's experience and gifts. Jesus is healer and companion,[27] accompanying one,[28] Christ, Sophia and Christa,[29] "Child of grace", "Emmanuel",[30] "Holy

---

[19] *Holy Rood House Community Prayer*, p. 8 and many other places.

[20] *Holy Rood House Community Prayer*, p. 9.

[21] *Holy Rood House Community Prayer*, pp. 9, 18–19, etc.

[22] *Holy Rood House Community Prayer*, p. 10.

[23] *Holy Rood House Community Prayer*, pp. 16–17.

[24] *Holy Rood House Community Prayer*, p. 104.

[25] *Holy Rood House Community Prayer*, p. 29.

[26] *Holy Rood House Community Prayer*, p. 33 and elsewhere.

[27] *Holy Rood House Community Prayer*, p. 13.

[28] *Holy Rood House Community Prayer*, p. 14.

[29] *Holy Rood House Community Prayer*, p. 73 and elsewhere.

[30] *Holy Rood House Community Prayer*, p. 80.

befriender",[31] "Home-gatherer",[32] "calmer of the distressed", "lifter of those who fall" and "carrier of the weak".[33] The risen Christ appears as "Holy Dancer", "soaring from the grave with cosmic rhythm".[34] The Spirit is "compassionate",[35] "inspiring",[36] "quencher of my thirst", "companion in my loneliness", "guardian of my soul",[37] "River Dancer",[38] "Cosmic Dancer",[39] "Holy Mover".[40] The Spirit is playful, the Spirit of adventure, and also veiled, visiting in surprise and newness and blazing in fire.[41] Holy Wisdom is acknowledged in the person of Christ and the Spirit. This is only some of the rich multiplicity of God language and imagery.

Liturgies at Holy Rood House also honour and include the work of many other feminist liturgists, so that the Community Prayer Book is the foundation text; but many other texts, hymns and songs are brought into the work of worship. Hymns by June Boyce-Tillman, Jan Berry and Brian Wren, amongst others, are often used, along with music from Iona and Taizé, while prayers by Janet Morley, June Boyce-Tillman, Jan Berry, the St Hilda Community and Nicola Slee (!) are often employed. New prayers, poems and blessings written by guests are also incorporated into worship, so that there is a sense that the prayer book is open and constantly being added to. Prayer and praise are not static but ever shifting and open to the blowing wind of the Spirit.

In all these, and many other, ways, the worship we experience at Holy Rood House is deeply educative and therapeutic, not in any heavy-handed,

---

[31]   *Holy Rood House Community Prayer*, p. 82.

[32]   *Holy Rood House Community Prayer*, p. 85—a good example of a term which is non-gender-specific but might well make us think of women who continue to do much of the home gathering and creating around the world.

[33]   *Holy Rood House Community Prayer*, p. 104.

[34]   *Holy Rood House Community Prayer*, p. 114.

[35]   *Holy Rood House Community Prayer*, p. 13 and elsewhere.

[36]   *Holy Rood House Community Prayer*, p. 90.

[37]   *Holy Rood House Community Prayer*, p. 104.

[38]   *Holy Rood House Community Prayer*, p. 129.

[39]   *Holy Rood House Community Prayer*, p. 131.

[40]   *Holy Rood House Community Prayer*, p. 133.

[41]   *Holy Rood House Community Prayer*, pp. 141–2, 145.

didactic way (as in many churches where "teaching" is understood as a primarily verbal, cognitive activity, very often in a form of instruction by male leaders), but in gentleness, in depth, in the congruence of all that happens here, and in ways which soak deep down into the depths of our being, both as individuals and as gathered community. Worship teaches and heals us, as it frees and sustains us, mostly when we are not aware that it is doing so, when we are open and receptive to receive the work of the Spirit within, between and around us.

I know that as Elizabeth moves on from leadership of Holy Rood House her legacy will live on in so many ways, and not least in the Community Prayer Book and the ways she has led worship, over decades, in the chapel, the garden and other spaces in the community. I know, too, that her work of gathering community and crafting liturgy is not ending, but is continuing at Hilda House, where I have been privileged to stay and see how a new house of gathering is taking shape; and I know that creative liturgy will be at the heart of all that happens in that place, alongside learning, conversation around the table, feeding and feasting, laughter and tears.

I cannot do better to end this reflection on the liturgical life of Holy Rood House, which Elizabeth has done so much to breathe into being and to nurture, than close with a blessing from the Community Prayer Book:

Glow and Flow Blessing

Now may every living being,
young or old,
living or far,
known to us or unknown,
living, departed or yet to be born.
May every living being
be blessed.

May the power and mystery go before us,
to show us the way.
Shine above us to lighten our world.
Lie beneath us to bear us up.
Walk with us and give us companionship,
And glow and flow within us to bring us joy.
Amen.[42]

---

[42]   *Holy Rood House Community Prayer*, p. 219.

6

Celebrating the audacious Elizabeth Baxter: Wine, women and song at Holy Rood House and Hilda House

Alison Jasper

I have known Elizabeth Baxter for a shorter time than many of the people who are contributing to this volume. My first visit to Holy Rood House was only a few years ago when she invited me to a meeting about liturgy and gender. But it was clear from the very beginning that here was someone of extraordinary vision and commitment, as the range of work and service apparent in Holy Rood House clearly demonstrated. Although the main work of the House focussed on healing and counselling, there was also an imperative for thinking theologically and for considering ways in which the liturgy could be made more welcoming to women. In two days of serious but companionable conversation, we discussed the language and the shape of the liturgy under the name of Vashti's Voices and the sign of the disobedient woman, recalling the wife who refused to act as dutiful royal consort/trophy bride at the beginning of the biblical book of Esther. Vashti is one of a number of biblical women who have chosen to flout the commandments of patriarchal authorities—not excepting some configurations of the divine. There was no doubt at all where Elizabeth stood, or that she was, audaciously for a woman ordained into the Church of England, on the side of those who felt profoundly let down by a church that still preferred to maintain an age-old paternalistic ascendency rather than set itself alongside the concerns of women and other marginalized communities.

But as the title of this piece suggests, this was a most enjoyable meeting—the first of many visits when I have felt warmly welcomed and have benefitted from the abundant food, beautiful setting, and ambient kindness of Holy Rood House. Though, inevitably, our work on that occasion did not produce the sea change in the liturgy that we are still hoping for, Elizabeth's initiative was an acknowledgement of the work that was still needed, and of her determination and desire to do all she could to take it forward. In Holy Rood House or at Hilda House, she continues to "stay with the trouble",[1] navigating a faithfulness to wider church communities with a tremendous energy and hope for change, and openness to what is new and different—in liturgical as in other contexts—in characteristic acts of faith and solidarity with people who are suffering and silenced.

Elizabeth has a gift for encouragement. I know there are many people connected to Holy Rood House and Hilda House who have found their own efforts and insights welcomed with open arms here and given scope for experiment and exploration. At times when I've had the privilege of sharing community life and worship in these places, new writers, composers, musicians and choreographers are drawn in, their contributions making the sacred space rich and vibrant, exciting and at times unexpected, without loss to the underlying rhythm and sustaining rule of meeting together for communal celebration and prayer. And everywhere there are books in abundance to inspire, educate and enliven. My own recent explorations of more welcoming and inclusive liturgies have owed more than a little to Elizabeth's warm encouragement; and I offer her back the following thoughts in gratitude for her help.

---

[1]   *Staying with the Trouble* is the title of a book by Donna Haraway, subtitled *Making Kin in the Chthulucene* (Durham, NC and London: Duke University Press, 2016), in which she describes her approach to the ongoing climate crisis in terms of finding better ways of living with as well as ameliorating the consequences of human exploitation. This involves a much more subtle and sophisticated appreciation of the ecologies of which we are a(n often destructive) part but which do not necessarily centre on human goals.

The disobedient woman

My first contact with Elizabeth was, as I say, under the sign of the disobedient woman in the Bible who refused to play the role assigned to her by a powerful king and lost her place as a result. Though Esther, who replaced her in the story, played a much subtler game and won both crown and a measure of control over King Ahasuerus, it is not Esther but Vashti who fronted Holy Rood House's liturgical venture. It was clearly a gesture of impatience. Though Vashti lost out in a material sense, it is hard not to applaud her refusal to be taken as a beautiful object, simply to be shown off. Today, a woman's voice is more likely to be heard, but there are still instances in which women struggle with a "malestream" approach and do not want to be forced just to manage male egos[2] in the way in which Esther clearly excelled.

When I sat down to write this piece and googled "disobedient women", two books appeared at the top of my list with this very title. They included a novel by Sangeeta Mulay (2022) set against a background of conservative forms of Hinduism,[3] and an extended piece of reportage by Sarah Stankorb, subtitled, *How a Small Group of Faithful Women Exposed Abuse, Brought Down Powerful Pastors, and Ignited an Evangelical Reckoning* (2023).[4] The setting in both cases is a culture or society framed by patriarchal assumptions, including the idea that there is a fundamental difference between men and women. Of course, there are some biological differences. But I am suspicious of fundamentalisms. The presumption

---

[2]   This is a theme taken up by the Nigerian writer Chimamand Ngozi Adichie in her book, *We Should all be Feminists* (London: Fourth Estate, 2014). Based on her own experience of growing up female in Nigeria, she suggests that a tendency to overprotect the egos of young boys means that they grow up finding it harder to cope with criticism and setbacks and this informs their relationships with women.

[3]   Sangeeta Mulay, *Disobedient Women* (Manchester: Fly on the Wall Press, 2022).

[4]   S. Stankorb, *Disobedient Women: How a Small Group of Faithful Women Exposed Abuse, Brought Down Powerful Pastors, and Ignited an Evangelical Reckoning* (Nashville, TN and New York: Worthy Publishing, 2023).

that fundamental differences exist between men and women is all too easily aligned with ideas such as men being physiologically predisposed to violence, or women having some important God-given purpose that is equal but different to that of men. These, so often, turn out just to be bad excuses for worse behaviour. At the same time, we have certainly been shaped *as if* these differences of gender are as important as the things that make us the same. In this context, liturgy can be a counterbalance to harmful patterns. Liturgy is more than the words or the actions in church on a Sunday. It motivates and informs how we occupy the world and live, every day.

Nevertheless, the disobedient woman who emerged from my Google search still has a highly ambivalent relationship with power and authority. High up on the list of links in response to my prompt was the story, recently novelized by Elizabeth Fremantle, of the seventeenth-century artist Artemesia Gentileschi, famed for her scintillating depictions of Judith beheading Holofernes from the Apocryphal book of Judith.[5] It is said that in her paintings on this theme, she portrayed herself as God's chosen instrument, the virtuous woman, Judith. The man who raped her when she was 17, while ostensibly teaching her to paint, was, correspondingly, the model for Holofernes. In the Apocryphal story, Holofernes was the unspeakably brutal Assyrian general sent by Nebuchadnezzar to wipe out the cities and nations that had resisted his attempts to invade, in a move he described as "disobeying" his commands. Gentileschi lived at a time in Europe when women's capacity to challenge power and authority was not much greater than that of the subjugated nations and tribes in the book of Judith. Her extraordinary talent could not outweigh the shame of her gender or her chattel status. Yet, she was, as one review puts it, "a survivor". Society demanded that she bow to its flawed authority, staying at home to "guard her virtue".[6] But, having gained a reputation as a woman once ruined, she owned her disobedience to social norms, establishing

5   Elizabeth Fremantle, *Disobedient: The Gripping Feminist Retelling of a Seventeenth Century Heroine Forging Her Own Destiny* (London: Penguin, Random House, 2023).

6   <https://www.independent.co.uk/news/ap-fremantle-roman-catholic-rome-caravaggio-b2389025.html>, accessed 3 April 2024.

an enduring artistic reputation as one of the finest painters in the school of Caravaggio. A living, responsive liturgy needs to handle concepts of the divine or the prerogatives of tradition with something of the same determination to move forward. And in our time, models of power and authority still have to be treated with caution. June Boyce-Tillman, a regular visitor to Holy Rood House, whose connections with this place predate mine by many years, is both determined and cautious in her hymn-writing, challenging routine references to God as "Almighty" in traditional hymn books, with her repeated references to the—female—configuration of divine Wisdom, and her "strong vulnerability . . . power and weakness entwined in God's heart."[7]

A more inclusive liturgy is the work of the people's imagination

The eucharistic liturgies currently used in the Anglican Church embody a pattern than can be traced back to the earliest Christian centuries. But, in respecting tradition, there is a danger of forgetting that theology and liturgy are works of the human imagination, practices to be undertaken in faith and hope, not just lists or laws to be followed blindly without any reference to the signs of the time. In the present urgency[8] marked by unconscionable human actions and consequent threat, but also by quite marvellous human ingenuity, we need new words, images and an intuitive capacity for grasping the implications of novelty as well as wisdom for addressing those aspects of life (and death) that are still predictable. In 2021, a small group of us organized an online conference on gender and liturgy, called *Responding to the Sacred*. In 2023, we followed this up with

---

[7]   June Boyce-Tillman, *A Rainbow to Heaven: Hymns, Songs and Chants* (London: Stainer & Bell, 2006), p. 60.

[8]   A term used by the historian of science, Donna Haraway, to describe the current situation of climate change.

a similar online conference on more inclusive liturgy.[9] Here are one or two examples of where the conversations were tending:

Cosmic thanksgiving . . .

As part of the first set of conversations in 2021, Lisa Isherwood and Marion Chatterley discussed the possibilities of moving beyond the walls of churches, often still framed in their architecture, administration and, of course, liturgical practices, by the needs of historically patriarchal cultures. In a figurative sense, Lisa Isherwood expressed a weariness with the focus on blood sacrifice. The word "eucharist" speaks to all the good we have received, not the least a home in the world in relationship with all its critters.[10] Isherwood was eager for something that expanded beyond the repeated references to torture and death, placing emphasis instead on eating together with human and other-than-human neighbours within a much larger, less human-male-centred, cosmic matrix. It put me very much in mind of celebrating the eucharist at Holy Rood House, with Elizabeth presiding at the altar in front of an open door into the garden, connections with both our neighbours and the other-than-human world outside, symbolized in this liturgical moment of crossing the threshold.

Out of the ruins . . .

In the second set of conversations in 2023, focussed on making liturgy more widely inclusive, Wren Radford and Heather Walton discussed the possibility of liturgy arising "out of the ruins". Remembering figurative and literal ruins—including the story of a fatal backward glance towards the beloved home of Lot's wife in Sodom, the blackened shell of Grenfell Tower and the abandoned seminary of St Peter's near Cardross—raised spectres of devastating loss, brutality, and moral and spiritual bankruptcy. Yet this was also a—liturgical—practice of memory and witness giving expression to grief, rage and protest as well as to the hope against hope

---

[9] *Responding to the Sacred*: YouTube link: <https://www.youtube.com/@Responding2Sacred>, accessed 3 April 2024.

[10] "In this book, 'critters' refers promiscuously to microbes, plants, animals, human and nonhumans, and sometimes even to machines." (Haraway, *Staying with the Trouble*, p. 169).

of resurrection. The artist Anselm Kiefer's endlessly repeated images of sunflower heads, shrivelled and unbeautiful, but full of seeds and the potential of new life, elicited that hope for us throughout the conversation. You can work it into your worship or thanksgiving and prayer however you like. It is a reminder of what is really at stake every day—not the least as Elizabeth and the Holy Rood House community labour to alleviate suffering and rebuild broken lives.

In the loop . . .
But the work of making liturgy more inclusive is not just about reaching for the stars. In one of the conversations in the 2023 conference, Paul Watson and Ruth Dunster talked about disability and about the decidedly unsexy matter of hearing loops. Paul is now deaf after an accident some years ago. He has good reason to understand that a properly serviced, functional hearing loop and a presiding minister who enunciates clearly, make any liturgical event more accessible and lessen the sense of isolation and exclusion that is often experienced by people with deafness and hearing loss. It's a little thing—the kind of small detail that Elizabeth, and her team at Holy Rood House, work hard at—as in using recyclable bin liners, alongside their much more ambitious plans for sharing the planet sustainably.

St Hilda of Whitby's ready response to a call by her bishop, Aidan, suggests that she was not a "disobedient woman". But she would still have had to be determined—if not audacious—to found and run monasteries in the seventh century! Along with all her friends, I am looking forward to more discussion and liturgical imagining at Elizabeth's new home and centre in Spittal, under the sign of St Hilda.

7

Theology and human flourishing: Another conversion?

Jonathan Baxter

Introduction

This chapter addresses the tensional relationship between the healing ministry of Holy Rood House and the damage wrought by life-denying interpretations of Christianity—in whatever form they take. Holy Rood House comes face to face with the shadow of Christianity when the Holy Rood community spend much of their time tending wounds inflicted by self-confessed and/or institutionally authorized Christians and *their* interpretation of Christianity. In conversation with Elizabeth—and previously, Stanley Baxter too—the question has often arisen: why remain in the church when the church does so much damage? Elizabeth's commitment to Holy Rood House answers this question by wrestling a blessing for the church despite its wounded and often wounding nature.

More-than-human

It's no longer acceptable to think of human flourishing without *first* setting the human within a more-than-human context—the recognition that humans are just one species among many, and that all forms of life have intrinsic value and agency.[1] Theology takes the more-than-human world as a given—albeit in a different register. The human is set within a trinitarian context; a deeply personal symbolism that offers the language of relationality—of Father, Son and Holy Spirit, for example—as foundational to human flourishing. But the language of trinitarian theology—and specifically its personal and gendered symbolism—begs the question: is this interpretative framework, this grammar of understanding, adequate to address the climate and ecological crisis? Where does the language of trinitarian theology sit within the meshwork of social, environmental and economic injustices? And does changing the language—to speak of Creator, Redeemer and Sustainer, for example—do anything more than change one metaphorical skin for another, leaving the wine undrinkable?

At Holy Rood House, these questions are a live issue. The new wine of understanding—the wine of more-than-human flourishing, for example—is of serious concern. Hence the two questions the community repeatedly ask themselves: what does it mean to be a Christian when the church is experienced by many as institutionally sexist, racist, classist and homophobic etc.? And what does it mean to practise an ecology of health[2] when our everyday wellbeing is predicated upon the suffering of

---

[1] The phrase "more-than-human world" was coined by David Abram in 1996. It refers to nature as a realm that includes and exceeds humankind. See David Abram, *The Spell of the Sensuous: Perception and Language in a More-Than-Human World* (New York: Vintage Books, 1996/7).

[2] The phrase "ecology of health" was coined in 2005 when formulating a framework for the Centre for the Study of Theology and Health—the educational wing of Holy Rood House. For its current (and somewhat modified) formulation, see <https://www.holyroodhouse.org.uk/studycentre.html>, accessed 3 April 2024.

others—the more-than-human world and those who are materially and politically disenfranchised?

In response to these questions, innocence is not an option. Hence the continuing significance of the Fall: it grounds us. But what do we mean by the Fall and is this language useful? To answer this question, I want to propose an analogy often used by artist-theologians like Jeremy Begbie when reflecting on the dialectic between tradition and innovation. There is, suggests Begbie, a generative tension between tradition and innovation; between the tradition one is schooled within and the innovation this makes possible.[3] But can the same be said of the tensional relationship between theological and ecological language? Or does ecology—when experienced through the climate and ecological crisis—finally burst the skin of God-talk?

The answer, of course, depends on one's sensibility. For some people, God-talk (*theo-logos*) is for ever a new language: a language that wrestles a blessing from the violence of a fallen world; of bodies that are mortal; of tragedies that befall us (including the climate and ecological crisis). For others, God-talk is a precursor to the Anthropocene,[4] a way of mis-fitting the world into an all-too-human frame—and this despite the fact that the symbolic language of God (including the language of Fatherhood and the language of Creator) is intended to signify *no* eternal personal principle

---

[3]   For an engaging example of Begbie's position (which is not, for the record, a theological endorsement), see <https://www.youtube.com/watch?v=UlR3bOsoAdA>, accessed 3 April 2024. For a more thorough engagement with Begbie's work, see Jeremy Begbie, *Redeeming Transcendence in the Arts: Bearing Witness to the Triune God* (London: SCM Press, 2018).

[4]   The term "Anthropocene" refers to the current geological age, viewed as the period during which human activity has been the dominant influence on climate and the environment. When considering this term in relation to the climate and ecological crisis, the concept has strengths and weaknesses. For a discussion of both, see Donna Haraway, *Staying with the Trouble: Making Kin in the Chthulucene* (New York and London: Duke University Press, 2016), pp. 30–57.

or source (which is another way of saying that God-talk intends to split the language of God-talk; the apophatic exceeds the cataphatic).[5]

This unsettling of theological language is played out gently in the prayers that Elizabeth has written for Holy Rood House.[6] Here the primary theme is one of personal and spiritual renewal through community. Or, more specifically, a recognition that God *is* community and that community is where healing can be found. Here pain, suffering and betrayal are openly acknowledged, but they are not the final word. Rather, God-in-Christ is *for ever* arising through our care of one another and the earth.

Post-communion prayer

The hope of Easter
has brought us to this table;
our feeding is our prayer for those who are not fed.
In solidarity we pray for those who are alone.

The lone singer before the dawn chorus
and the one who has no song.

Through community
we meet with the song writer,
and our songs come together

---

[5]   For readers unfamiliar with these terms but interested in the wider topic, see Keith Ward, *God: A Guide for the Perplexed* (Oxford: One World Publications, 2002/3). Cataphatic language uses positive descriptions and statements to deepen our understanding of what we mean by God—God as Father, God as Creator, God as Lover etc. Apophatic language takes the opposite approach: it articulates what God is not, i.e. it "approach[es] the infinite by denying everything finite" (p. 46). Taken together these terms form a complementary pair.

[6]   See Elizabeth Baxter, *Holy Rood House Community Prayer* (Thirsk: Holy Rood House Publications, 2017).

with the song of the birds;
our Christic crescendo
as we rise with Christ into action for justice.

Alleluia. Christ is rising.
There is hope for the world.[7]

Here, in the difference between the more familiar yet absent "Christ has risen" and the less familiar "Christ is rising", we have a good example of the generative tension between tradition and innovation. "Christ has risen" suggests an act wholly accomplished. "Christ is rising" suggests a process underway. The tension between them is eschatological; both now and not yet.

In this prayer, we also have a good example of the praxis of Holy Rood House: of rising with Christ into action for justice; and how the Holy Rood community go about this task. First, hope is found in the Easter story (a historic event and Christic rupture which sets the community on its way). Hope, in this context, means entering into communion with one another through the Sacrament of the Eucharist and other acts of Christic hospitality. At Holy Rood House, this includes the everyday practice of "welcoming the stranger" (the latter more commonly referred to by the Holy Rood community as "guests") through acts of friendship, psychotherapy (including creative arts therapies), counselling, theological reflection and time set aside for self-care. Primary among these acts of hospitality—perhaps the centre around which they spiral—is the daily rhythm of Holy Rood House, expressed in its liturgy and the sharing of food at mealtimes. Here the daily liturgy—culminating, symbolically, in the Sacrament of the Eucharist—and the everyday practice of mealtimes blur (as they did on the road to Emmaus). Hence mealtimes at Holy Rood House repeat the Sacrament of the Eucharist, but with a difference: a life less scripted, charged with the tension of a *becoming* community,

---

7   *Holy Rood House Community Prayer*, p. 111.

including all of the uncertainty and disintegration that this becoming entails.[8]

Significantly too, in the imagery offered by this post-communion prayer, the becoming community includes "the song of the birds". Here the song writer (the triune God), the guests around the table (not one but many) and the birds (representatives of the more-than-human world) come together in a "Christic crescendo / as we rise with Christ into action for justice". Justice for one another; justice for the earth.

And it's here, in this more-than-human context, that I suggest Holy Rood House—and, more broadly, the Christian healing ministry—is called to innovate: where "our songs come together / *with the song of the birds*" (my italics). What this coming together sounds like, looks like, tastes like, smells like, feels like and moves like is another way of asking what Christian healing entails in a time of more-than-human crisis. Might it entail taking on the challenge of personal and political redemption—the act of being saved from error—when understood through the loss and damage of an ecologically devastated but still becoming world—a world in which human history (or herstory) is not the only story being told?

This personal and political redemption also includes a form of theological redemption: the renewal of our minds through the renewal of our language, as God is reconfigured—or newly configured (once again)—as radical hospitality and solidarity with the more-than-human world. What this means is more than the healing of broken bodies—albeit that is part of the task. It also means the healing of a potentially dysfunctional God-talk, i.e. the death and resurrection of a crucifying language, transformed into a language more fructifying.

In the context of feminist liberation theology—which is clearly where Elizabeth situates her ministry—the healing of God-talk involves the

---

8   My emphasis on disintegration and its relevance for the becoming of community owes a debt to Sara Maitland's exploration of a big-enough God, who (sic), like a butterfly, first needs to be destroyed to be resurrected. See Sara Maitland, *A Big-Enough God: Artful Theology* (London: Mowbray, 1995), p. 171. This emphasis also acknowledges the often-painful psychological journeys that many guests undertake in the context of their engagement with Holy Rood House.

redemption of God, i.e., the foregrounding of theology as a theology of mutual relation: one that celebrates a more radical and pre-discursive relationality.[9]

> For in the beginning is the relation, and in the relation is the power that creates the world through us, and with us, and by us, you and I, you and we, and none of us alone.
>
> By this power we are pushed further than we dare to imagine we can go. By this power, we are en-couraged to live together. By this power we are en-abled to see and know that we are encouraged and enabled constantly to god. By us, with us. Through us, this power is re-leased.[10]

In this quotation by Carter Heyward, we have a glimpse of what life at Holy Rood House is all about—or what it strives to be about. And as

---

[9] See Isabel Carter Heyward, *The Redemption of God: A Theology of Mutual Relation* (London: University Press of America, 1982). The ecological implications of Heyward's work are given more explicit narration in later publications, including Heyward's essay, "Turning to the Animals: Another Conversion"—from which I borrow for my title—published in her collection *Staying Power: Reflections on Gender, Justice and Compassion* (Cleveland, OH: The Pilgrim Press, 1995/2000), pp. 101–11. Given my reference to the pre-discursive it is also worth noting the relational developments within psychoanalytic theory and practice, where emphasis has shifted from a classically Freudian (and patriarchal) reduction of religious experience— as always already symbolic and *masking* a deficit—to an object relational investigation of the mother-infant dyad as integral to establishing the grounds of *unnoticed* "infinite boundless support" (Michael Eigen). For an overview of these developments, see James W. Jones, *Religion and Psychology in Transition: Psychoanalysis, Feminism, and Theology* (London: Yale University Press, 1996) and for specific engagement with Eigen's concept of "infinite boundless support" or a "boundless supporting unknown", see Michael Eigen, *Flames from the Unconscious: Trauma, Madness and Faith* (London: Karnac Books, 2009), pp. 11–28.

[10] Heyward, *Staying Power*, p. 172.

with Heyward, Elizabeth's contribution to Holy Rood House—expressed in the following community prayer—calls us into these acts of godding (albeit presented, here, in more traditional trinitarian language).

(From) Additional Easter Prayers

God of all life and empowerment,
who through the resurrection of Jesus
opened a new way
out of the tombs of oppression
into a garden of beauty.

Grant that we may no longer cling
to our grave clothes;

the familiar comfort that holds us back;
but call us out

and empower us
to be alive to one another
and to the earth,

so we may bear witness to the movement of the Spirit
and the flourishing of the whole world. Amen.[11]

Deep incarnation

Taking this movement as our task, our calling, I now want to turn from "the flourishing of the whole world" to a more localized consideration of the power of mutual relation. And I want to do this by asking a question about the entanglement of Holy Rood House with its wider ecology.

As well as the bricks and mortar of Holy Rood House and the people who make up its becoming community, Holy Rood House is set within

---

[11]   *Holy Rood House Community Prayer*, p. 120.

generous grounds. Presently these grounds are laid out as "a garden of beauty" (to echo the above prayer). This includes providing a home to a variety of animals—goats, chickens, other resident and migratory birds, frogs, pond skaters and snails etc.—all of whom bring joy (and sometimes frustration) to their human co-residents. Food is also grown within the grounds and integrated into the meals provided for, and by, the community.

But the question I want to ask is this: how can the grounds of Holy Rood House become *more* than a beautiful garden, albeit a garden offering inspiration and food for the Holy Rood community? In short, if the birds, and the wider ecology of which we are a part, have their *own* song—not *our* song but *their* song, please note—how best can the Holy Rood community hear it into speech—especially now, when this song includes a cry of extinction?[12] And how might this cry of extinction—this *cri de coeur*—transform the healing ministry of Holy Rood House?

This isn't the place to give a detailed response. Rather, as Elizabeth steps down from her leadership role at Holy Rood House, the wider Holy Rood community will take up the challenge of addressing this and other questions as they continue on their journey. But I do want to suggest a direction of travel, one that moves beyond the *rhetoric* of a beautiful garden to a deeper *practice* of incarnation—a way of living in the world as if the earth *really* mattered.

This direction of travel is deeply ecological, but in practical terms it needs a form. And the form I'd like to propose is that of permaculture—a sustainable culture of earth care, people care and the fair share of resources.[13] By adopting a permaculture approach to ecological practice,

---

[12] For a more extended reflection on this all-too-summary statement, see <https://fivedials.com/reportage/climate-change-is-us-the-sixth-extinction-is-us-we-are-at-the-heart-of-all-of-these-issues-julian-hoffman-interview/>, accessed 3 April 2024.

[13] For an accessible introduction to permaculture, free to download and containing lots of useful links, see Andrew Millison's *Introduction to Permaculture*: <https://open.oregonstate.education/permaculture/>, accessed 3 April 2024. For a more in-depth look at social permaculture, see Looby Macnamara, *People and Permaculture: Designing Personal and*

Holy Rood House would be taking another step on its own healing journey, adding the practice of permaculture to its daily rhythm. In practical terms this would entail regenerating the grounds for both human *and* more-than-human flourishing. It would also put into practice a particular way of understanding our ethical relationship to the earth, so that the practice of incarnation—as a practice of Christian healing—becomes a *local* planetary task—not just something we aspire to in the abstract.[14]

This differs from the current theological emphasis on the concept of "deep incarnation", where, for the most part, the driver remains cognitive—a sincere attempt to understand and to justify how a loving God relates to the suffering of Creation (both the suffering built into the evolutionary process and the suffering caused by the climate and ecological crisis specifically).[15] Yet as with all theological reflection, the concept of deep incarnation is best worked through in practice. And the practice of permaculture—as a practice of incarnation—is one (but only one) way to do this.

So, in honour of Elizabeth's 30-plus years of working to pioneer, and working alongside, the Holy Rood community, I'd like to conclude by quoting another of Elizabeth's community prayers.

Collective Planetary Well-Being (East Meon: Permanent Publications, 2012/ Revised edition 2019).

[14] For an alternative, but complementary, exploration of this challenge, see Catherine Keller, *Political Theology of the Earth: Our Planetary Emergency and the Struggle for a New Public* (New York: Columbia University Press, 2018).

[15] For a useful overview—noting the origins of the concept and subsequent developments—see Denis Edwards, *Deep Incarnation: God's Redemptive Suffering with Creatures* (Maryknoll, NY: Orbis Books, 2019).

(From) Communion by Extension

These gifts come from the earth,
and through the eating and drinking of them
we feed on Christ who walked this earth
and dwells in us by faith.[16]

And the final question, or set of questions, I want to ask follow naturally: what does it mean to "feed on Christ" in the context of a climate and ecological crisis? Is Christ—and the wider symbolic language of trinitarian theology—sufficiently nourishing to sustain the deep ecological conversion that the climate and ecological crisis calls for? In short, how might the Christ who "walked this earth / and dwells in us by faith" deepen our own sense of incarnation—as resident or alien in a more-than-human world?

Only time will tell, but Elizabeth's legacy is clear. Perhaps it's time to resolve our ambivalence.

---

[16] *Holy Rood House Community Prayer*, p. 188.

Creative writings from Holy Rood House

Morning Anticipation

Car is encrusted with frost as dawn starts to break.
Hints of light on the eastern horizon.

Along the valley, mist hovers over the river
Shrouding the low-lying land in its ephemeral veil.

Above the hills are fluffy clouds suffused with pink,
Reflecting rays of the yet-to-rise sun.
Is this a shepherd's warning, or a glimpse of glories to come?

Between the peaks a thin duvet of bright, white cloud
Hovers over the greening grass of God's upland garden,
Evaporating slowly from its overnight caress of earthly life.

Dazzling sun surmounts the horizon.
Warming rays dispel mist and frost.
A new day has dawned!

Helen L. Leathard

Shadow of Psalm 23

Shadows creep and weave down from the dark gold sky,
Cover my feet as serpents bold, yet I will not die.
Day has lost its fearsome heat and moon is rising high,
My heart's in silver slivers, yet I will not die.
Your hand will reach to guide me and your watchful eye
Admonish my self-righteous soul, yet I will not die.
My tears are pearls of ice, cold streams of life flow by:
My thirst is quenched but harshly, yet I will not die.
Your breath a gentle wind now, my fears take wings to fly
Up to your dancing stars: my spirit will not die.

Jenny Kartupelis

Sophia's Sea

Based on a reading about wisdom from Apocrypha

Our gift is wisdom from the deep
Reflecting up through waters clear;
As we swim through seas of sleep
It finds, enfolds us, holds us near.

Like shadows on the sand below
Show ourselves not as we know,
But as a shape that yet might be
Or maybe past, left in that sea.

Jenny Kartupelis

I am a wave

*At a Summer School on change and transition I took part in a creative
writing workshop in which participants were asked to choose one or two
pictures from the selection, to use as inspiration for their writing. One of a
number of options was to write something beginning "I am ... ". My mind
was focussed on my recent transition into retirement, and the pictures
that appealed to me were of ripples on water reflecting light and of waves
crashing on rocks, and I wrote the following:*

I am a wave at the edge of the ocean, full of power and unseen energy,
impelled by the wind and pulled by the moon. Out of the depths I
climb up the shore slope, bubbling with excitement towards sun and
sky. Suddenly the surface tension breaks, and I burst forth in a cloud of
spray, glistening as I hover in the still air, only to fall, to caress the coastal
rocks with my moist embrace.

Some of my neighbours were dashed harshly against those rocks of
change, where sea meets land in strange exchange. Power of propulsion
meets strength of stillness with transformative trauma at the interface.
What can survive this clash of nature's titans? Energy is always conserved,
but where does it go? Motion meets stillness in a roar of exhilaration and
disintegration.

I, the coherent roller of a wave, disperse into glistening droplets, my
energy spent in eroding the yielding rock into grains of sand. My parts
seem greater than my whole as I dance in the sunlight, but where do I
go from here? Gravity draws me down, back down to earth! My droplets
coalesce, our mutual attraction causing rivulets to stream down the steep
side of the resilient rock—into a pool. Drop calls to drop, and we start to
dance to a new rhythm—the rhythm of the gentle breeze that whispers
round the rocks. Now ... I am a different wave:—a ripple in a rock pool.

Helen L. Leathard

Love Elemental

I am Wind,
I blow wherever I will;
From fiercest gale
To gentlest breeze,
My endless breath of air
Giving and receiving life
We con-spire
Together forever we love.
Let me fill your sail.

I am Fire,
I give life her warmth
And I consume
And purify
Wherever I burn.
I reach the farthest
Corners of the world
Where I am eternal love.
Let me set you ablaze.

I am Water,
I sustain and nourish
And give life his energy.
I find every level
In all beings;
No place is beyond me,
Each tiniest drop
Pure love.
Let me drink your tears.

I am Earth,
From me you are made
Each particle
Of golden dust;
And even the very last one
Can never be blown away
If I create the next universe
In loving memory of you.
Let me be your rock always.

My name is Love
And my twin is you
Together we belong
Our worlds are one.

David McDonald

It takes just one flower

It takes just one flower, a flower in bloom
In a tiny vase on the windowsill
To make a sanctuary of a room
And a heart more at peace, strangely fulfill'd.

It takes just one smile, a welcoming smile,
As you hesitate on your way down the stair,
Fearing and hoping all the while
Might you just have something to share?

It takes just one touch, a gentle touch
On your arm as you enter, feeling unable
To meet all these eyes: are they asking too much?
A touch that says, please join us at table.

It takes just one brush of hen's warm feathers
When you sit on the bench to feed her some corn,
To tell you this place is yours and is hers,
To feel all its hope in the pale shades of dawn.

It takes just one flower, a flower and a bee
To breed all the seeds of the summer's day,
That day when you start to heal and to see
That yourself is enough to find the way.

Jenny Kartupelis

The "Ivy Tree"

Sun is glinting on golden berry bunches,
And gleamingly reflected from glossy leaves of ivy
Adorning the trunk of a fir tree.

Is this synergy, symbiosis or parasitism?
How do trunk and suckered tendrils relate to each other?
As host and guest or for mutual benefit?

What happens underground?
Roots entwine with hidden filaments of fungal mycelium—
A microcosm of the wood-wide-web of life.

Helen L. Leathard

The sacrament of non-doing

Having used labyrinths previously to seek answers to perplexing questions, during a Garden Quiet Day I headed to the one in Holy Rood House Garden, starting by standing on the threshold to conceptualize my quest to explore the sacrament of non-doing.

Walked slowly;
Soft bed of pine cones nurturing fungi.
Are they parasols?
Need to check later.
Snap a photo to aid memory.

Journey on to the centre with its guardian cherub.
There the pine bed calls me to rest awhile.
Semi-supine on a soft bed
Enfolded in a cosy coat to gaze upwards,
or inwards with eyes closed.
This feels like non-doing!

Bathed in scent of pine,
Serenaded by sound of birdsong.
Beyond the trees birds fly
Fluttering or gliding, alone or in flocks.
Entranced by tracery of twigs above.

A squirrel stirs in the branches,
Scuttling about before descending
Headlong, flattened against the trunk,
Gripping with clasping claws
Exquisitely camouflaged when still,
Visible only when moving,
Surveys the stranger below.
Satisfied that no harm threatens,
Squirrel ascends with amazing agility,
To disappear once again.

Attention returns to self.
Lying not only on pine needles but also cones
Sensitivity heightened in repose,
Perceive gentle massage with each breath.
Blissfully relaxing.
Forest bathing in the scents, sights, sounds and touch of nature,
Dwelling in the sacrament of non-doing.

Helen L. Leathard

Frog watching

In the Walled Garden pond,
Movement stirs among the ferny green fronds,
Arms stretch. Legs stretch.
Noses and eyes rise through the surface.
Vigilant, yet curious about the creature on the bank—watching them.

Stillness of the frogs is reflected
In the stillness of their human observer.
Necessarily so, because . . .
The slightest sound or movement triggers
The sudden submersion of the aquatic amphibians.

Position adjusted, camera now at hand,
I resume a stillness that entices
The re-emergence of my new-found friends.
Appraising gaze greets appraising gaze
Lingering lovingly in a timeless mutual embrace.

Camera clicks to capture an impression
Of this memorable moment;
And frogs flee!

Helen L. Leathard

And when that time comes

And when that time of reckoning comes,
That time when all the known is shaken,
Our image in the mirror cracked,
When we are spilt, and all trust taken:
Who then will be there for us?

And when that time of danger comes,
The dreaded monster from the deep
Rises cold eyed with broken talon,
Woken from its watchful sleep:
Whose love then can rescue us?

And when that time of healing comes,
To see our image whole at last,
Accept our variegated truth
In the smooth and mended glass:
Then we'll step out to the waiting world,
The door left ajar for another guest.

Jenny Kartupelis

8

Radical Apostolic Women: Sent by God to aid human flourishing

Helen L. Leathard

"Thinking outside of the box" and "pushing at boundaries", while remaining rooted firmly in its Christian foundation, are characteristics of the ethos of the Holy Rood House community that have nurtured and inspired me over the past 25 years. Elizabeth's passion for feminist theology in general and avoidance of referring to God as masculine have been particularly influential in my own spiritual, theological and ministerial development. It is to that passion that I now pay tribute through delving into the apostolic contributions of two women who engaged impressively with Jesus, before explaining why Elizabeth, through her leadership and ministry at Holy Rood House, might also be recognized as a radical apostolic woman, following in the footsteps of those impressive forerunners. Elizabeth's influence gave me confidence to use my analytical, scientific inclination to explore creatively the encounter of the Samaritan woman with Jesus at Jacob's Well, as part of my preparation for ordination, 12 years ago—the style of writing reflecting that academic context. Continuing with that approach of analytical and creative interpretation of biblical and non-canonical texts, I also offer a reconstruction of elements of the life and apostolic ministry of Mary Magdalene.

Sychara: Apostle to Samaritans

Introduction

According to the Gospel of John (4:1–42), while taking the usual three-day walking route from Judea to Galilee through Samaria,[1] Jesus, fatigued by the journey, was sitting beside Jacob's well near the city of Sychar. About noon a woman came to draw water. The author did not name her, but I will give her the dignity of a name: Sychara, a feminized version of the name of her city.

The cultural norm was for women to draw water in the cool of the early morning, not in the heat of the midday sun, so we might wonder why Sychara came to the well so late. We might also wonder who observed these events that are reported only in John's Gospel. Had John remained there with Jesus while the other disciples went into the city to buy food, or did he pick up the story as it was referred to later? If the latter, why did the writers of the other Gospels not include it?[2] Did they deem it of insufficient importance, or omit it deliberately because it magnified the role of a foreign woman in Jesus's mission? Whatever the reason for it appearing only in John's Gospel, we must be aware that the dialogue as we have it is not necessarily in its original form, but in a form that enabled John to make the theological points that he wished to draw from the events. These focus on purity regulations, living water, multiple marriages and Jesus's prophetic insights and missionary success.

Exegesis

According to verse 7, Jesus asked Sychara for a drink. At first glance, it seems that this involved making a dramatic break from Jewish custom and purity laws but, according to Barrett, although it was most unusual for there to be a conversation between a Jewish man and a Samaritan woman, the purity regulations (Niddah 4.1, cited by Barrett) that precluded Jews from using utensils "together with" (Barrett's translation)

---

[1]   C. K. Barrett, *The Gospel according to St John: An Introduction with Commentary and Notes on the Greek Text* (London: SPCK, 1955; 9th impression, 1972), p. 193, citing Josephus Ant. xx, 118.

[2]   Barrett, *Gospel according to John*, p. 191.

Samaritans, on the assumption that Samaritan women were always unclean (menstruating), were introduced in AD/CE 65 or 66 and so were not applicable during Jesus's ministry.[3] It seems, therefore, that the parenthetical note in verse 9 is a late editorial addition by John.

There was, therefore, nothing untoward in Jesus asking her for a drink in the heat of the day in the arid land. Most likely, this was a way into a conversation through which Jesus could pursue his mission to some people who were, at least in part, estranged from their Israelite heritage because they worshipped other gods in addition to YHWH.[4] This aligns with Jesus's mission to the lost sheep of Israel (cf. Jeremiah 50:6; Ezekiel 34) and contrasts with his initial reaction to the Syrophoenician woman (Mark 7:24–30) who was not of Israelite descent.

Clearly, Sychara recognized Jesus as a Jew and, being aware of difficulties between Jews and Samaritans, questioned his request. Jesus did not reply directly but took an opportunity to continue with his missionary endeavour by introducing the subjects of God and "living water". Here there was scope for misunderstanding because "living water" could be understood as referring to running water, obtainable from a well that accessed an underground stream.[5] Instead, Jesus interjected that, if she had been aware that she was experiencing a divine visitation, Sychara would have requested a gift from God. Here, according to Barrett, we have the conflation of two metaphors.[6] First, that Jesus "supersedes" the Jewish use of water for cleansing with "living water" for drinking. I wondered if this might be interpreted as leading to inner purity; although there is some tension between this notion and Jesus's teaching that it is not what goes into the mouth that defiles a person (Matthew 15:11). More convincingly, Jesus is drawing on the Old Testament usage of "living water" as a metaphor for divine activity (Jeremiah 2:13; Ezekiel 47:9), expressed explicitly as the Holy Spirit in the Torah.[7]

---

[3] Barrett, *Gospel according to John*, pp. 190, 19.4

[4] René Kieffer, "John", in John Barton and John Muddiman (eds), *The Oxford Bible Commentary* (Oxford: Oxford University Press, 2001), p. 968.

[5] Barrett, *Gospel according to John*, p. 196.

[6] Barrett, *Gospel according to John*, pp. 190, 195.

[7] Barrett, *Gospel according to John*, p. 195.

Sychara was, however, still thinking in material ways: she pointed to Jesus's lack of means to draw water, living or otherwise, from the well, and asked him where he got the "living water". Here it becomes clear that Sychara has no reservations about debating with Jesus. She is on home ground, and he is a thirsty traveller. She is well-informed about the history of the well and the status of Jacob as an ancestor of all Israelites, both Jews and Samaritans. If he can offer something greater than life-giving water from the historic well, is this visitor somehow greater than their shared ancestor? Sychara is clearly educated, and both willing and able to converse engagingly with the stranger. Is she someone who comes to the well regularly, or not? Is she a lady of some status who has come to the well unusually late because a servant is sick and has failed to fetch enough water at the usual time?

Jesus replied (verse 14) by enlarging on the properties of "living water" in contrast to well water: "living water" would be continuously refreshing and, by welling up within, it would give eternal life. This living water sounded highly attractive, so Sychara requested it, addressing Jesus respectfully as "Sir" even though she is still presented as thinking materially—keen to be relieved of thirst and of the chore of carrying water. Hence, Jesus moved on the conversation, revealing his prophetic insight by reference to the men in her life: she has had five husbands and the man she is now with is not her husband (verses 16–19). According to Barrett, rabbis (including Jesus) did not approve of more than three marriages, even though any number was legally admissible;[8] so Sychara might have been in a marriage that was legal according to Mosaic Law but not according to Rabbinic or emergent Christian standards. Equally she could have been living in the household of a male relative. What is actually important here is the demonstration of Jesus's supernatural knowledge that leads Sychara towards an understanding of Jesus as the Messiah—a tentative suggestion that he affirmed immediately (verses 25–6), causing her to return to the city and attract a crowd of people to come to see him (verses 28–30). Evidently, she was a very influential woman.

---

[8]   Barrett, *Gospel according to John*, p. 197.

According to Elizabeth Schüssler Fiorenza, this dialogue aligns with a Johannine tradition ascribing Jesus's mission to the Samaritans primarily to a woman.[9] She compared Sychara's testimony with that of Andrew (John 1:40-2), and her insightful conversion experience with that of Nathanael (John 1:46-9), and went on to explicate the way in which faith and revelation interact dialectically in the conversation that led to Sychara becoming a missionary of Christ.

In the meantime, Jesus's (male) disciples had returned with food. He engaged with them in a food and harvest-based conversation (verses 31-8) that paralleled his "living water" conversation with Sychara, but it seems that they did not pick up on his deeper meaning as she had done. In remarking on this, Robin Griffith-Jones discerned that "the Samaritan woman met Jesus and saw more deeply into the truth of Jesus than Jesus's own disciples saw".[10]

Somewhat disturbingly, in verses 39-42, we see Sychara's role being diminished progressively. Initially many Samarians from Sychar believed in Jesus because of her testimony. They persuaded Jesus to stay with them for two days, during which time many more came to believe in Jesus as prophet, Messiah and "Saviour of the world", with a deeper understanding than that of the Jews in Jerusalem.[11] Sychara's testimony was more than amply confirmed, and yet her role in Jesus's mission was diminished by the author reporting people as saying to her: "It is no longer because of what you said that we believe" (verse 42).

Conclusion

In this exegesis, the use of hermeneutics of suspicion and remembrance, based in feminist theological methodology, has yielded a view of Sychara as an influential, educated and spiritually perceptive woman who served

---

[9] Elizabeth Schüssler Fiorenza, *In Memory of Her: A Feminist Reconstruction of Christian Origins* (London: SCM Press, 1983), p. 327; citing Rudolf Bultmann, *The Gospel of John* (Philadelphia, PA: Westminster, 1971), pp. 175ff.

[10] Robin Griffith-Jones, *Mary Magdalene: The Woman who Jesus Loved* (Norwich: Canterbury Press, 2008).

[11] Kieffer, "John", p. 969.

exceedingly well as Jesus's missionary to the Samaritan people of Sychar. With some prompting, she grasped Jesus's metaphorical teaching about his Messiahship in a way that his male disciples did not, and led many citizens of Sychar to an understanding of Jesus as Saviour—putting these Samaritans ahead of the Jews in Jerusalem. Even though the author tended to diminish her importance, she clearly played a significant role in the formation of an early Christian community in Sychar and provided a valuable model of Christian spirituality through her theological awareness and readiness to bring people to Jesus as God's Messiah.

Mary Magdalene: Apostle to the Apostles

Introduction " . . . go to my brothers and say . . . " (John 20:17)

The three synoptic Gospels report Mary Magdalene as one of the women who went to Jesus's tomb early in the morning when the Sabbath was over and found it to be empty (Matthew 28:1; Mark 16:1; Luke 24:10). The Gospel according to John (20:14–18) provides a further account of her being the first person to be greeted by the risen Christ, and sent by him to tell his disciples of his living presence and anticipated ascension. We do not know when Mary started travelling with Jesus's disciples, but if we make a connection between Luke's (8:1–3) introduction of her as a healed woman among his supporting, female travelling companions with Mark's (1:39) account of Jesus casting out demons in Galilee, we can discern that Mary could have been a follower of Jesus from early in his ministry.

Mary's life

In drafting this exploration of Mary Magdalene, I am taking inspiration from Paula Gooder's "stories" of *Phoebe* and *Lydia*[12] to create a meaningful narrative of Mary's life, faith and ministry, based on the little material

---

12   Paula Gooder: *Phoebe: A Story* (London: Hodder & Stoughton, 2018); and *Lydia: A Story* (Hodder & Stoughton, 2023).

we have in the canonical Gospels, fragments of the *Gospel of Mary*[13] and what I understand, from wider reading, of the context of her life.

In the canonical Gospels, Mary is described by Mark (16:9) and Luke (8:2) as a woman from whom seven demons had gone out, so we might compare her with Legion (Mark 5:1–15), a Gerasene man who was living an immensely troubled life until he was cleansed of "unclean spirits" and, thereby, healed by Jesus; but there is no evidence that Mary was as severely ill as he was. We can, however, speculate that she had been a troubled teenager, perhaps suffering with what would now be recognized as catamenial epilepsy and bipolar disorder with some features of psychosis—ailments that rendered her unattractive for marriage but were not utterly incapacitating—so she remained single and lived in her parental home in Magdala, a Galilean village between Tiberias and Capernaum.

One day, when Jesus was healing and teaching nearby, she had been taken by her parents seeking her healing; and their faith was rewarded. In the presence of Jesus, she was relieved of the neurological and psychological mental turmoil; she was calm and capable. She emerged into sane adulthood and became a keen follower of Jesus, sometimes taking provisions for him and his disciples as they travelled around Galilee, and intermittently joining the group to journey to Jerusalem for the major Jewish festivals (Mark 15:40–1). She knew that when she was near Jesus she was in a safe space; and she really enjoyed listening attentively to his teaching.

And so it was that she became an integral part of the group of disciples that accompanied Jesus on his final visit to Jerusalem, lodging in Bethany and travelling daily to the temple. Then, on the evening of the "Last Supper", she remained in Jerusalem to help prepare the Passover meal in the guest room of a wealthy supporter of Jesus. Was it Joseph of Arimathea or Nicodemus (John 19:38–9)? There Mary watched Jesus wash his disciples' feet and heard his farewell discourses recorded in

---

[13] *The Gospel of Mary*, introduced by Karen L. King, translated by George W. MacRae and R. McL. Wilson, and edited by Douglas M. Parrott, in *The Nag Hammadi Library in English,* 4th revised edition (Leiden: EJ Brill, 1996), pp. 523–7. Because of the brevity of this piece, I do not refer to specific pages.

John's Gospel (Chapters 13–17). It is hard to imagine the turbulence she experienced when she grasped that the end of his earthly life was imminent. Nevertheless, she remained faithful, witnessing his crucifixion and entombment, and returning to his tomb at the first opportunity. Jesus's sending of Mary to announce his resurrection to the disciples is the last time she is mentioned in the canonical Gospels, so I now turn to *The Gospel of Mary*.

The Gospel of Mary, first extant section

The first extant section of *The Gospel of Mary* reports a discussion during one of Jesus's resurrection appearances, possibly one of those reported in the Gospel according to John (20:19–29), or a similar occasion prior to his ascension. I am not qualified to provide a scholarly exegesis of the fragmented text, but I can offer an insight into Mary's apostolic role, based on Karen L. King's introduction, and the translation by George W. MacRae and R. McL. Wilson (1996). *The Gospel of Mary* reports a discourse that does not appear in the canonical books of the New Testament. In it, Jesus was being questioned about the fate of matter and (by Peter) about the nature of sin. Jesus's response is not easy to comprehend. If I have understood it correctly, Jesus replied that there is no sin other than that arising from human wrongdoing; and that he (the Good) came to restore every nature to its "root"—its healthy, untainted state.

Jesus seems to have sensed disquiet among his listeners and told them to "be of good courage" and, if discouraged, to be encouraged in the different forms of nature. It is understandable that this would distract them from being discouraged, but it is not clear whether "nature" here refers to what we think of as nature (gardens or countryside) or is something more psychological. Jesus then encouraged them, saying: "Peace be with you. Receive my peace to yourselves," using that familiar greeting before warning them not to be led astray but to follow him (to follow the example he had provided) and go out and preach the gospel of the kingdom authentically—a command that is consistent with the ending of Matthew (28:18–20).

Jesus then departed, leaving the disciples grieving and weeping—fearful of being arrested, tortured and crucified as Jesus had been. It was then that Mary Magdalene showed her outstanding faith and leadership qualities, telling the disciples not to grieve but to be resolute because the grace of Jesus would be entirely within them to protect them. Rather than despair, they should praise Jesus's greatness "for he has prepared us and made us into men". Being addressed to male as well as female followers, this must refer to a psycho-spiritual transformation that would enable all to function effectively as apostles within the culture of the time, rather than an alteration in the biological sex of the women.

If the narrative elements of the Gospel of Mary are in chronological sequence, these events could have taken place at Jesus's first resurrection appearance in the Upper Room, with Mary's account adding to what we know from the canonical Gospels.

The Gospel of Mary, second extant section

The second extant section has two main features. One is the record of visionary dialogue with Jesus (the Saviour) through which new teaching is imparted about the soul and its ascent beyond the bonds of earthly life—a report that, for reasons given below, seems to have been given by Mary to the disciples in the days between Jesus's ascension and Pentecost. The other provides insight into the sometimes-tense relationship between Mary and Peter—a tension that is implied also in the Gospel of Thomas (saying 114) where Simon Peter is reported as saying to the disciples: "Let Mary leave us, for women are not worthy of life."[14]

Taking the visionary dialogue first, let us envisage another gathering of the disciples in the Upper Room. After Jesus's appearance to convince Thomas of his resurrection and, therefore, divinity, the disciples had dispersed, with the fishermen returning to their boats in Galilee (Matthew 28:16–20; John 21:1–23), where Jesus had appeared to them as foretold. Then, being faithful Jews, as Pentecost approached they had returned to Jerusalem. Taking comfort in "walking down memory lane", they had revisited the Garden of Gethsemane and Mount of Olives, from where Jesus bade them farewell as he ascended (Luke 24:50–1; Acts 1:9–12).

They returned to their accommodation (staying with friends in Bethany or the Upper Room) and, as they sat reminiscing, Peter turned

---

14   *The Gospel of Thomas*, in: *The Nag Hammadi Library in English*, p. 138.

to Mary for inspiration. Having noted that Jesus loved her more than other women, he asked her to recall what she could of Jesus's words that they did not know. Mary's account of her vision in this section is not easy to understand, partly because several pages are missing and partly because of the nature of the insights that are revealed. It seems most straightforward to review the vision in two parts, separated by the missing pages of extant text.

First part: We return to the narrative at the point where Mary, when invited by Peter, opened her recall of a visionary dialogue by greeting Jesus, saying: "I saw you today in a vision," to which he replied that she is blessed because she did not waver at the sight of him. It seems likely, therefore, that this vision occurred soon after her first encounter with the risen Christ near the empty tomb. Why else would he commend her for not wavering at the sight of him? She would have been much less likely to be troubled by seeing him in later resurrection appearances such as those in the Upper Room in the company of others, or subsequently.

So, let us infer that, after taking her news to the disciples (John 20:18), Mary returned to the tomb for a time of contemplation, and apprehended a visionary encounter with her beloved healer and teacher. As if to reassure her further, Jesus had continued by saying that "where the mind is, there is the treasure". Her mind had not wavered and so she found the treasure of insight and wisdom.

Regardless of whether she saw him with the eye of her body or the eye of her mind, because her mind focussed on him, she would perceive the treasure of his teaching. She grasped the opportunity to ask whether visions were seen through the soul or the spirit (presumably alternatives that were subject to debate in their culture) and was instructed that neither of those is correct, but it is the mind, which exists between soul and spirit, that perceives visions. Further enlightenment on this topic is curtailed because the text is missing.

Second part: Where the text resumes, Mary has moved on to relating a dialogue with a soul that was ascending. From the sentence that follows the dialogue, it can be inferred that the ascending soul was that of "the Saviour", so her enlightenment was coming directly from Jesus, through conversation with him and through visionary observation. Her strong desire for him to remain with her is expressed in a forceful accusation:

"Why do you lie, since you belong to me?" The closeness of their relationship is attested in the Gospel of Philip, where it is justified by a parable that implies that Mary sees the light of Christ while others remain in darkness.[15] The lie, we might discern, is Jesus's statement in the garden by the tomb when he had told her there was no need to cling to him because he had not yet ascended (John 20:17).

For 40 days, Mary had been comforted by the risen Christ's repeated appearances. She had never seen him descending to make those appearances, but now she saw clearly that he was ascending. She thought he was committed to belonging to her and perceived his ascension as a betrayal. The soul's (risen Christ's) response was that he had seen her and been watching over her at times when she did not recognize him (and, by implication, he would continue to do so). But it must have been gut-wrenching for Mary to see the soul depart "rejoicing greatly"—as Jesus might well do as he finally returned to his home in heaven. That was not, however, the end of the vision, which continues by describing the soul's ascent to freedom from the binding of earthly powers to attain immortality in eternal silence—a silence that was reflected in Mary's silence as she reached the end of what Jesus had revealed to her.

The account of Jesus's revelations to Mary had been solicited by Peter, but her silence was broken by an antagonistic intervention from Andrew, inviting those who were gathered to comment on what she had revealed, because he was not inclined to believe that Jesus (the Saviour) was the source of these "strange ideas". Peter joined in the dissent, questioning the possibility that Jesus would have spoken with "a woman" in their absence and without their knowledge. (He had clearly forgotten the time Jesus spent with the Samaritan woman at Jacob's well!) Were they inclined to turn their attention to Mary? Did they believe Jesus preferred her to them?

Despite being distraught because of their reaction, Mary responded powerfully. Did they really think she would have intuitively invented these revelations and lied about Jesus? This prompted Levi to intervene in support of Mary. Levi (Matthew, the Levite-turned-tax-collector, as I understand him) had sometimes felt an outsider among the disciples,

---

15   *The Gospel of Philip*, in: *The Nag Hammadi Library in English*, p. 148.

not being one of the Galilean fishermen. He stayed with the group because of allegiance to Jesus, not through friendship with those who had been called first—a bit like Mary but for different reasons. He was not, however, lacking in self-confidence, and unhesitatingly reminded Peter of his tendency to be hot-tempered. He was appalled that Peter should contend with Mary as if he were debating, as Jesus had done, with the oppositional Jewish leaders in Jerusalem. He appealed to the wisdom of Jesus in honouring Mary, and questioned Peter's authority to reject her. Levi's perception was that Jesus knew Mary very well; and that was why he loved her more than he loved them. Rather than doubt Mary, they should be ashamed of their relative inadequacy. They should "put on the perfect man", acquiring graciously the gift of characteristics Jesus had striven for years to bestow upon them, so that they could preach the gospel exactly as he had taught them.

After that admonition (and a short break in the text), the disciples, at last, grasped the nettle of becoming apostles and went forth to proclaim and to preach the words of the gospel. It would be fascinating to know if the missing text referred to the coming of the Holy Spirit at Pentecost, but that remains a mystery. What we can be confident of is that Mary Magdalene was a devoted disciple of Jesus through much of his earthly ministry, and she continued to communicate with him in visions for many days after that first resurrection embrace in the garden near his temporary tomb. Sustained by her perception of his ongoing presence within and around her, Mary informed, encouraged and inspired the male disciples through those tumultuous weeks after Jesus's crucifixion until they "put on the perfect man" and became effective apostles.

Elizabeth Baxter: Apostle of Human Flourishing

Introduction

Excited by the ethos created by Elizabeth and Stanley Baxter at Holy Rood House, I soon became a regular visitor, and Consultant to the Centre for the Study of Theology and Health (CSTH). Summer schools, Hildegard Lecture weekends, research and study days became regular fixtures in my diary. I soon discovered what a force of nature Elizabeth was, with her passion for inclusivity, gender equality, community living, feminist theology, and the importance of safe space in house and gardens as being fundamental to health and healing. Her apostolic tendencies were manifest in many ways, and I describe here only those with which I am most familiar.

Publications

Elizabeth was keen for material from CSTH events to continue to reach a wide audience following the 2007 publication of *Wounds that Heal*, edited by Jonathan Baxter.[16] I was preparing to become Editor of *Chrism, the Journal of the Guild of St Raphael*, and suggested using *Chrism*, with its circulation of 1,000 copies twice-yearly, as a possible way forward. With the support of the Guild Council, a meeting was duly convened, through which Elizabeth and Stanley, Bishop George Hacker (the retiring editor) and I agreed details of a collaborative venture—a venture that proved fruitful for all concerned and still continues.

Elizabeth's aspirations to further disseminate good practice developed at Holy Rood House were manifested in the publication of *Holy Rood House Community Prayer*,[17] which is an invaluable prayer resource for many and various occasions, using language that is compassionate and inclusive, and avoids reference to God as masculine—all characteristic of Elizabeth's sense of justice as being fundamental to health and healing.

Prayer

A profound belief in the efficacy of prayer has been a defining feature of Elizabeth's fearless pursuit of developing Holy Rood House for the good of all. Daily community prayers in the chapel with weekly Eucharistic services, the provision of chaplains, and confident appeals for prayer support for particular initiatives are hallmarks of the profound Christian faith that has underpinned her determination to persist with aspirational ambitions even when progress was slow. One example is the development

---

[16] Jonathan Baxter (ed.), *Wounds that Heal: Theology, Imagination and Health* (London: SPCK, 2007).

[17] *Holy Rood House Community Prayer* (Thirsk: Holy Rood House Publications, 2017).

of a carer's suite to provide convenient residential accommodation for people with physical disabilities and their enablers.

Connecting chapel and garden

Another visionary project was the linking of chapel and gardens through the replacement of a solid wall with floor-to-ceiling sliding glass doors and the construction of a patio. As, at Elizabeth's instigation, the community's "ecology of health" project developed, the ability to move freely between the chapel and its scenic environment, and to meditate in the chapel with a full view of the beauty of nature, has proved to be a tremendous asset.

Purchase of Holy Rood House and Gardens

One of the greatest threats to the holistic functioning of Holy Rood House was the decision of the owners to realize part of their asset by selling a substantial part of the gardens for housing development. Elizabeth was horrified by that devastating possibility and set out, with immense grit and determination, to raise what seemed an impossibly huge sum of money to purchase the whole of the house and gardens. Through prayer and persistence, she succeeded, and a tremendous asset has been preserved for posterity. Garden Quiet Days are restorative manifestations of that success, that I have been blessed to attend recently; and I close this tribute to Elizabeth's apostolic zeal with a reflection arising from one such day, led by her.

God's Garden at Night[18]

In the night, sounds are distant.
Grass is tinted with frost.
The full moon's silvery light bathes all.

Trees are leafless, skeletal sentinels,
Rooted in the earth:
Grounded, anchored, nourished.

We, too, start and end in dark: journeying from womb to tomb.
From protective nurture . . .
To the gateway to resurrection into spiritual eternity.

There we move beyond the earthly rhythms of day and night,
Of our rotating planet orbiting its sun,
To the infinity of cosmic spacetime.

Stars are viewed through the lens of time travel.
Are they still there?
Was the sky above Gethsemane like this, on that fateful night?

Jupiter hangs over the goat shed,
Prompting pondering of star over stable long ago—

A planetary conjunction over Bethlehem,
Marking the incarnation of God in a special babe:
Emmanuel,
God with us!

---

[18] Helen L. Leathard, November 2023; inspired by meditative reflection "The Winter Garden at Night" by the Revd Canon Adrian Botwright, a volunteer chaplain at Holy Rood House, who contributed to the Garden Quiet Day programme led by Elizabeth Baxter.

9

Storytelling while walking: Feminist theologies and healing

Jane Craske

"The community becomes a place of storytelling where each person's story is valued and nurtured as a story of the beloved."[1]

Connections with Holy Rood House

"I have journeyed to this place
—this space—
where silence is possible.

I watched
fishes absolutely still
leaved and resting
perfect in their environment.
And they allowed me to be calm."[2]

I became acquainted with the work of Holy Rood House: Centre for Health and Pastoral Care not long after Elizabeth and Stanley Baxter began their ministry in Thirsk. Elizabeth spoke about the work at what

---

[1]   Elizabeth Baxter, "Beloved Community: A Glimpse into the Life of Holy Rood House", in Jonathan Baxter (ed.), *Wounds that Heal: Theology, Imagination and Health* (London: SPCK, 2007), p. 20.

[2]   Fragment of a poem written at Holy Rood House, November 1997.

I think must have been the British and Irish School of Feminist Theology Summer School in Durham in 1994. I was inspired at the time, and also in subsequent visits to Holy Rood House, by the vision of healing ministry allied with the creation of a justice-seeking, ecologically aware community, deeply attentive to individuals and living on a global map. I was encouraged by the explicit valuing of professionalism in varied therapeutic work, and the intention to overcome dualisms in the vision of Christian healing. It seemed so much more expansive than any approaches to Christian healing I had previously encountered. Given the context in which I heard Elizabeth speak and my own research interests, it was also clear that explicitly feminist approaches were valued in the vision and work being developed at Holy Rood House.

All those strands have continued to shape the work of this Centre for Health and Pastoral Care. Not only that, but theological enquiry also became even more explicit through the creation of the associated Centre for the Study of Theology and Health, digging at the roots of Christian accounts of healing which remained mired in a dualistic separation of physical and spiritual, or in deeply difficult accounts of sin and forgiveness, for example.

I have visited Holy Rood House as a guest a number of times over the subsequent 30 years. As with many others, I have appreciated generous hospitality in all the forms in which it is embodied in the community. It has been for me personally a place of healing and retreat, often at times of transition where, in a community context with its rhythms of prayer, activity, shared food and conversation, I could attend to God, seek space, write and move on. Elizabeth Baxter has herself described a "threshold theology" emerging from the praxis of Holy Rood House, in which she explored the listening community, where connections can be made, as a place of storytelling, in embodied ways.[3]

In December 2003, I was able to give a paper at a study day in the Centre for the Study of Theology and Health. The day overall focussed on "Pain, Possibility and Promise: A Theology of Relational Health"; and I explored the theological education context in which I was working at the

---

[3]   Baxter, "Beloved Community", p. 20.

time.[4] As a Methodist minister, I have worked in Circuit appointments in four different geographical contexts, as well as being a tutor in theological education in two different institutions, latterly at the Queen's Foundation for Ecumenical Theological Education in Birmingham.[5] In those varied contexts, some of those I have ministered alongside have similarly found Holy Rood House to be a helpful, exploratory space.

When I was invited to contribute to this volume, I was asked in connection with my interest in feminist theology, or in feminist perspectives (plural) brought to bear on continuing exploration of Christian theological traditions. Much has happened in that field during the past 30 years, i.e., since Elizabeth and Stanley Baxter took on the work which this book celebrates. I aim to briefly trace and comment on some of those changes, and then to explore the links between that work and the work of Holy Rood House. It is significant in that context that I write in the year in which the Methodist Church in Britain will be celebrating the fiftieth anniversary of the ordination of women to presbyteral ministry.[6] While the ordination of women to particular ministries in Christian churches of various traditions is only one marker of the ways in which things change over time, it remains a significant marker, and I note the link to Elizabeth's own ordination to priesthood in the Church of England in 1994, enabling her together with Stanley to model a shared priestly leadership that grounded the work of the Centre for Health and Pastoral Care for many years.

---

[4]   Jane Craske, "Not in the Abstract: Feminist Practices of Theological Education and the Bearing of Pain", unpublished paper given first at the Feminist Theology Seminar at the Society for the Study of Theology conference, 2003.

[5]   <https://www.queens.ac.uk/>, accessed 3 April 2024.

[6]   The Methodist Church recognizes two orders of ministry, presbyteral and diaconal. Up until 1974, the Methodist Church in Britain had not ordained women to the presbyteral ministry of word, sacrament and pastoral responsibility, though women had been in diaconal ministry, in the Deaconess Orders of various Methodist Churches in Britain, since the 1890s.

Thirty years of feminisms

Feminism can be defined as the commitment to the full personhood of women. It has been a label (though not the only label) under which a challenge has been issued to all that keeps women as second-class citizens across the world. The limitations placed on women's roles and identities in various societies have been named and noted at many points in human history. In the modern period as it applies to the West, and especially since the mid-twentieth century, feminism sought transformation for women's lives through liberal notions of equality, then through a Marxist-inspired focus on liberation, and for some through a focus on sexual difference and a re-valuing of the female/feminine. All of those perspectives, part of what has often been described as second-wave feminism, help us to see the value of talking not so much of feminism as of interrelated *feminisms*. That has become more and more important as challenges have been issued about whose voices and experiences have been represented by the work of some feminists, and whose have not. The sharpest critique came first from Black women, charging white feminists with racism.

In all those feminisms developed between the 1960s and the 1990s, there were many voices by the end of the 1990s, at least, implying that the battles had been won. Natasha Walter, writing *The New Feminism* in 1998, agreed that young women (at least in the British/Western context in which she was writing) were able to do more and expecting to do more than ever before. Yet the reality of the broader social picture was still of continuing gender inequality, especially material inequalities.[7] Younger women of that time, naming these continuing inequalities, began what was often labelled third wave feminism.

In April 2012, Laura Bates began the "Everyday Sexism" project, in what has sometimes been labelled a fourth wave of feminism.[8] She sought to give voice to what she and other women continued to experience as sexism and harassment. The Everyday Sexism project still collects the ordinary stories of sexism that bedevil women, across the world. The

---

[7]   Natasha Walter, *The New Feminism* (London: Virago Press, 1999 [first published 1998]).

[8]   <https://everydaysexism.com/>, accessed 3 April 2024.

project has sought to offer support and to educate. It has publicized many incidents, ranging from those which have been frustrating and belittling in their continuation of stereotypes, or discriminatory in personal and structural settings, through to terrifying physical assaults. The project has taken many forms, for instance pointing out ongoing sexualization in the fashion or music industries, or developing better approaches to dealing with harassment and assault, with an emphasis, too, on suggesting avenues of support for a wide range of women in different cultures and contexts.

In addition, in recent years, the #MeToo movement has uncovered deeply disturbing experiences from harassment to sexual assault, rooted in many different industries and workplaces, beginning with the film industry.[9] While the Everyday Sexism project and the #MeToo movement both began with a focus on women's experiences, they have also opened the way to others, of different gender and sexual identities, to name the forms of harassment they have suffered. At the same time, there has been increasing attention given to the construction of masculinities, again differently inflected in different contexts, not least with attention given to intersectionality with race.

Even in the most recent weeks, as I have been writing this piece, there have been stories of online abuse of female sports pundits and presenters.[10] The evidence in these Western/European contextual examples is of ongoing misogyny and backlash when it seems advances are being made for women. The examples could be multiplied and varied in a range of contexts across the world, with most media attention in recent years probably given to the situations in Afghanistan and Iran. The story is of some advances and also of a pernicious persistence, which takes different cultural forms, of attitudes and actions that endanger women and girls, and not them alone. There remains a deep need for places in which these ongoing experiences can be attended to.

---

[9]   <https://metoomvmt.org/>, accessed 3 April 2024, a global movement to end sexual violence.

[10]   <https://www.bbc.co.uk/sport/football/68001449>, accessed 3 April 2024.

Thirty years of feminist theologies

Feminist theologies, from the 1960s onwards, mirrored many of the perspectives and concerns of broader feminisms, looking at how women's voices were (or were not) included in Christian traditions and communities, seeking the equal leadership of women, and also asking questions about distinctiveness, with new theological and liturgical language, images and perspectives. At times, separate Christian spaces for women, or for those who were women-identified, emerged.

A volume of the journal *Feminist Theology* from May 2023 celebrates the groundbreaking feminist theological work of Rosemary Radford Ruether, who died in 2022.[11] Ruether's work encompassed a wide range of themes, developing over time, and can stand as an example of others' work. She explored the theological resources that could be used to reshape Christian doctrine.[12] She supported a Women-Church movement responding to liturgies and practices that harmed women and others spiritually.[13] In the 1990s, she developed an emphasis on the oppression of women *and the earth*.[14] In the 2000s, she focussed on work in relation to world religions. In all her activism and scholarship, she was concerned to develop conversations with women theologians from across the world.

Short summaries of "feminist theology" or language of "women's experience" (in the singular) have been problematic from the time that different perspectives on feminism were being developed, not always harmoniously, in the 1970s, throughout the 1980s and beyond. In the field of feminist theologies, Jacquelyn Grant's *White Women's Christ*

---

[11] *Feminist Theology* 31:3 (2023), celebrating the life and work of Rosemary Radford Ruether.

[12] Rosemary Radford Ruether, *Sexism and God-Talk* (London: SCM Press, 1983).

[13] <https://www.religion-online.org/article/the-women-church-movement/>, accessed 3 April 2024.

[14] Rosemary Radford Ruether, *Gaia and God: An Ecofeminist Theology of Earth Healing* (London: SCM Press, 1992); (ed.), *Women Healing Earth* (London: SCM Press, 1996).

and Black Women's Jesus, from 1989, explicitly critiqued white feminist theologians' work, as she noted their concentration on gender to the exclusion of race and racism, and therefore their inability to draw on Black women's experiences or speak into their contexts.[15] The theological voice that Grant and other African American women developed became womanist theology. Subsequently, the voices have diversified so much further. Nicola Slee comments on the myriad forms of theology that could be named: "To narrow the focus to my own field of feminist theology itself, the forms bifurcate and multiply at a dizzying rate: womanist, *mujerista*, Asian and African women's theologies have been joined by new discourses around gender and the search for new masculinities. There have been backlash, post-feminism, post-Christian and post-denominational feminist theologies."[16]

Slee herself explores the field of feminist practical theology, building on the work of others, through the metaphor of "fragments" in her collection of essays, *Fragments for Fractured Times*, from which the previous quotation is drawn. It is important to note the attitude that is taken to these developments: are they regarded as destructive fragmentation, or a rich and creative diversity? Slee argues for a "dynamic toing and froing"[17] between the fragmentation and the drawing together of voices and contexts as the best response to these developments.

Feminist Theology journal, which is the product of the already-mentioned British and Irish Feminist School of Theology, has published in recent editions articles on the religious and cultural concerns and practices of very specific contexts: on particular women in history; on the ways in which some theologies and practices continue to be male-focussed; and on new perspectives in the light of new questions around gender and sexuality, not least trans and intersex experiences and the questioning of male/female gender binaries. At best, careful attention is being given to the specificity of a much greater range of experiences.

---

[15]   Jacquelyn Grant, *White Women's Christ and Black Women's Jesus: Feminist Christology and Womanist Response* (Atlanta, GA: Scholars Press, 1989).

[16]   Nicola Slee, *Fragments for Fractured Times: What Feminist Practical Theology Brings to the Table* (London: SCM Press, 2020), p. 12.

[17]   Slee, *Fragments*, p. 13.

The ongoing feminist theological journey has to be one of humility and making connections between different contexts.

What, though, of the ways in which churches have engaged with these increasingly diverse theologies? Are they ignored or taken for granted? In some mainstream Christian churches in Britain, over the past 30 years more women have come into ordained leadership; in others there are still issues of exclusion from some key roles on the grounds of gender. I still find, however, that many women entering preaching and teaching ministries or ordination training have a story of how they have had to come to terms with certain expectations, or histories, or biblical passages, in a way men don't. Every time I think we are finally through all that, another woman, considerably younger than I am, tells her story of exclusion or limitation, or people's expectations of her as a woman.

However, I also hear all-too-similar stories, differently inflected, from those of Global Majority Heritage backgrounds, who argue that similar issues of exclusion are being repeated, often more overtly, in relation to racism. There are also experiences to be heard in relation to those with different abilities, those who are neurodiverse and those who have suffered heterosexism and transphobia in the churches. The challenge, here too, is to recognize what has happened to many women, while also attending to the voices of others who experience exclusion.

My own experience has been not so much hostility to women in particular roles but of hostility to overtly feminist theological ideas in churches. In the church I know best, this is true at the local level, where even a commitment to using inclusive language about people still seems to be a novelty. In 1992, the Methodist Church in Britain produced a report on inclusive language and imagery about God,[18] which was adopted by the church's governing conference, highlighting the need not simply to use inclusive language about people but to broaden the images we use for God. While the recommendations have been implemented in connexional (whole-church/national) contexts, and worked through in relation to newer liturgical resources, the report has had much less purchase on the worship led week-by-week in Methodist churches.

---

[18] "Inclusive Language and Imagery about God", Agenda of Conference (Methodist Church, 1992), pp. 462–79.

The latest "Inclusive Language Guide" produced by the Methodist Church[19] takes a much broader approach to encouraging attentiveness in our language; and it may be a different route to challenging language that imposes narrow, "normative" perspectives while offering positive alternative terms and strategies.

In 1995, a report on the experience of women presbyters, two decades after they had first been ordained, was presented to the Methodist Conference.[20] Entitled "A Cry of the Beloved", it included stories of both the acceptance and rejection of women in that form of ministry; the voices of some women who had experienced discrimination, sexual harassment and abuse were heard. The report also used a feminist theological lens to critique the practices of the Church. However, the report and its recommendations were not adopted by the Conference, which many at the time saw as a response to the explicitly feminist perspective. While many of the recommendations were in fact revisited and reshaped before being accepted in a revised form by the following year's Conference, it remains an interesting example of the clash between a mainstream church and explicitly feminist voices. Again, however, all-too-similar concerns have been raised about experiences of discrimination and the abuse of power by increasing numbers of ministers of colour. The dynamics are not simply about questions of gender, though they may be expressed in that particular form for some.

Throughout this period, I could rely on Holy Rood House to be a space where feminist theological exploration, liturgies and practices were part of the *healing* focus and simply taken for granted by women and men. A good number of British feminist theologians and liturgists have themselves been associated with Holy Rood House.[21] Elizabeth Baxter's own interest in the Wisdom/Sophia tradition has infused liturgical experimentation and creativity and drawn others into new perspectives.

---

19   <https://www.methodist.org.uk/about-us/news/the-methodist-blog/the-inclusive-language-guide/>, accessed 3 April 2024.

20   "A Cry of the Beloved", the report of the Commission on Women Presbyters and the Church, Agenda of Conference (Methodist Church, 1995).

21   Nicola Slee, Mary Grey, Elaine Graham, June Boyce-Tillman, Jan Berry and Elizabeth Baxter herself, to name just some of those most involved.

"The biblical image of Wisdom/Sophia at the crossroads is particularly helpful and inspiring for women"[22], she wrote in 2007. The project on hymns and healing, led by Jan Berry, has been another rich example of the feminist-inspired liturgical creativity encouraged and celebrated at Holy Rood House.[23]

From "bearing the pain" to safe enough spaces for storytelling: The work of Holy Rood House

In the paper I presented at Holy Rood House in 2003, "Not in the abstract", I used Rebecca Chopp's book *Saving Work: Feminist Practices of Theological Education*[24] as a lens through which to examine a course I was then teaching called "Women and Theology". The course included but was not limited to explorations of feminist theologizing. I found that my explorations with the varied groups of students with whom I worked at the time led to my wanting to add an earlier stage to Chopp's list of practices for feminist theological education, one for which my metaphor was "bearing the pain". The pain I watched many students "bearing" was to do with acknowledging what the church had been for some people, especially for many women, with dissonance between their own continued presence in the church and the rejection they had sometimes experienced. It was also the significant struggle of rethinking, of looking again, of creating anew. Pain-bearing was not a place to stay, but it was part of the journey which needed to be acknowledged.

---

[22] Baxter, "Beloved Community", p. 22.

[23] Jan Berry and Andrew Pratt (eds), *Hymns of Hope and Healing: Words and Music to Refresh the Church's Ministry of Healing* (London: Stainer & Bell, 2017).

[24] Rebecca Chopp, *Saving Work: Feminist Practices of Theological Education* (Philadelphia, PA: Westminster John Knox Press, 1995). Chopp explored narrativity (hearing the stories), ekklesiality (creating places of grace) and theology (reshaping Christian traditions) as feminist practices of theological education, with the key purpose of theological education being transformation. See p. 3.

The work of healing is related to pain: understanding it, bearing it (which relates to naming it), living with it, moving on and transforming it, not always in a one-way or linear fashion. The naming of pain, not least in the work of hearing stories, has been at the very heart of the work at Holy Rood House. In the *face2face* project, led in its early stages by Barbara Glasson, the focus has been on giving attention to those who have experienced sexual abuse. From careful listening to the stories of individuals, often those who had not been heard before, especially women, though never exclusively so, emerged new theological and spiritual insights. These were explored in Glasson's *A Spirituality of Survival: Enabling a Response to Trauma and Abuse.*[25] Not least of the significant insights is the naming of God as the "silent, listening God . . . We are mostly far too busy to have any sense of the God who is listening to us."[26] Our listening is rooted and held by the listening God.

In a more recent book, Glasson continues to name the need for this practice, in the creation of safe spaces to listen: "One positive action for peace-making would be to make small safe spaces for honest conversations . . . The theory is simple, the reality costly. The holding of such a thing would require a massive inner space for the ones that held it, but the result could be transformational."[27] Holy Rood House is dedicated to the holding of safe enough/as safe as possible spaces for listening, for paying attention. This practice is at the heart of healing and transformation. To use a different theological word, it is part of the ongoing work of God's salvation, that word so deeply linguistically and conceptually related to health and healing. In that sense, Holy Rood House practises *ekklesiality*, to use Rebecca Chopp's term: places of grace in which storytelling and dialogue happen for the purpose of transformation and liberation.[28]

[25] Barbara Glasson, *A Spirituality of Survival: Enabling a Response to Trauma and Abuse* (London and New York: Continuum, 2009).

[26] Glasson, *Spirituality of Survival*, p. 14.

[27] Barbara Glasson, *Peace is a Doing Word: Prayer Patterns for Peacemakers* (Durham: Sacristy Press, 2022), p. 52.

[28] Chopp, *Saving Work*, Chapter 3, "Places of Grace: The Practice of Ekklesia", pp. 45–71.

I have returned to storytelling as metaphor and activity time and again in my own work, for instance in reflecting on Philip Pullman's *His Dark Materials* trilogy, where the telling of true stories of ordinary lives liberates people from the world of the dead.[29] Storytelling involves choosing, shaping and making meaning: far from being simply a record of the past, it is a mode of re-creation. It is a way of developing agency, not least for those against whom power has been misused. If we can create safe enough spaces for listening and storytelling, we begin to work in the areas of discernment and accountability: themselves key practices and formative experiences in the field of theological education I am part of.

The creation of safe enough space at Holy Rood House is rooted and grounded in loving attention, embodied listening, and the many and varied practices of hospitality. It is not least significant, however, that these practices sit alongside the modelling of female leadership, of shared leadership and the building of community.

Storytelling while walking

Feminist perspectives, I believe, offer something positive and difficult to theology and to the church. But they are not the only perspectives to do that. Feminist voices are not the only ones the church needs to hear. There are critical questions to be asked about whose visions and perspectives are most easily shared in the churches—a whole set of concerns about whose voices are heard in what contexts, whose stories are told, whose aren't, and what the effects of that might be.[30]

As well as telling stories, other metaphors I have worked with over time, as in the quotation above, are "perspectives", "seeing visions" and "hearing voices", mixed as these metaphors are. As with the image of "fragments", I hope we can find richness in the diversity that results—and actively seek such diversity, rather than sitting only with perspectives and

---

[29] Jane Craske, *Being Human: In Conversation with Philip Pullman's* His Dark Materials (Peterborough: Inspire, 2007).

[30] Jane Craske, "Seeing Visions, Hearing Voices: The Consequences of Feminist Perspectives in Theology", *Epworth Review* 26:3 (1999), p. 19 [12–24].

stories that are familiar to us or are spoken by people like us. However, there is more to say about the complexity and conflicts of this.

Beyond the telling of stories, sharing experiences, there is more work to be done. Feminist scholars found relatively early on that they needed to unpack the notion of "women's experience", too often written in the singular, as if all women had the same "experience". "Experience" itself is not a simple category philosophically; storytelling involves selection, shaping and creation. In so many settings, as people tell the stories of their experience, and need those stories to be heard, there is the unsettling discovery that stories can be contradictory and even competing as they are set alongside each other. The tensions can be considerable at this point.

Can the tensions become creative? Beyond storytelling there is the need for further exploration and reflection, examination and retelling. As individuals and in community, exploration can lead to our finding links, acknowledging distinctions and difference, and noticing how relative power is used. At the Queen's Foundation, where I currently work, the renewing of our mission statement led to an important conversation about whether to choose "inclusive" or "diverse" to describe Queen's and its aims. We settled for "diverse", in part because "inclusive" seemed too settled a word, not bearing witness sufficiently to the tensions. In a recent publication celebrating the work of Nicola Slee, the editors in their introduction wrote of Queen's that it "has consistently sought to be a place where difficult conversations are possible, even if partial and faltering".[31] At times, keeping the explorations and conversation going between varied voices, in very many settings, is difficult. It is painful, and the need for healing is evident. But this is not a matter of ignoring or dispelling the tensions: "Crucially, while tensions remain, we can never lose a sense of the provisional, shifting and unstable nature of our theological work."[32] This is, for me, a hugely important assertion

---

[31]   Ashley Cocksworth, Rachel Starr and Stephen Burns (eds), *From the Shores of Silence: Conversations in Feminist Practical Theology* (London: SCM Press, 2023), p. 11.

[32]   Heather Walton, "Registering: Theology and Poetic Practice", in Cocksworth, Starr and Burns (eds), *From the Shores of Silence*, p. 70.

about the value of the "provisional" in human experience as well as in theological work.

The language of healing leads to a comparable exploration. When "healing" is translated as "cure", or as a process with a predetermined outcome, the result can be damaging. Even language of integration or wholeness can be difficult if those terms are interpreted as a set and settled end, or if they do not allow space for a more fluid account of identity.

So, might walking be one more metaphor to consider? Walking, if we analyse it, is a matter of unbalancing and rebalancing; if we are to take more than one step, and keep walking, then that unbalancing and rebalancing has to continue. In walking, we are always both unbalancing and rebalancing, in order to move forwards. For many people, beyond the stage of learning (and falling over and picking oneself up), walking seems to come very naturally and is an unconscious practice. It may have to become the focus of more attention if something impairs our ability to walk, when the actions that enable us to let go of one form of settled balance and move one more step have to become conscious again—as when someone is learning to walk again after an accident, or a hip replacement operation (where I saw it most often, in hospital chaplaincy). The brain needs to be retrained if we are to walk "unconsciously" again. Walking is not simply stable, but a fluid and provisional movement.

Walking can also be a mindful practice, and a shared activity, too. I have picked walking as my metaphor, though there may be more skilled balancing needed in running, or cycling, or skating, because there is something important about the slower pace. Storytelling while walking can be a powerful context for exploration. This is, though, still a metaphor, which does not depend for its usefulness on our physical capacities.

One of the most valuable aspects of the vision of healing that Holy Rood House offers is the commitment to overcome binaries and dualisms, not least the competing dualisms of physical/spiritual, or individual/corporate. To me, the work of the community at Holy Rood House is about life and flourishing, with an acceptance of fragility and mortality; it is about transformation for the individual, set within a particular place, with a global and cosmological reach, because the Sophia-God is found at the centre and on the margins, as the margins are recentred. Where relationality is the key, connections can be found between fragments and threads, so that the stories and perspectives of many enable the creation of something beautiful and new. Where relationality matters, there will also be tension and conflict, and our brokenness is not simply "fixed". Healing may be more a matter of constant balancing, unbalancing and rebalancing, in the face of trauma and overwhelming, and also in the midst of joy and transformation.

This vision is not of Holy Rood House as a settled space, but as a space that instigates and nurtures the ongoing activities of listening, exploration, discernment and the seeking of wisdom, embodied in hospitality, practical response and care. It involves attending to those present and looking out for those not present. Holy Rood House will not be the right space for everyone, so there are important questions to be asked about how other spaces can be encouraged. In these many ways, it may be that the insights, mistakes and complexities of feminist theologies over the past 30 years have still more to offer to the work of healing.

> There will still be struggle
> Still light and dark together
> Interweaving of frustration and joy.
> All repeated.
>
> But it will not be the same situation:
> Uniquely, in this place
> I will have moved on.[33]

---

[33] Fragment of a poem written at Holy Rood House, November 1997.

Holy Rood House and "Living in Love and Faith"

Christina Beardsley SMMS

Elizabeth's commitment to a church that fully embraces everyone has shaped the ethos of radical welcome at Holy Rood House. At Elizabeth's request, I presented a paper with the above title for the Holy Rood House Consultants' Symposium, held on Monday 6 September 2021. Given that sexual orientation and gender identity continue to be controversial subjects in both the church and the wider culture, and that inclusion is dear to Elizabeth's heart, I have expanded the paper for the purposes of this festschrift in her honour, and updated it in the light of recent events.

The Church of England and sexuality

The contemporary church's poor record in relation to people marginalized by their gender, race, sexuality, social class, physical or mental disability, as well as survivors of abuse, continues to cause harm and dismay.

During the last 30 years, people's sexual orientation, and more recently, gender identities, have been the focus of intense disagreement and controversy in many Christian denominations. More recently, UK denominations like the United Reformed Church, the Methodist Church and the Scottish Episcopal Church have made progress towards equality by enabling their clergy to conduct same sex marriages in church, while respecting the consciences of those clergy who are unable to officiate at such ceremonies on theological grounds. The Church in Wales has also moved in this direction by authorizing the blessing of same sex couples in its churches.

The Church of England, by contrast, has been slower to address the needs of same sex couples, and has even appeared hostile and unwelcoming. The House of Bishops' pastoral guidance on Civil Partnerships in 2005, and Same Sex Marriage in 2014, discouraged public blessings in church, leaving informal prayer to the clergy's "pastoral discretion". This meant that clergy who wished to bless couples publicly had to turn them away or disobey their bishops. Church of England clergy and ordinands have been permitted to contract same sex civil partnerships—which are assumed to be celibate—but not same sex civil marriages.

It is only very recently that the Church of England's governing body, the General Synod, has been permitted to discuss "issues in human sexuality"—the Church of England's euphemism for homosexuality. Instead, the Church of England has spent the past 30 years commissioning reports, or facilitating conversations, but with little outcome in terms of policy. This has led to considerable frustration, with people commenting that "the ball was being kicked into the long grass" or of "the can being kicked further and further down the road".

One reason offered for this delay has been the dynamics within the Anglican Communion, complicated by the Archbishop of Canterbury's role as one of its four "instruments of communion (unity)". Yet only since Lambeth 1998, when careful preparatory work on sexuality was set aside, has homosexuality become such a defining "issue" in the Anglican Communion. Communion participants like Phil Groves, for example, have identified a Western politicizing of Global South leaders in this matter, and the sidelining of affirming voices within the Global South itself.[1]

The Church of England's latest attempt to address sexuality and relationships, identity and marriage, the Living in Love and Faith (LLF) project, remains ongoing, and has reached a critical stage. The House of

---

[1]   The affirming position among Global South churches is articulated in T. Brown (ed.), *Other Voices, Other Worlds: The Global Church Speaks Out on Homosexuality* (London: Darton, Longman & Todd, 2006).

Bishops has, as of January 2024, authorized Prayers of Love and Faith to be used with same sex couples within existing public worship but has yet to commend this suite of prayers for use in "stand-alone" services (as agreed in principle at the November 2023 General Synod). Also awaited is the promised Pastoral Guidance which will replace—and many hope will overturn—earlier episcopal guidance preventing clergy and ordinands from marrying someone of the same sex.

To the anger and distress of many, including General Synod members who voted for change, on 25 January 2024, the two new lead bishops for LLF, Helen-Ann Hartley, Bishop of Newcastle, and Martyn Snow, Bishop of Leicester—who hold different views on relationships and sexual ethics—announced their intention to seek General Synod's commitment to "reconciliation, humility and repentance, honesty and transparency, and freedom of conscience" before "the general sense of direction" can continue.[2] Given the depth of the divisions expressed about the use of the Prayers of Love and Faith, in and beyond the General Synod, this proposal appears naïvely optimistic and potentially disruptive of due process and governance.

Why this subject?

My first stay at Holy Rood House was as a Trustee of Changing Attitude, England, which worked (and still works, though nowadays as an informal network) for the full inclusion of LGBTI+ people in the Church of England and the Anglican Communion. I was the first of several transgender trustees, and it is this perspective that I have brought to my role as a House Consultant. From August 2017 to January 2019, I was also a consultant member of LLF's Coordinating Group, but I found it impossible to continue in that role and set out my reasons in a *Church Times* article at the time.[3]

---

[2]   <https://www.churchtimes.co.uk/articles/2024/26-january/comment/opinion/living-in-love-faith-and-reconciliation>, accessed 3 April 2024.

[3]   <https://www.churchtimes.co.uk/articles/2019/1-february/comment/opinion/dr-christina-beardsley-why-i-left-the-bishops-sexuality-project>,

Principally, I failed to see how LLF would be able to reconcile the intensely held and increasingly polarized views around sexuality and gender that exist in the Church of England. I questioned this attempted reconciliation because of its inherent inequality and lack of attention to the power imbalances that exist. Once again LGBTI+ people's lives were under scrutiny rather than addressing how and why the Church's current practice was proving harmful to LGBTI+ people. These are behaviours I have documented, with collaborators, in a trilogy of books.[4]

When Elizabeth invited me to write a paper for the September 2021 Consultants' Symposium, the question she posed to me was, "Where is Holy Rood House situated relating to conversations around 'Living in Love and Faith'?" In this revised and updated version of the paper I've expanded the section about trans people, whose lives have become the subject of a toxic media "debate" in the few intervening years, a disturbing trend that Elizabeth and I have continued to discuss.

How LLF came about and what has emerged

The Church of England's Living in Love and Faith project, or LLF, to adopt the usual abbreviation, arose in the aftermath of the unexpected February 2017 General Synod decision not to "take note" of the House of Bishops' proposals in GS 2055, "Marriage & Same Sex Relationships after the Shared Conversations".[5]

GS 2055 was an attempt to maintain the Church of England's position that marriage is only possible between a man and a woman, and that

---

accessed 3 April 2024.

[4] C. Beardsley and M. O'Brien, *This is my Body: Hearing the Theology of Transgender Christians* (London: Darton, Longman & Todd, 2016); C. Dowd and C. Beardsley, *Transfaith: A Transgender Pastoral Resource* (London: Darton, Longman & Todd, 2018); C. Beardsley and C. Dowd, *Trans Affirming Churches: How to Celebrate Gender-Variant People and their Loved Ones* (London & Philadelphia, PA: Jessica Kingsley Publishers, 2020).

[5] <http://www.tgdr.co.uk/documents/229P-GS2055.pdf>, accessed 3 April 2024.

the weddings of same sex couples should not be celebrated in church. Churches, however, would be encouraged to exercise "maximum freedom" in their ministry of welcome to lesbian, gay, bisexual and trans (LGBT+) people. Specifically, this would require "a fresh tone and culture of welcome and support", as well as teaching and pastoral guidance. Like most compromises it pleased no one. For those who had expected change, same sex couples would still be treated differently from heterosexual couples, and the Church of England's discrimination against LGBT+ people was left unaddressed.

When General Synod debated GS 2055, several speakers pointed out that LGBT+ people were not a category "out there" who needed to be welcomed into our churches, but rather, fellow congregants, as well as family members, or colleagues. Some affirming members of Synod also boycotted an afternoon session in which case studies about LGBT+people in the life of the Church were to be discussed, arguing that this objectifying and problematizing of people's lives was unacceptable. For these and other reasons, the "take note" motion was lost in the House of Clergy. General Synod had proved unwilling to even acknowledge the bishops' proposals.

In response to this unprecedented outcome, the Archbishop of Canterbury issued a statement, which said, "No person is a problem, or an issue. People are made in the image of God. All of us, without exception, are loved and called in Christ. There are no 'problems', there are simply people."[6] To address "the real and profound disagreement" expressed in the General Synod debate, Archbishop Justin expressed the need for "a radical new Christian inclusion in the church. This must be founded in scripture, in reason, in tradition, in theology; it must be based on good, healthy, flourishing relationships, and in a proper 21st century understanding of being human and of being sexual."

It emerged later that the archbishops envisaged interdisciplinary teams of scholars who would consider human sexuality, relationships and marriage through the lenses of the Bible, history, the biological and social sciences, and theology and doctrine. In fact, some people had already

---

[6] <https://www.archbishopofcanterbury.org/statement-archbishop-canterbury-following-todays-general-synod>, accessed 3 April 2024.

been recruited for these workstreams, because GS 2055 had proposed "a substantial new Teaching Document on marriage and relationships", but, in the light of the General Synod vote, the emphasis changed. As well as adopting a new name, *Living in Love and Faith,* LLF began to understand itself as a pedagogical process, focussed on learning as much as teaching.

The LLF book, published in 2020, reflects that shift by combining theological essays with stories and conversations. It does not draw specific conclusions, which led Oliver O'Donovan, in a mainly favourable review, to describe it as "classically post-modern".[7] John Barton, on the other hand, has questioned this impression of openness, pointing out its "biblicism", namely, its assumption that "the Bible has to be the first port of call" on moral issues.[8] Diarmaid MacCulloch has criticized "pervading distortions caused by historical myopia in *LLF*"[9], a view confirmed by historian consultants, like Helen King, whose contributions are largely missing from the LLF book.[10] Another critical review, by Adrian Thatcher, highlights the book's failure to embrace biblical criticism, and its superficial understanding of marriage, gender and church culture.[11]

In "An Appeal", which concludes the LLF book, the bishops acknowledged their divisions over the ethics and lifestyle of opposite sex relationships, and around gender and pastoral provisions for trans

---

[7]   Oliver O'Donovan, "Mapping the Terrain for Engagement on Human Sexuality": <https://covenant.livingchurch.org/2020/11/10/mapping-the-terrain-for-engagement-on-human-sexuality/>, accessed 3 April 2024.

[8]   John Barton, "The Bible in Living in Love and Faith": <https://modernchurch.org.uk/prof-john-barton-the-bible-in-living-in-love-and-faith>, accessed 3 April 2024.

[9]   Diarmaid MacCulloch, "Living in Love and Faith": <https://modernchurch.org.uk/prof-diarmaid-macculloch-living-in-love-and-faith>, accessed 3 April 2024.

[10]   Helen King, "Living in Love and Faith: Doing History": <https://modernchurch.org.uk/prof-helen-king-living-in-love-and-faith-doing-history>, accessed 3 April 2024.

[11]   Adrian Thatcher, "Living in Love and Faith": <https://modernchurch.org.uk/adrian-thatcher-living-in-love-and-faith>, accessed 3 April 2024.

people.[12] This is slightly surprising, as the July 2017 General Synod, including the House of Bishops, had voted by a significant majority to recommend a ban on sexual conversion practices, and to welcome and affirm trans people in the life of the church. That was just six months after the GS 2055 debate, when the General Synod had been engaged in its own Shared Conversations about sexuality, and greater understanding seemed to be emerging. As the July 2017 General Synod ended, an Anglican Communion observer, whose province had already voted to marry same sex couples in church, told me that he thought that the Church of England's General Synod was itself ready for that debate, but momentum was lost, as energy, time, and money were poured into LLF.

What is at issue?

Three years later, in the LLF book, the bishops were agreed—unsurprisingly—that the "most pressing" questions they faced were around same sex relationships. The LLF course, which parishes were encouraged to run, was even more direct, claiming that same sex marriage was the key issue that now confronts the Church of England. Since the book's publication, the Methodist Church voted in August 2021 in favour of permitting same sex marriage, and the Church in Wales approved same sex blessings in September 2021.

Alongside the LLF book and the LLF course is the LLF website. There one can access numerous scholarly articles that lie behind the book, and a library of film stories, illustrating the range of relationships and people to be found among the Church of England's congregations, including same sex couples, trans people and gay people who have married someone of the opposite sex or chosen to be celibate because they believe the Bible requires it. A disclaimer explains that inclusion in the film library need not imply conformity with the Church of England's current teaching. The production of this quantity of resources in just over three years

---

12   Church of England, *Living in Love & Faith: Christian Teaching and Learning about Identity, Sexuality, Relationships and Marriage* (London: Church House Publishing, 2020), p. 422.

was a remarkable achievement, but the lack of signposting about the way forward has been a disappointment. That LLF was never intended to reach decisions on contested matters has only strengthened the impression that the project was an exercise in delay.

It has taken a further three years, during which the General Synod elections were hotly contested, and a highly polarized demographic elected, before General Synod was permitted to debate LLF. When it did so, in February 2023, it was not the hot topic of same sex marriage identified by the LLF course book that was on the agenda, but the Prayers of Love and Faith, a suite of resources designed for use with same sex couples who were already partnered or married.

In the LLF book, the bishops had claimed, as they had for some time, that they were divided over same sex relationships, but numbers were never mentioned. Was the split 50–50, 60–40, or something else? We weren't told. In 2023, however, percentages emerged, as the bishops voted in the General Synod debates and the voting figures were leaked from meetings of the House of Bishops (mainly diocesans) and the College of Bishops (diocesans plus suffragans and area bishops). The most recent figures, authorizing the Prayers of Love and Faith, indicate that the House of Bishops is roughly two-thirds in favour of this change; while leaked numbers showed an even greater percentage within the College of Bishops in favour of same sex marriage.

After more than six years of the LLF project, those opposed to the Prayers of Love and Faith complain that the theological basis for their introduction has not yet been demonstrated. Theologically, there is always more work to be done, but there are specific lacunae which Holy Rood House is well equipped to address.

Holy Rood House: Theology, sexuality and gender

The critiques of the LLF book by John Barton, Diarmaid MacCulloch, Adrian Thatcher and others demonstrate that the Church of England has further theological, spiritual and pastoral work to do, specifically, by engaging with a wider range of creative theological thinking and pastoral theology that already exists in this area. "Radical, new, Christian inclusion", which sounded so promising, was left undefined by the archbishops, and LLF has not attempted to define it. A definition is urgent.

Even though the bishops identified same sex relationship as the key issue, the LLF book did not provide a theological rationale in favour of same sex marriage. Bishops like Steven Croft[13] and John Inge[14] would do so ahead of the 2023 General Synod debates, though same sex marriage was not the substance of those debates, albeit underlying. Adrian Thatcher's critique indicated the need for a better understanding of gender, and his latest book highlights Christianity's problematic relationship with the body, especially the female body.[15] Given its long engagement with feminist theology, Holy Rood House has much to offer in this area.

As a consultant adviser to the LLF Coordinating Group I advocated for a queer theological perspective on LLF, arguing that a queer theologian should review the LLF book prior to publication. Alex Clare-Young, who replaced me as a consultant adviser to the Coordinating Group, expressed the same view, but our "advice" went unheeded. Perhaps Holy Rood could assist in encouraging the application of this and other theological lenses "from the margins".

There is growing concern about the extensive discrimination and the emotional and spiritual abuse experienced by LGBT+ people in our churches. Changing Attitude, England has for some time argued that these destructive patterns of behaviour have theological roots. Discerning how faith and belief influence these harmful and complex dynamics calls for insights from counselling and therapy, as well as theology and spirituality. Holy Rood House's integrated approach to the human person represents a unique blend of theory, skill and practice that could contribute to this sensitive area of work.

---

[13] Steven Croft, Bishop of Oxford, "A Letter to the Diocese of Oxford", <https://mailchi.mp/oxford.anglican.org/pastoral-letter-llf-synod-vote-feb-23>, accessed 3 April 2024.

[14] John Inge, "An open letter from Bishop John", <https://www.cofe-worcester.org.uk/an-open-letter-from-bishop-john.php#_edn19>, accessed 3 April 2024.

[15] Adrian Thatcher, *Vile Bodies: The Body in Christian Teaching, Faith and Practice* (London: SCM Press, 2023).

Holy Rood House: Embodiment/healing

An emphasis on a learned clergy, and on learning generally, has been a historic strength of the Church of England, but sexuality, relationships and marriage are not simply intellectual matters, topics for scholars, study and group discussion, which has been the LLF model. Sexuality, relationships and marriage are about our bodies as well as our minds, our emotions as well as our thoughts, flesh as well as spirit. As Bishop Rowan Williams recognized long ago, our sexuality is bound up with "the body's grace".[16] LLF acknowledged the value of embodiment by including people's stories in its book, course and film library resources, but this emphasis is more difficult to sustain now that the process has moved to the synodical arena of motions, amendments, standing orders and debate.

Having spent a decade (1989–99) exploring dance as part of my spiritual practice, I was thrilled, on my first visit to Holy Rood House, to find a booklet in the chapel with a dance version of the Eucharist.[17] On a subsequent visit with the Sibyls—the nationwide group for Christian transgender, non-binary and intersex people, their partners and allies— we danced this Eucharist. Holy Rood House's commitment to healing and the theology of healing could assist the Church of England to adopt a less cerebral, more embodied approach as it seeks to develop new policies about human relationships.

---

[16]   Rowan Williams, "The Body's Grace" (1989), <https://www.anglican.ca/wp-content/uploads/2010/10/the-bodys-grace.pdf>, accessed 3 April 2024.

[17]   Elizabeth Baxter, "Dance", in *Eucharistic Services for Holy Rood House and Hexthorpe Manor* (n.d.), pp. 37–44.

Holy Rood House: Brave space or safe space

To avoid potentially harmful risks associated with discussing contentious matters across theological and ecclesiastical difference, LLF's Pastoral Advisory Group developed a set of Pastoral Principles[18] designed to maintain respectful, non-judgmental listening by participants when LLF is discussed in parishes, deaneries and synods. These Pastoral Principles work in some settings, but the hostile framing of certain questions posed at General Synod shows that the culture they promote is yet to be embedded at that level of the Church of England's governance. My own recent research, with others, into the experience of LGBT+ clergy, has also shown that in ecumenical settings, like the ministers' fraternal, some Church of England clergy have refused to welcome clergy from another denomination who are trans or in a same sex marriage, as if theological rectitude excuses one even from politeness and civility towards those with whom one disagrees.

Meanwhile, the Church of England's protracted and increasingly polarized disagreements about sexuality and gender identity have led to calls for alternative structures, like those put in place following the 1992/3 decision on women's priestly ordination and the 2014 decision to consecrate women as bishops. It seems that the longer the church has spent talking about sexuality and gender, the less inclined people become to engage with one another across difference. Those opposed to change now wish to dissociate themselves from those who advocate for it. Many LGBT+ people and their allies seek to avoid such confrontations, having learned, from earlier shared conversations, and appeals for "good disagreement", that being open about their lives or views risks rejection by those who "disagree".

My impression is that earlier optimistic talk about "brave spaces", where people might articulate their embodied experience to those who profoundly disagree with them, is receding, though the need may still exist, perhaps more than ever in a climate where groups are avoiding

---

18   Pastoral Advisory Group, *Pastoral Principles for Living Well Together*, <https://www.churchofengland.org/sites/default/files/2019–02/PAG-PP-website.pdf>, accessed 3 April 2024.

each other. Holy Rood House could be a venue for these difficult and uncomfortable conversations. Hardly a "neutral" ground, yet more than just a brave space: a place where those who differ might reach deeper understanding and healing. I know from my own visits to Holy Rood House that it has long been a refuge for those who need a safe space, a private space even, where they can simply be together with others of similar experience: a place of mutual acceptance away from the scrutiny of others.

Sadly, many people do not feel safe in our churches. Too many lives have been damaged by churches promoting themselves as welcoming to all, but which subsequently prove unaccepting or un-affirming of those who are not heterosexual or who are gender diverse. It's more important for Holy Rood House to maintain its reputation as a safe space than to be a brave space, unless it feels especially called to the healing work of reconciling the theological fissures in the church. Set somewhat apart, and with its own distinctive ethos, it is an ideal safe place where people can be refreshed and energized to enter brave spaces elsewhere.

Feminism and trans people (but mainly trans women)

The Church of England's painfully slow pace of change in terms of gender and sexuality, compared to the wider society in which it exists, means that its deliberations have often been overtaken by events. Trans people were included in the LLF project, but when its resources were published in 2020, same sex marriage was seen as the key issue for the Church of England to address—which is probably correct—with the pastoral care of trans people a matter of disagreement among the bishops, but less pressing.

Yet, even as LLF was underway, a perfect storm about trans people was brewing in wider society. Much of the controversy has followed the dissemination of misinformation about trans people's lives and experience, promoted by wealthy foundations and private interests keen to maintain the current culture wars at the highest level of intensity. This cultural shift has been dramatic. In 2014, black trans actress Laverne Cox appeared on the cover of *Time* magazine, next to the headline

"The transgender tipping point". Cox was starring in the Netflix drama *Orange is the new Black*, and the implication was that trans people had become mainstream. Earlier decades of shame and ostracism were over. As Christine Burns noted a few short years later, within five decades UK trans people had undergone "a journey from the shadows".[19] Thanks to UK equality legislation like the Gender Recognition Act of 2004 and the Equality Act of 2010, we were able to live openly, without fear of prejudice. We'd stepped into the light, but the acceptance proved short-lived: just over a decade, and then the onslaught against us began.

The subheading of the Laverne Cox *Time* magazine cover was "America's next Civil Rights Frontier". But frontiers can be dangerous places and the pushback against trans people in both the US and the UK has been massive. Examples are legion: the numerous attempts to introduce so-called "bathroom bills" into state legislation in the US, aimed at preventing trans people from accessing the toilets of the gender in which they are living. The controversies about trans athletes—but predominantly trans women athletes—in sporting competitions. Radio and television "debates" about trans people with no one trans in the studio to speak about their experience. Alarmist headlines suggesting that gender diverse children and teenagers are being "rushed" into transition, while the therapeutic services that support them are reviewed and then curtailed. The appointment of people with anti-trans views to government equality posts and organizations. Little wonder that the 2023 International Lesbian, Gay, Bisexual, Trans and Intersex Association Europe (ILGA-Europe) annual "rainbow map" of 49 countries across Europe showed that the UK—which led the table in 2015—had dropped to seventeenth place.

A Google search of the UK media between August 2018 and August 2019 has also revealed a staggering 878 articles about trans people—a mere 0.6 per cent of the population—in 365 days, and the onslaught has continued. This kind of media pile on doesn't happen by accident. It is a well-funded and orchestrated campaign. The UK is currently experiencing a torrent of negative propaganda—"the spreading of ideas, information,

---

[19]   C. Burns (ed.), *Trans Britain: Our Journey from the Shadows* (London: Unbound, 2018).

or rumour for the purpose of helping or injuring an institution, a cause, or a person"—about trans people. One example will suffice. According to the media, proposals to reform the legal recognition of trans people is a potential threat to same sex spaces. This is a fabrication. Gender recognition reform is about legal paperwork, documentation that trans people are never required to produce in public. Same sex spaces are regulated by the Equality Act, and contain proportionate exemptions, which can exclude trans women, for example, from women's refuges, in specific circumstances. The alleged conflict between trans (women's) rights and women's rights has scant social foundation, but this hasn't prevented it from being a media hot topic.

LGB without the T

The anti-trans bias of the UK media, and the rapid propagation of false narratives about trans people, has also caused a split in the LGBT+ movement. There are now LGB groups, firmly and pointedly "without the T", which are based on the mistaken idea that young people are being pressured into gender transition, and which argue that lesbian and gay people are being erased by an ideology determined to "trans away the gay". The LGB-only position, though still a minority one, is another example of the tendency—like requests for structural division in the Church of England, mentioned above—of groups to isolate themselves and avoid interaction with those with whom they disagree.

After decades of collaboration within LGBT+ alliances, the emergence of LGB organizations without the T, albeit small and few, has been a puzzling, even troubling phenomenon. A key question to pose to these groups is whether they are, as they claim, thoroughly pro-LGB, or does their ethos, literature and campaigning tend to be anti-trans, to some degree? For a line is surely crossed once a group or individual misrepresents or even denies the experience or reality of someone simply because they are different.

This othering of trans people, which has been normalized in UK society over the past five years, has tapped into an older strand of feminist opinion about trans women, infamously articulated by Janice

Raymond in *The Transsexual Empire*, first published in 1979. Raymond was a pupil of feminist theologian Mary Daly, so there is a potential theological link here as well, but the understanding and professional care of trans people has changed vastly in the intervening decades. Gender incongruence, once stigmatized as a pathology, is now seen as a normal human variation; and despite the impression created by the current culture wars, most feminists are not trans exclusionary; just as most LGB people are not trans exclusionary. A minority are, and those who are exclusionary make their case extremely vociferously. Anything Holy Rood House could do, perhaps through feminist theological reflection, to address this rift in feminism and within LGBT+ networks would be much appreciated.

Conclusion

Elizabeth, I salute you. For all that you have given to Holy Rood House and to the wider church. For keeping us focussed on what matters, and not allowing us to shirk the challenges involved in working for justice. Thanks to you, and shaped by feminist theology, and insights into embodiment and healing, Holy Rood House could be a rich resource to the Church of England, currently at a crossroads on the journey to equality in so many areas. A trusted, confidential place, Holy Rood House can be, in turn, and as needed, both a brave space for difficult conversations and a safe space for those who are wounded. Drawing deep from its feminist theological wells, it could even help to heal society's current stigmatizing of trans people, especially trans women.

The little that becomes enough: Reflections on hope as character, community and culture[1]

David Gee

I have sometimes wondered what churns in the spirit of guests who walk up the steps to Holy Rood House for the first time. Often distress, I imagine, sometimes despair, certainly uncertainty. And yet, it strikes me that their trauma defines them no more than their courage to bring their distress in and let it be met. They may come feeling broken, but in coming in at all they are also not broken, as the door jamb is their witness.

I have wondered also how it feels to leave after a few days, to turn from the company of care, walk down those steps again, and rejoin the motorway home, often alone. It may be painful to leave solidarity behind, feel it pale with distance. And yet its experience leaves its trace, perhaps as a kind of confidence that although one may be alone, one is also not alone—that, for having come into a community of belonging, one can go out into the world again a little more ready to meet it.

For the searching spirit, these two threshold-crossing moments form a pair. We could even say they form a rhythm, to which one first "comes in" to the refuge of care, then "goes out" again, readier to face the future.

The same twofold movement bookends Mark's Gospel (1:17) account of the disciples: not the 12 men alone but the whole throng, all who hear "Follow me" and do, following after they know not quite what, becoming

---

[1] This chapter was originally published in shorter form as *Truth's tilt* on the hopeswork.org blog.

the people they know not quite yet that they mean to be. They have come into company, sharing a journey that will waken their minds, open their hearts, cultivate their spirit. They fumble, feeling lost, but find themselves on the way.

After the coming in, the going out . . . After the crucifixion has broken the disciples' high hope of a world redeemed, three women gather at the tomb to mourn their friend in grief and gratitude, only to find he has risen and gone out into the world once again (Mark 16:1–8). What are they to do? To do likewise, and not be alarmed, for although the future is filled with dangers their courage will be met. This has been the point all along. And so they go, "trembling and bewildered",[2] into the day.

As they go out, I wonder what little they have that may be enough to face the world as they find it. I wonder the same of the guest making their way home from Holy Rood House on the A1(M). I ask the question also of myself, as an activist alarmed by a foreclosing future prophesied by one climate statistic after another, by the rise of new machines made to think in our place, by the endless invention and reinvention of violences.

Hope

To wonder what may be enough is to wander onto the ground of hope: not that unaffordable confidence in tomorrow that we call optimism, but the will to face what needs facing today and to meet the future as it comes. This hope has us hang loose from predictions, asking instead who we mean to be now, and how to live our way into the future, even one filled with dangers. And for this hope, the "enough" in question is not so much for wishing the life of the world into wholeness, but for meeting it as if its living pieces still matter.

The question—what is enough to meet the day?—has accompanied the human story from the first. It gets thrust with the most force—and the least justice—on those whose high dreams have been wrenched away by every kind of violence, people who have suffered damage both temporal and spiritual. Such trauma can abandon the soul to barren indifference.

Bible quotations are from the New International Version.

But if hope does not die in the deluge, it may yet dive more deeply. When it surfaces, it has changed.

Listening to people who have come through such crisis undefeated, I have often heard described the same radical reconstitution of their hope. After violence swept in to uproot their ingenuous faith in the future, in its place grew a new, deep fidelity to life here and now. Where future-oriented expectations had fallen down, present-centred conviction stepped up.

I first noticed this in Natalia Ginzburg's account of the bombing of her family house in the Second World War.[3] The bombing had left a child bereft of her home and yet the young Natalia wrested a difficult blessing from the rubble: the wisdom to distinguish what can and cannot be relied upon. Even bricks and mortar could not protect without doubt. "[W]e can no longer trust any of these things," Natalia wrote later, "because once, suddenly, we had to leave them behind."[4] For a child, this must have been an anguished discovery indeed, and yet learning it was a step forward, for it is true.

As violence threshed away Natalia's unquestioning trust in the world around her, a new commitment dropped like a seed into fertile ground: "Perhaps this is the one good thing that has come out of the war. Not to lie, and not to allow others to lie to us."[5] When I first read this, I had to pause. It was a new thought for me that a commitment may be more than something we choose, but also something we discover, even in the rubble—perhaps especially in the rubble.

Natalia's words, I think, point to the possibility that our high but shallow-rooted hopes may stand in the way of the real thing, until a difficult moment of disillusion, as the sweeping away of illusions, leaves the ground open for new conviction to grow. Then, hope as passive presumption gives way to hope as passional commitment. *Our hope is that care will prevail* becomes, perhaps: *Our hope is to care. People can be trusted* shifts to: *We mean to trust. Let us turn this crisis around* morphs into: *Let this crisis turn us around.*

---

[3] Natalia Ginzburg, "The Son of Man", in Marjorie Agosin (ed.), *A Map of Hope: Women's Writings on Human Rights* (New Brunswick, NJ: Rutgers University Press, 1999).

[4] Ginzburg, "The Son of Man", p. 4.

[5] Ginzburg, "The Son of Man", p. 5.

Tilt

I like to imagine the three disciples similarly charged with intention as they leave their friend's empty tomb and go into the world again. None goes out quite the same as they came in, but go they do, less certain of the future though more sure that they meet the world as they mean to. Hence the root meaning of "disciple" as a person under discipline, which for these disciples is to sustain a conscious, lifeward tilt.

After all, the disciples of Mark's story are not out to do whatever they like. These are people of faith, seized of a hopeful purpose that, though freely chosen, will not easily let them go. They may not know what to do, may lack answers they wish they had, but as their spirit leans towards the life within and around them, they do know which way to face.

Such discipline of self-constraint is bound to change who these individuals are and how they meet the world. It is bound, in other words, to season their character and enrich their relationships. Just as Natalia Ginzburg emerged from her crisis into a new discipline of truthfulness, I have heard others talk of their hope as the desire of care, the openness of thoughtfulness, the humility of prayer—all these and more. These are commitments of spirit, which can lend character new bearing, in all senses of that word: directedness, composure and holding something of value.

Just as significant, I think, is that hope walks in company. As the disciples of Mark's story first set out, the same new commitments that begin to shape their character also gather in the community of the emerging church and inspire the stories it begins to live by. By the story's end, when the three women go out of the tomb into the day, nothing suggests that their hope is a private endeavour. Hope's work—and its song—are held in common in the character, community and culture of these inspired people-on-the-way.

Compare this with this similarly inspired account of the 1990s British roads protests from Phil Pritchard, one of thousands who climbed the trees in solidarity with our wild spaces against the machinery of anthropocentric aggression:

There was a sense in me of urgency, purpose. I felt I was part of an immune response, protecting life on Earth: an antibody defending life. We took on the dominant culture, challenged the destruction of Sites of Special Scientific Interest, Scheduled Ancient Monuments, put our bodies, emotional wellbeing, and freedom on the line. The protests were characterized by "noisy defeats and quiet victories", as one commentator said.

What are they doing now, those 1990s roads protesters? Many I meet are nurturing a love of the natural world in young people, sometimes by setting up food growing projects in schools. Lots are involved in building a network of skilled, agro-ecological farmers who produce food with short supply chains and leave space for nature. Others are campaigning for better public transport and safer provision for cyclists. Some have stepped into the world of academia and local politics.[6]

This, for me, carries the ring of a disciple's journey too. It attests to the same lifeward tilt and the conviction to which it gives rise, and to passionately enacted commitments of character, community and culture.

Turn

In the face of the runaway urgencies that now besiege our future, Phil's story, like Mark's, proffers an equally urgent invitation to hold the commitments of hope in common, reaching over the many borders that divide who is in from who is out. The story of Holy Rood House is another such invitation. Indeed, stories like these must number in the millions worldwide, yet they remain marginal, a prophetic provocation to the norm but not the norm itself.

By way of wondering why, one can ponder a place that seems to lack hope and ask what makes it so. I am not thinking of the war in Ukraine, or Gaza, or some other calamity. If hope is a kind of work, these places

---

[6]   Phil Pritchard, "Singing Hearts: A Reflection on the Roads Protests of the 1990s", published on the hopeswork.org blog, 2024.

manifest it in abundance through thousands of brave daily practices of mutuality and care. Human rights defenders resist violence from all sides of the wars; neighbours share scarce resources and face dangers together; almost everywhere reigns an unspoken consensus that children and elderly come first.

By an apparently hopeless place, I mean one where hope's work and its song are altogether harder to find. I think of my childhood hometown right in the middle of Middle England, caught up in the fiction that the more comfortable life gets, the more successful it becomes. In the years of my childhood, you could watch news of the Falklands War at six and switch to *Sale of the Century* at seven thirty without a twinge. Today, the chemically perfect lawns and parked-up SUVs, some marketed as "Zen cocoons"[7]—all well defended by a millionaire MP—still belie the same flimsy haven far from the fray. At the extreme, it strikes me as a culture facing away from life's essential vitality—numbed, anxious, rootless, adrift, in every way expensive, and still widely coveted.

This contrast is obviously too neat. I do not really imagine a place of unswerving, hopeful action "over there" and one entirely bereft of it "over here". But by these examples I do mean to suggest two opposing leanings that do much to structure our lives and societies. One tends towards the life in and around us, reaching outwards over the frontiers of exclusion, as well as inwards to the life that is right here in all its intimate particularity. The other, its shadow, shrinks back to defend what and whom one knows against all else. Both tendencies, held in tension in probably every human heart, emerge as radically human, radically divergent responses to a future filled with dangers.

If this description is fair, then the tension between these two leanings holds the future in the balance. How well we heed the life around us, how assuredly it draws our devotion, has perhaps never been more vital, more so than how much we know or have or do. As matters stand, our societies show signs of swinging the other way, cowed behind walls, rattling nuclear sabres, pushing back the boats, cheerleading strongman leaders who preside over all the anxiously antagonistic insularity with a winning smile.

---

[7]   Pritchard, "Singing Hearts".

It suits the powers that be that our care for life unfamiliar to us may atrophy. The impulse to care at all is deliberately disparaged, not least in the shouting headlines of billionaire media barons who frame every outcast as a threat. I think too of advertising which, in the words of marketeer-turned-artist Darren Cullen, "takes a mother's love for her child and uses it to sell bleach".[8] All flimflam, we know, but these are such dominant lies, which so mesh and merge with daily life that they begin to pass unnoticed. Left unchecked, the daily consumed lie consumes daily life in turn, leaving our societies truncated in care, certainly impoverished in hope.

This is spiritual violence, which the deep hope of Natalia Ginzburg, Phil Pritchard or indeed Mark's disciples defies. By committing to tell the truth, Natalia faced down the sham that is war. With steadfastness and song, Phil and his tribe of all-comers confronted the pretence that societal advancement means shoving the humane and the wild aside. The disciples, too, having accepted the invitation to "follow me", began a long turn away from a violent social order. And how many guests have crossed the threshold of Holy Rood House seeking refuge from some spiteful god, carrying a buried intuition that it too is a lie?

Choose

I have become fascinated about whether the tilt and turn of such deeper hope can be precipitated more widely, coming in from the margins to occupy the common ground on which communities and societies stand. What might lead us collectively to favour a future more generous?

I can think of nowhere this question had to be faced more squarely than in the Eastern bloc during the Cold War, after decades of state communism had colonized the minds of the people with a particularly brute charade. In every high street, tin lilies hanging from every lamppost would tinnily spout every Soviet anthem to every passer-by. From each greengrocer's window, the same sterile poster would call the world's

---

8   Darren Cullen (2015), "Advertising" [artwork], <https://www.royalscottish academy.org/artworks/7574-darren-cullen-advertising-2015/>, accessed 3 April 2024.

workers to faux unity. Informants would watch from street corners to report the least deviance. People still danced, dreamed, fell in love, but as time passed, they grew meeker, suffocating under a grey circus of control that seemed set to last for ever.

In fact, the seeds of the regime's downfall were growing unseen. The more the system prised apart the lives that people meant to lead and the lives that they were made to lead, the more it built a subversive charge in them. The more the people acquiesced and did what was expected of them, the more a cost to the conscience mounted and agitated the soul: *I am not being the person I mean to be; we are not being the people we mean to be.* In sum, the more the game made the people play along, the more it imperilled itself.

Despite the system's apparently total control, despite the people's outwardly hopeless predicament, the Czech playwright and dissident Václav Havel (2018) wrote with startling confidence that "the lie" cannot for ever imprison the "essential aims of life".[9] It was precisely because daily life was being diminished to absurdity, Havel believed, that people would have to reckon with who they are and how they live—with what their own truth asks of them. Eventually, the scales must tip. Then something "snaps", as Havel put it, and the choice of saying "no" must be faced, of denying the lie and risking an "attempt to live within the truth".[10]

Much of Havel's account matches, I think, our collective predicament today. If some glimmer of a brave new world cannot invite us forth in hope, perhaps what can is the daily experience of living under norms so hostile to human and ecological dignity, so anathema to the elan of life itself, that they become unbearable. Not unbearable to everyone, perhaps, but to enough of us in the social sea-swell that the tide may start to turn.

It can happen. Havel's confidence in "the power of the powerless"[11] was vindicated a decade later when Czechoslovakia's people, exasperated with the Soviet lie, finally threw off its yoke. Even had the Velvet Revolution

---

[9]   Václav Havel, *The Power of the Powerless* (London: Vintage, 2018), p. 34.

[10] Havel, *The Power of the Powerless*, p. 37.

[11] Havel, *The Power of the Powerless*, p. 1.

never come, Havel's hope would still have been worth the work. But come it did. And anything that has happened once can happen again.

In my own early journey as an activist, I can recognize something of the existential turn that Havel describes. When I was seven years old, I happened upon a CND poster showing a gigantic mushroom cloud, captioned with a few words whose meaning lay beyond me: *Do not go gentle into that good night / Rage, rage against the dying of the light.*[12] I remember staring at the monochrome image a long time, learning a lesson for which I have the words only now: the world is not safe.

As I understand this moment, the poster achieves nothing by itself, and nor can the waiting openness of the child. But when the two come together—when Dylan Thomas's words tilt towards the uncomprehending child and the child tilts towards them in turn—then a moment of unsettling truthfulness lands. This was not my doing, nor the poster's, but the encounter between the two precipitated a vital movement of the spirit. It disturbed the life of the lie.

The psychology of the moment is significant here, I think. The child has not gained understanding so much as lost an illusion that had kept them from seeing their world clearly. That moment of disillusion leaves them with a choice. They can try to keep calm and carry on, anxiously smothering the life that newly stirs in them. Or they can make room for it in their unease and allow their failing knowledge of the world to give way a little further. In other words, they can double down on the domesticating spectacle of the lie, or allow it to break, rather as a spell breaks, and step into a new, feral thoughtfulness.

Today, I remember that moment not as a singular epiphany but as one of a long and slender thread of *precipitating encounters*—some fleeting, some enduring, all unexpected—which have tugged me willingly and unwillingly towards a life more thoughtful. Nothing has snapped. Perhaps like you, I feel just as caught between an attempt to live within the truth and the life of the lie, as if saved and damned all at once. The only change I count is that now I know which way I mean to face.

---

[12] Dylan Thomas, "Do not go gentle into that good night", in John Goodby (ed.), *The Collected Poems of Dylan Thomas: Centenary Edition* (London: Weidenfeld & Nicolson, 2016).

Practise

So, returning to the three disciples at the end of Mark's story, who step out into the world with a deeper feeling for who they are, who they are not, and who they mean to be, knowing that the future must be lived into. Bewildered as they are, filled with grief and with gratitude, they go out into the day because it has become the only way to go.

In Mark's book, the story ends there, with a beginning. It is a beginning that looks significantly our way as if, as the disciples go out, they glance back at the reader to ask, "Well? Coming with us?" For we too stand on the threshold of the day that must be met, knowing that it will make demands we do not foresee. That day is a guest's journey home from Holy Rood House. That day is the rubble-strewn ground where Natalia Ginzburg's childhood home stood just yesterday. That day is also the long, slow, downward slide of humanity's self-absorbed, self-denying ecocide. Will we go out to meet it? How? What is the little we have that may be enough?

The disciples go out to meet the world charged with intention. They go out in company, walking in the companionship of a hope held in common. And though they go out in uncertainty, they will keep telling one another the story they belong to, so as not to forget which way to face. In these ways, the disciples go out clothed in spirit, broken and also unbroken, still vulnerable before violence but preserved against the lies on which it trades.

To hold to the way, they will have to carry, like recipes, the practices that cultivate their character, community and culture. Since these are religious people, the cupboard is not bare. *Religare* means in essence to "go through again": gather again around the sacred, draw on its aid, tell the story over, utter the prayer once more, commit anew, relieve, refresh. In antiquity as now, religion's spiritual rhythm invites its disciples to come back in, and then encourages them to go out, a little fitter to face the day again.

When religion does not offer this—when it degenerates, as it often does, into a confusion of comfort and condemnation—practices that restore and revivify us in our commitments may still be cobbled together regardless. Phil Pritchard recalls the DIY "music, song, and camp culture" that kept gathering up the roads protesters into their love of life, salving their grief and anger at the destruction they could not prevent. In communist Czechoslovakia, people flocked to absurdist theatre to laugh out loud at the life of the lie, and illegally passed *samizdat* poetry from hand to hand, insisting on freedom of the spirit. It seems to me that these practices too may belong to *religare*, as the spiritual clothing-and-reclothing that has enabled communities of care to go out once more and meet the day in hope.

Once again, this thought will trouble any notion of hope as a private journey. Hope needs its places of rough-edged fellowship to "come into" for refuge, remembrance and revitalization. Be they the countercultural netherworld of theatre, the suddenly sung song around the campfire, the natural temple of the wildwood or river, these are small republics of hope that occupy a place in time and space where the life of the lie has no dominion.

By the norms of the times, these are marginal places—Holy Rood House is one—though what they do belongs to the heart of things. Among those who gather there, Life comes as itself, and as promised. And though such places may be messy, falling short of themselves, they yet share what Wendell Berry (1990) has called a "hearable wholeness", showing that the practices of conscious hopefulness are also those that lean towards flourishing, and have not given up on its possibility.[13]

As I imagine the three women leave the empty tomb to meet their future, I think of all our fellowships of hopeful practice that "attempt to live within the truth". Truth, that is, not as the steady accumulation of right answers to what the world needs, but the deepening and broadening of care. The women encourage in me personally the consciously vulnerable wisdom of bewilderment, for violence is indeed bewildering, but also the charged intention to take life's side, nonetheless. Am I coming with them? I want to.

---

[13]   Wendell Berry, "A poem of difficult hope", in *What are People for?* (Berkeley, CA: Counterpoint, 1990).

Allow

All these stories—the courage of the disciples, the sensibility of the roads protesters, the defiance of Natalia Ginzburg, the faith of the Cold War dissidents—fill me with a feeling for hope at work in the world. And yet they also share the same bleak astonishment at life's continual violation, as its witnesses, though also, with all of us, as its unwitting agents. I think of Peter's bitter tears (Mark 14:66–72) the moment the fact landed with him, as the same has with me, that he had already had a hand in the violence to come on the morrow.

And yet, is the shock of violence really the thing that brings hope to life? Violence may astonish, but only by subtraction—by the gaping absences it leaves behind. Its necrotic action lacks the vital means, it seems to me, to turn our company of humanity to attention and care. It may be that the creative force powering hope is found not in knowing violence as theft, but in already knowing the life it violates as gift. Peter's tears issued from his shame, but his shame issued from his love, which had been there all along. In the end, those were tears of care.

As I write, here at home on my boat, the sun scintillates off the river in spate, dazzling the frozen flood plain beyond. Many days, our nearest star passes me by as a mere stage-light for our straitly human drama, but in an occasional moment of attentiveness I have felt its promise warming through me, urging me outwards from my narrower self. This too is an astonishment, one that makes itself available every morning should I care to notice. When I remember to remember, I am left a little more undone, a little more awake to a breathing world that will, if I allow, keep tilting me its way.

I am left for now with this: an attempt at truthfulness more than denies the lie; it also learns to love the life the lie diminishes. Why else would we labour to crack the brittle spectacle open, but that we have already begun to move with the life of the world it hides, hoping to meet its teeming vitality with our own? Could this be the little that becomes enough? Learn the songs of the birds, favour the outcast's story, it is not too late. Tilt head, heart and hand towards the life that moves in you—commune, create.

Theological humanism and human flourishing

David Jasper

This essay will be an attempt to offer a very personal reflection on the experience of being an Anglican priest at a time when the church as an institution is clearly in decline and all too often seems to be stuck with a structure, a theology and assumptions that offer little by way of escape and recovery. I begin with a remark made about myself by David Fergusson, Regius Professor of Divinity at the University of Cambridge, made in 2022, expressing a position which I am sure Elizabeth will immediately recognize, though it came as rather a surprise to me.

> Though critical of the institution[1] and often displaying a radical theological scepticism, David has remained within the household of faith . . . . Though labels are always hazardous and of limited use, I would judge David to represent a Christian humanism that is much needed today. In this, he points us towards the end of the church.[2]

The last phrase can, of course, be read in two quite different ways, and perhaps both are appropriate. For the end of an institution in any

---

[1]   In my case the Scottish Episcopal Church.

[2]   David Fergusson, "Foreword", in Bridget Nichols and Nicholas Taylor (eds), *The End of the Church? Conversations with the Work of David Jasper* (Durham: Sacristy Press, 2022), p. vi.

recognizable form does not at all mean the end or conclusion of the church. Yet a great deal of baggage to which we are often deeply—and sometimes oddly—attached must be shed along the way. But it is the phrase "Christian humanism" and its implications which I wish to explore further here, although I would prefer to change it slightly to the broader term "theological humanism".[3]

I take my start from the thinking of Charles Taylor in his landmark book *A Secular Age* (2007),[4] in which he follows the shift from "Western Christendom" to the contemporary "secular age", suggesting that this is not so much a radical change but rather a rediscovery of forms of "religion" which are less institutional and more private and individual than hitherto. Religion—and this includes Christianity—has not vanished but has been transformed, and the churches have failed to adapt to this change. I remain absolute in this assertion, and its spirit is embodied in a remarkable way in the life and ministry of Elizabeth Baxter. In her, we see that it is possible to be loyal to the church and its beliefs while not being dragged down by its institutional limitations. Rather we find that a devotion to humanity held within the love of God is at the heart of all life—a deeply held theological humanism.

In this essay, I will explore, in a rather personal manner, an aspect of this change by examining how today we might seek a condition of human flourishing through a reflection on the nature of theological humanism and its practical outcomes. The term "theological" rather than simply "religious" is important as I would contest that a significant reason for the decline of the churches has been their almost total abandonment of the theological project which properly sustains them, and a retreat into what David Klemm and William Schweiker have called "hypertheism". This is the condition in which the imposition of dogma or the retreat into forms of fundamentalism or administrative absolutism render religion simply authoritarian with the resultant and inevitable curtailing of freedoms. It

---

[3] In these reflections, I am especially grateful for the thinking of David Klemm and William Schweiker in their fine book *Religion and the Human Future: An Essay on Theological Humanism* (Oxford: Blackwell, 2008).

[4] Charles Taylor, *A Secular Age* (Cambridge, MA: Harvard University Press, 2007).

occurs when a church identifies God with its own interpretation of the nature of God.

The opposite of this Klemm and Schweiker call "overhumanization", in which raw human power is employed to shape reality without any recourse to the transcendent, and the result is ultimately totalitarian systems of government and the exploitation of natural resources in the service of human beings. The present ecological crisis is a direct result of overhumanization. Such things are seemingly unimaginable but can happen all too easily. Witness the shadow that hangs over the USA today.

Between these two extremes of the religious and the secular, both of them finally deadly for human flourishing, I seek a middle way which is grounded in the freedom to explore the integrity of life for all people and ultimately all creation. It takes its beginning from the permission granted to the other to be themselves and this is extended in the imperative to oneself to know what it is to "be". This is much more than the philosopher Kant's famous Enlightenment dictum *"Sapere aude!"*—which roughly means simply "grow up" or learn to use your own understanding.[5] That too easily becomes a pathway towards overhumanization. It is closer to St Augustine's celebrated statement at the beginning of the *Confessions*— "My heart is restless until it finds its rest in God." In brief, my humanity cannot flourish until it is transfigured (an important word) by finding itself in the wholly other—in short, the divine. The path of true being is a restless one, exemplified in the life of pilgrimage which the Celtic Church placed at the heart of Christianity. In their search for integrity the Celts laid no great stress on ecclesiology but rather on the community that was living, changing and endlessly hospitable.[6] Such a form of being makes no absolute claims for itself but acknowledges the other in their otherness in a form of what the Italian philosopher Gianni Vattimo has called "weak theology". But such weakness is never to be dismissed lightly, for in it lies also great strength.

---

[5]   The phrase is from Horace, *Epodes* 1, 2, 40, and means literally "Dare to be wise". Immanuel Kant, *Political Writings*, ed. Hans Reiss (Cambridge: Cambridge University Press, 1977), p. 54.

[6]   See further Ian Bradley, *The Celtic Way*, new edition (London: Darton, Longman & Todd, 2003), pp. 70ff.

This theological humanism that I am beginning to explore requires a persistent exercise of the imagination upon which faith finally rests. Many years ago, the theologian and bishop (a breed of church person now all too rare) Ian Ramsey used to insist on the importance of modelling for exploring the proper nature of both human and divine activity,[7] and his books on the subject have accompanied me for more than 50 years since the early days of my own ministry. So, allow me to explore three models, not necessarily theological, of the context in which human flourishing may take place.

The first finds its beginnings for us, though it is undoubtedly much older than that, in the first chapters of Genesis: the model of the garden. Just for one moment in Genesis, Chapter 2, there is an idyllic vision of a garden provided by God and maintained by Adam in perfect harmony. "The Lord God took the man and put him in the garden of Eden to till it and keep it" (Genesis 2:15). A little later, Adam is joined by Eve, both naked and unashamed, a tiny community that is celebrated in John Milton's *Paradise Lost*—just for a moment. Contrast this with the desecrations of the natural world by modern exploitation—forests felled, the earth gouged for minerals and oil, the atmosphere poisoned by toxic industrial fumes. And none of us are innocent, and we cannot say that it is not our fault. Every Sunday I drive my car, fuelled in part by petrol, to church, where I praise God for all creation. The word "integrity" is insistent here—for human flourishing is dependent on the integrity of *all* creation. And none of us can do it alone, for we are creatures of community and dependent upon one another if we are truly to be ourselves. And so to the second model—the school.

Human beings flourish when they are given the opportunity to learn and grow, and where people are deprived of education the results in society are quickly all too clear. Of Jesus himself we are given a glimpse in Luke's Gospel of a human being who as a boy "increased in wisdom and in years" (Luke 2:52)—he had to learn, like everyone else. How far we are succeeding in the exercise of teaching the next generation seems very unclear, but it is quite evident that as flourishing human beings we need

---

[7] See, for example, Ian T. Ramsey, *Models for Divine Activity* (London: SCM Press, 1973).

to be educated and to learn the broad art of theological humanism. We should recall that bishops are, essentially, not administrators but teachers of the faith. In the Scottish Ordinal of 1984, the newly consecrated bishop is one who is called under Christ's authority to "*teach* and enable others to bear witness, so that God's Word may enlighten the people of God and heal the nations". In Mark's Gospel the first thing that Jesus does after the initial gathering together of his disciples is to enter the synagogue in Capernaum and *teach* (Mark 1:21). On his second missionary journey, Paul lectures and *teaches* at the ancient university of Athens, the Areopagus (Acts of the Apostles 17:22–31). As we have failed in the first model, the garden, how far have we succeeded in the second model, the school? An old friend of mine who taught for some 30 years at his university in the United States once said that he firmly believed in the university as an institution which was there to make the world a better place. But, he concluded, "I'm least happy about the fact that after my three decades in higher education our society appears to be in worse shape than ever. I take this personally."[8] As a teacher myself I know what he means.

But it was the same teacher, Robert Detweiler, who also taught me one of the most important lessons which can be applied not only to teachers but to everyone else as well. It is an inevitable part of being human and it is a paradox, but in order to flourish we need also to learn to be a failure. Robert describes a great novelist who was also a scholar-manqué, and there is many an academic (myself included) who would fain have been novelists. But I have failed in this. The best book in recent years on this subject is Beverley Clack's *How to be a Failure and Still Live Well*.[9] The secret, of course, is what about us we honestly admit to ourselves, for in any community the first person you have to learn to live with is yourself.

My third model has its origins in literature. It is that of the stage on which we are all players and actors. But I am not thinking only of

---

[8] Robert Detweiler, in David Jasper and Mark Ledbetter (eds), *In Good Company: Essays in Honour of Robert Detweiler* (Atlanta, GA: Scholars Press, 1994), p. 448.

[9] Beverley Clack, *How to be a Failure and Still Live Well* (London: Bloomsbury, 2020).

Shakespeare's (or rather Jacques') great speech from *As You Like It*, but of all of us. For indeed we are all called to learn and play our part on the stage of life in the company of others, and indeed, in order to flourish we need to learn many parts and adapt to different dramas. For the stage offers us both tragedy and comedy as well as sometimes melodrama. Tragedy can be a hard context in which to flourish but we need to be reminded that, from time to time, we, too, are called like Kent at the end of *King Lear* simply to soldier on without pressing for all the answers, accepting things as they are. Sometimes the world is too large for us, but that does not mean that we cannot continue to pursue human flourishing and freedom within religion and without requiring it to supply all the answers to life's mysteries and, sometimes, tragedies.

One way of managing this is to follow the example of the ancient Greek and Roman thinkers known as Stoics. They were essentially fatalists, who thought that everything was fixed and therefore all you could do was to accept whatever happened with as little concern as possible. Happiness is a state of *apatheia*—a state to be maintained in the face of bereavement, accident, human violence and all manner of malevolence or disasters as they occur to us. Perhaps the clearest example of such stoicism in more recent European thought is the thinker Arthur Schopenhauer, and he certainly is *not* a good example for my vision for human flourishing. Indeed, Schopenhauer's gloomy pessimism simply drains life of all real meaning. Quite different from this is the "passionlessness" or *quies* of the ancient desert mothers and fathers, who fostered a form of inner tranquillity in the face of all that life could throw at them, yet who were sustained not by fatalism but by a faith in a transcendent possibility that lies at the very heart of theological humanism.[10] Any reader of the *Sayings of the Desert Fathers* will know that there is a quiet sense of humour in the remarkable characters of these ancient men and women—a belief that life, in the end, is a comedy in the best sense of the word, and not a tragedy. All, indeed, shall be well.

And now to gather a few important terms together as we seek to focus a little more clearly on the key term, theological humanism. The history of

---

[10]   See Thomas Merton, *The Wisdom of the Desert: Sayings from the Desert Fathers of the Fourth Century* (London: Sheldon Press, 1960), p. 8.

humanism in Western culture since the Renaissance has been important in sustaining the sense of freedom in the broadest possible expression. At its worst this freedom can be smothered by overhumanization when human beings make the mistake of taking too much upon themselves and forget the "other". We see in our present world the dire effects of such arrogance and, ultimately, totalitarianism. But it was Martin Luther (though he was no saint, for which I am grateful) among others in the great rupture of Western Christendom that we know as the Reformation, who affirmed the freedom in the other in his statement that "a Christian lives not in himself/herself, but in Christ and in his neighbour".[11] The point is that the "other" is both divine and human and the two are inextricable: for truly to live in Christ is also to live in one's neighbour, and vice versa. And this lies at the very heart of the integrity and dignity of life—to find one's freedom through the other, who is both and at once divine and human. The Christological echoes are clear enough. But what I am saying is hardly new. You can find it in the writings of the Jewish philosopher Martin Buber, and it is there also in the Gospels themselves. The freedom of human flourishing rests, then, not in solitariness nor even in any kind of "private" relationship I may claim to have with God—but in a community that does not finally separate the human and the divine. The dignity that this reveals in human life is sadly lacking in certain current world leaders—and the consequences of that lack are all too obvious and call us to ever-greater activity.

This sense of community at the heart of human flourishing encourages us to examine further the term "integrity" as I have been using it in this essay. We often speak of the sanctity of human life, and although this expression has much value it also needs to be taken with some care. It has, in my view, not been particularly helpful in debates about assisted dying or, particularly in the United States, such moral questions as that of abortion, where it has been used to render very complex issues oversimple and finally oppressive. For there are indeed moments demanding hard decisions and compromises or when the right thing may be to lay down one's life—and as Christians we have a supreme example of that. For

---

[11] Martin Luther, "The Freedom of a Christian", in *Martin Luther: Selections from his Writings*, ed. John Dillenberger (New York: Anchor, 1961), p. 80.

example, it may be that I am called to an act of *sacrifice* for the sake, perhaps, of my children.[12] And so, I prefer the term integrity of life, which recognizes that my life is indeed a great gift that has been given to me as part of the complexity of creation and it is to be held in balance with that, and sometimes in its service. My existence is with and for the other and for others.

Furthermore, as a *Christian* humanist, that existence for the other can never exclude others who profess a different faith or indeed, none. I have been fortunate to live extended periods of my life in different cultures, in India and in China, and what is quite clear to me is that as one lives and makes friends with people whose lives are often lived and governed very differently from one's own, the differences gradually become far less clear and certainly far less important while friendships grow in importance. This is not to deny real problems and issues but still one can begin to live, or one should learn to live, with difference and yet with proper integrity. All too often it is the unknown and the unfamiliar that one fears for no good reason, and we see this frequently in our own society, as in a recent newspaper report describing an incident in which asylum seekers in England were rejected by local people when they tried to enter a village pub. The response, though the guests were well behaved and courteous, was chilling. "It's obvious—think of a horror film. The fear is what might happen—the unknown and lack of control."[13] Is this the society we seek to live in, one which fears and hates the other even before it is known?

Such fear of the unknown other is utterly counter to the theological humanism that I am tracing here. There is, of course, always risk, but in the restlessness of the heart that seeks God there is more importantly a care for the other that translates into a care for all people and for the world, and a recognition of the dignity of the other within all the complexities of experience. I am not suggesting for one moment that

---

[12] The word "sacrifice" properly means an offering to God. It may perhaps be said that there are circumstances when, for God's sake, I give my life for others such as my children. See John 15:12–13: "This is my commandment, that you love one another as I have loved you. No one has greater love than this, to lay down one's life for one's friends."

[13] Reported in *The Guardian*, 31 December 2023.

this is easy, but at the same time the driver for such care is a sense of the highest good, recalling Anselm's ontological argument in the *Proslogion* that "God is a being than which none greater can be imagined". This is dependent, of course, on Anselm's idea of perfection—that is the absolute changelessness of God to which, in the valley of the restless human soul, we aspire. But it is the human possibility and the vision of perfection viewed in the resurrection life that draws us in care for the other, despite all failings and fallings away. For the Christian humanist what might happen is not finally to be feared—but to be anticipated in hope and with love. No darkness can finally overwhelm that light of love.

It has become general practice today, especially within the field of hospital chaplaincy, to draw the term "spiritual" into secular usage. Indeed, it might further be remarked that the primary definition of the word "spiritual" in the *Oxford English Dictionary* concerns that which is "pertaining to, affecting or concerning, the spirit or higher moral qualities". This, however, is sufficient only to a degree, yet it is important in its emphasis on moral qualities. But theological humanism as it relates to the fundamental concern of human flourishing requires a further term that necessarily carries us beyond the purely secular. Rather than "spirit", I choose to enlist the term "soul" as more appropriate for my argument—and more scriptural. In the Greek of the New Testament, the term $\pi\nu\varepsilon\tilde{\upsilon}\mu\alpha$ (*pneuma* – "spirit") gives way to the more elusive $\psi\upsilon\chi\eta$ (*psuche* – "breath of life", "soul"), seen as being the object of divine grace and eternal salvation. Thus, at the end of the Epistle to the Hebrews we read, "Obey your leaders and submit to them, for they are keeping watch over your souls" ($\psi\upsilon\chi\tilde{\omega}\nu$) (Hebrews 13:17). The term soul as descriptive of the essence of human being acknowledges the necessary relationship with, and capacity to embrace, the divine as fundamental to our humanity. It avoids the dualism of body and spirit that has been part of Protestant thinking, the notion of "soul" reflecting the essence of what it is to be human under God, including the embodied self. In the words of Klemm and Schweiker:

> The classical Christian humanist conception of the human
> capacity for the divine was a longing for completion in light of
> the fallibility and incompleteness of human existence.[14]

The fact that this conception links us to and requires the Christian theological models of Christology, the atonement, sacrifice and resurrection does not exclude other possible models for religious humanism in other traditions with which we share our common humanity. But to explore that is beyond the limited scope of this essay.

For this essay must be concluded with the proper acknowledgement of the work and ministry of Elizabeth Baxter as a wonderful instance of theological humanism and a vision, put into practice, of the integrity of human life in Holy Rood House, Thirsk which, in a number of ways, provides a garden for the soul reflected in the natural garden for plants, animals—and the human beings who tend it. Its whole drive is towards human and natural healing and flourishing, not least in the library that encourages the life of the intellect, its richness in feminist theology being of particular note. To stay in Holy Rood House is to participate in a community that celebrates hospitality and recognizes the centrality of theology in its conferences on Christian life and teaching.

In the work of Holy Rood House, there is a vision that has a necessary logic of perfection that enables, or better requires, Elizabeth to take risks and live by faith and hope, without which there can be no true charity. Of course, the challenge to the perfection and harmony of the Garden is present in the first chapter of Genesis, and the fact that the gardens of nature and the human soul are endangered is due not least to the imperfections of restless humanity. Throughout the history of Christianity, drawing the model from Jesus Christ himself, the heart of the matter has always been found in people who are at once on the edge and yet at the same time at the very heart of the vision of theological humanism. It is to them that we turn to ensure, in spite of all, the condition of human flourishing on earth and under God.

---

[14]   Klemm and Schweiker, *Religion and the Human Future*, p. 91.

A reflection on the creative arts as a healing process, and the creative arts at Holy Rood House

Elaine Wisdom

And if there come the singers and the dancers and the flute players, buy of their gifts also. For they too are the gatherers of fruit and frankincense, and that which they bring, though fashioned of dreams, is raiment and food for your soul.

Kahlil Gibran[1]

The creative arts have been an integral part of the ethos and philosophy of Holy Rood House since its inception; they are a theological imperative in the work of the house and the healing process. From humankind's earliest beginnings, imagery and imagination have been used in the sacred process of life, including the healing of emotional wounds which so often have repercussions on our mental and physical wellbeing. A part of that early imaginal thinking was a holistic view of humanity, connected with the natural and cosmic context in which life was lived. Our imaginative creative impulse is integral to us as human beings and part of our inner healing process. It is fundamentally linked with our spirit, and to what could be called the "dream space", that unconscious domain where dreams originate. Dreams are part of our unconscious

---

[1]   Kahlil Gibran, *The Prophet* (London: William Heinemann Ltd, 1926/1972), p. 45.

imaginal life and are powerful tools for healing which ancient cultures, such as Australian Aboriginals, continue to access.

We are told in the Gospel of John (8:3–11) that Jesus bent down and began to write on the ground with his finger. Making marks on a surface with a finger or other tools is an ancient activity. At Cresswell Crags in Derbyshire, images are scratched into the rock of the caves that sheltered the prehistoric people living there 12,000 years ago. We don't know why the marks were made, but some of those early scratched images can still be recognized today.

And recognition seems to be something that making marks helps us do: recognizing, acknowledging and perhaps putting parameters on the world as experienced. We have the same need today as those ice-age ancestors of ours. It is an activity that can be immensely helpful in addressing trauma, loss, conflict, crisis—the wounding marks inflicted on us by life. For this reason, making prints is a powerful metaphor for the marks life has left on us, and the marks we make on life.

Today, the act of creating an image in a chosen medium for healing, using the imagination as both aid and antidote to memory, is called art therapy. We are creative because we are human. The making of images, engaging the imagination to help the healing process, is therefore seen as an ancient practice, using touch as the basic tool. The making of an image thus becomes an embodied experience which can allow one to reconnect with, for example, a dissociation or distortion of touch in trauma or abuse. Therapy can be undertaken for a variety of reasons, but fundamental would be the desire to find freedom from past events which hold us captive: disempowering trauma or present circumstances.

In our Western culture, there may be apprehension about what will happen when we engage with our creativity in this way. We often consider ourselves to be unartistic or non-creative. But we are creative because we are human, and we all have a sense of colour which can be a helpful starting point. In the art room at Holy Rood House, that initial burst of colour can bring with it an immediate response of liberation and empowerment, and a joy too infrequently felt in life: a stirring of the sense of a possibility of beginning again.

One of the therapist's functions is to act as a witness to what has happened in the past and to bring the individual to this space at this time, and what is now happening in their lives. To support and walk alongside as a growing awareness of self emerges. The dark areas or "shadow self" are unrecognized by many of us and therefore untapped as the potential source of energy it can become. It has been said that this "shadow self" is 90 per cent gold if recognized, worked on and transformed. The therapist tries to provide a safe and boundaried space, the *temenos* of the art room, in which recognition and growth may be facilitated.

However encouraging the therapist tries to be, they may only partly alleviate the anxiety of stepping into the unknown and uncertain territory of creative expression. A place perhaps never before travelled into, or if attempted at school, told we "have no talent" and immediately disempowered. Small children have no such inhibitions, happily drawing on any surface they can find with whatever comes to hand. So, these first hesitant steps into new and potentially frightening terrain are acts of great courage, comparable to the heroic journeys of ancient myth. The controls one has tried to exert over the management of crisis and trauma, the quasi-security these attempts at controlling and managing fractured lives can give, are slowly left aside as one begins a journey into a place where feelings and experiences can begin to emerge and be expressed safely. The power of expression realized and embodied in the image can begin to unblock atrophied channels of feeling, opening up the possibility of subsequent steps to enable the process of change and healing. In this sense, the created image has been likened to the ancient Hebrew idea of the scapegoat, which symbolically carries away those perceptions and ideas which are no longer helpful to us, allowing them to be released and freeing us from them.

Some may consider the journey too risky because it means leaving the security of what is at least known. Old stereotypes and patterns of coping die hard, and there may be a desire to cling onto these obsolete patterns rather than letting them go. This may also be part of the core difficulty experienced with whatever is troubling us, so the active engagement with art materials and the making process may help clarify this and allow its articulation for perhaps the first time in our conscious lives.

The process of art therapy works partly by reaching the places in our memories and psyche that words alone cannot reach. Images may emerge from the psyche or be made as an expression of a past event that is causing us to live in a dysfunctional way because there seems no alternative. In the art room at Holy Rood House, we work in ways which may at first appear random and abstract. Working fast on large sheets of paper with paint but without the use of conventional paintbrushes, we use instead ready-made "tools" such as toothbrushes, lollypop sticks, old plastic cards and fingers. This is partly because, for many, holding a conventional paintbrush can cause a barrier to their creativity as stereotypes of "good art" come into play. What I call the "Leonardo effect". A trinitarian process is used, with a first painting made by pouring three colours of paint chosen by the maker onto a sheet of paper, from which a first print is taken so the maker has a record of the original work. The original painting is then worked into using the method described above, and finally a second print is made from the worked-into painting. This is often the most revelatory of the three images and constitutes the final image of the process. Sometimes, these are worked into again.

The process is designed to help people relax, free up and hopefully have fun with the activity of painting, regaining if only for a short time the ability to play like children. The process may also help them connect to their "inner child", an important personage in the healing process. The speed and abstract nature of the process can provide a direct route for many to areas of the mind and heart often kept apart or split off from daily life.

Creative activity is often likened to what is Divine. A holistic connection that our culture finds difficult to embrace. Music, art, dance and drama are things children instinctively find absorbing and necessary for their wellbeing; and it is the same for adults—clearly seen as beneficial in the recent Covid-19 pandemic. The safe, *temenos* space of the art room—and indeed the whole of Holy Rood House—is integral to the creative healing process, establishing a safety that allows one to feel unsafe as the journey progresses. What is made in the art room can make it possible for a new or different reality to frame the story of oneself: one's experiences, hopes and dreams. The art-making process can also help change the way we look at, and therefore experience, the past. The life of the imagination is a powerful dynamic, a relationship with "making" using colour, texture, shape and mark-making. To imagine a new possibility for oneself allows it the potential to become future reality. If we can imagine a different reality, it is more likely to happen. Michelangelo said of his sculptures that he did not impose anything, but simply revealed the figure within the block of marble. Thus, rapport with the materials sees its potential and possibilities and can be a metaphor for our own lives and the possibilities within us.

Jesus encouraged and empowered those around him to become the best they could be, and there are many examples in the Gospels. One such example is the story of Zaccheus (Luke 19:1–4), who took the actively imaginative step of climbing a tree in order to see Jesus, and had his life transformed as a result. Images made in art therapy can often help the maker to see more clearly, thereby enabling change.

Paint, because it flows, can be seen as a paradigm of the psyche. Sometimes it is only possible to manage pouring the paint before the process becomes overwhelming. The struggle to contain and control the chaos, pain and fear of a life become moribund is sometimes seen and felt all too painfully in the act of pouring paint. We opt for paralysis as less painful. But next time, the pouring and the mark-making, interacting with the paint, may become more of a possibility. This slow and, for many, painful process may somehow allow the possibility of an inner movement to be recognized, integrated and allowed to happen over time, enabling new possibilities of a different kind of life. It can be transformational; and it is always a metaphor for change.

In the art room, the object made becomes a third element in the conversation and can "speak" as much to the therapist as it does to its creator. It becomes part of the spoken contribution within the creative process, helping draw together and illuminate those aspects of life that have been split off or buried as too shameful or terrifying. The artwork in this sense becomes the "scapegoat", as mentioned above. We see this sort of release into greater freedom many times in the Gospel stories, where lives are taken up and a beginning made to live more fully. Taking up our beds and walking where before paralysis had seemed the only option.

Recorded in Jeremiah (18:3–4, Jerusalem Bible) are the words, "So I went to the potter's house and there he was, working at the wheel. But the vessel he was making came out wrong, as may happen with clay when a potter is at work. So, he began again." The creative arts and therapies can all make a profound contribution to living life more fully and sometimes, when necessary, to beginning again. They allow a reimagining of life's potential and possibilities in an actively embodied way of making it more possible. Nurturing a creative outlook may also benefit an attitude to and engagement with life, both helpful and necessary to its living.

Jesus said, "I have come that you may have life, and live it to the full" (John 10:10, NIV). Holy Rood House continues to provide a unique space in which this can begin to happen for so many people who come and stay.

> Then Mary slipped through the door and stood with her back
> against it, looking about her with excitement, wonder and delight.
> She was standing inside the secret garden . . . Mary always felt
> that however many years she lived, she would never forget that
> first morning when her garden began to grow.[2]

_____

[2]   Frances Hodgson Burnett, *The Secret Garden* (The Reprint Society, 1957), p. 33.

When psychology meets theology

David McDonald

I first met Stanley and Elizabeth Baxter in 1994 at a national conference for Christian Healing Homes, where I was a speaker, and they invited me to become a consultant to Holy Rood House. Here, I will discuss what engaged us at that conference, and our thinking and conversations over the years about reforms needed in the patriarchal church, seeking a common integrated gender-equal theology against a background of an evolving consciousness of the panentheistic nature of community. Time and space do not allow a scholarly researched essay, but I offer a synopsis of my talk and continuing thoughts, and a condensation of some of the discoursed ideas and experiences we shared, as a tribute to their work and as a memento for Elizabeth.

The talk that I gave, frequently quoted by Stanley and Elizabeth when introducing me at workshops and conferences at Holy Rood House, was "The Shadow Side of Jesus". I would often expound on this in illuminating the nature of the work that went on in the community they were facilitating: the light-bringing counselling and therapy, the creativity, the healing and worship as truly living and loving God and one another.

We are familiar with the shadow side of human personality, aspects that are kept in the dark, consciously or unconsciously, which are usually seen as negative, but which may also contain repressed or lost positive qualities.[1] Disavowed aspects of self are often projected onto others,

---

[1]   William Miller's *Your Golden Shadow* (San Francisco: Harper & Row, 1989) describes the discovery and fulfilment of the undeveloped self, using Jung's

individually and collectively, where negative and destructive elements may become very damaging to self and others. A casting of the self's dark attributes externally may range from othering through to scapegoating, harming interpersonal relatedness and diminishing our humanity. At best, it is an individual measure for self-survival. At worst, collectively, it is genocidal.

In the context of a "sheep-and-goats" division, I would not be suggesting that Jesus defensively promoted himself as whiter than white by painting those who were against him as blacker than black—such was the posturing of the self-applauding hypocrites. Sheep and goats can make their own choices, according to free will, and can jump or be helped over the fence (may the metaphor be understood).

Positive qualities unrecognized or disallowed in oneself may be projected in idealizing others, leaving one lesser as a person. Healing, in the idiom of psychotherapy, would entail recognition and reclaimed ownership of negative and positive part-selves in "soul recovery", repair and restoration of healthy relationships—with oneself as well as with others and the environment. The ongoing work of "bringing to light" what is in the shadow, raising to awareness and supporting continued consciousness in reflective thinking, linking, connecting, communication, righteous thought and action, is itself redemptive.

My understanding of the personality of Jesus is that he could embrace and integrate the dark negative side of humanity—and become the containment of sin for us—while also living out the positive side fully in the light: the unwavering unconditionally loving and nurturing feminine, and the protective benevolent law-giving masculine together as God-given archetypes to shape us in the divine image intended for us. Jesus knew this and, regardless of gender, he showed how each of us as a whole person has both feminine and masculine attributes—for such is the nature of God. I will examine this again later.

Aside from the concept of the human shadow, expounded by C. G. Jung, including the unconscious natures of the feminine in man, and the masculine in woman, I had pondered much over a Divine Shadow

---

view that the essence of the shadow is "pure gold" through the awareness of choice—as in "Free Will" bestowed by God on humankind.

after reading Jung's "Answer to Job".[2] This had been a shocking and controversial interpretation of the nature of God: the God, named Yahweh, who allowed or even allegedly inflicted suffering upon the most dearly beloved of creatures. And what a thing to contrive: for his "Only Begotten Son" to suffer the most humiliating and painful death after an unblemished life of obedience![3]

For Jung, the Archetype of Deity is the totality of opposites, which accounts for all of its attributed power and glory and omniscience.[4] "God's tragic contradictoriness"[5] is expressed in allowing the Satan side to cruelly devastate Job's life. Stories of amoral behaviour by the jealous wrathful Yahweh had been described since time immemorial. What kind of Supreme Creator would banish humans from Paradise with a mandatory death sentence, reject Cain as to make him an accursed fugitive and condemned murderer, bring a deluge to wipe out all creation apart from the one and only obedient family chosen to survive with all mating species to replenish the earth, and horrifically traumatize Abraham's son, who might never trust his father again . . . and so on?

One truth, and the rest is dogma

Dogma derives from Greek and Latin terms referring to agreed opinions, philosophical tenets, thoughts believed to be true, collectively accepted and firmly held. There is the shadow side, often driven by human egocentric motives which may not accord with divine intention for the common good. I do not suggest that dogma must be untrue if there can only be one big Truth. Dogma may indeed be sometimes untrue, and

---

[2]   C. G. Jung (1952), in *Psychology and Religion: West and East*, Collected Works Vol. 11 (London: Routledge & Kegan Paul, 1973), pp. 357–470.

[3]   But we are familiar with "A Method in the Madness".

[4]   Concise summaries of Jung's assessment of Yahweh and struggle with the concept of the Godhead can be read in *The Handbook of Jungian Psychology*, edited by Renos Papadopoulos (London: Routledge, 2006), Chapters 4 and 13.

[5]   C. G. Jung, *Memories, Dreams, Reflections* (1963), ed. A. Jaffé (London: Fontana, 1995).

it is often unproven, but there are many smaller truths as sure as night follows day. There are consequences to thoughts, words, and actions whether freely chosen, or coerced, or arising out of the deeper mind unconsciously. Dogma is usually laid down with good intentions, with reasoning and understanding for rules and practices, to keep us safe, to guard us from temptation and offending, to preserve the common good. But there is a well-known maxim: "Rules are for the obedience of fools and the guidance of wise men."[6] This gives us licence to challenge dogma—and it may be necessary where we need to restore Wisdom to her rightful place. We certainly have seen this at work, constructively, at Holy Rood House.

We have learned not to take literally all that we read in the Bible, but to see allegorical narratives for the representations they are—and Jesus was a master of storytelling, imagination and metaphor.[7] But why should men paint Yahweh so monstrously, and instil a terrible fear of God? And why should men hold the first woman, Eve, responsible, in league with the devil, for the Fall of humankind in Original Sin. These questions we could keep revisiting. The answers seem to be "power and control".

In Genesis, God is alleged to show his firstborn, perfectly innocent, immortal human son and daughter the Tree of Knowledge of Good and Evil and tantalize them with its forbidden fruit which, unsurprisingly, they eat—and then to curse them both and the very soil with perpetual adversity while they await death. Even the serpent, the cleverest of wild creatures, is cursed by its Creator. What is all that about?

Jung took the view that God actually manipulated the first couple into this abysmal outcome. Whether or not it was a paradoxical challenge to bring about this aim, the omniscient God would have already known the natural human disobedience expected with that injunction regardless of any outside influence. Serpent, which had hitherto been an ancient symbol of Wisdom and Healing, becomes here, allegorically, not only the

---

6   Quote attributed to Group Captain Douglas Bader, RAF fighter ace in World War II, who often saw the advantages of taking risks in defiance of rules.

7   What ludicrous hypocrisy to feel self-righteously impelled to remove a speck of sawdust from another's eye when there is a plank of wood in one's own (Luke 6:41–2).

intelligent voice of normal doubt and disbelief, but also the smart cunning element in human nature that will always find a way to compromise the law for its own gain.

A weaving serpentine adaptation is seen, par excellence, in the becoming of the human ego-consciousness, I-ness, starting from a birth into the world of conflicting opposites. It has to come to reconcile, if possible, subjective loving–hating experiences of the self, and objective good–evil perceptions of the other. There are repeated vicissitudes between polar experiences as the developing ego winds its way onwards in discovery and in making sense of this new world, the self and the other. The fall from idealization, through disillusionment to denigration is a constant to-and-fro, while the infant mind as self is repeatedly recovering a blissful safety when being held and loved, and forming over time a constancy of the other and their connectedness. This is the "download and installation" of trust from which hope emerges as the first virtue and begins the building of resilience. Benevolent, consistent reliability of the primary caregiver is paramount to forming a secure attachment relationship as the prototype for ongoing interpersonal faith in the goodness of self and other and, ultimately, in the cosmos as the kind and nurturing container of everything. The human attachment pattern is the scaffolding for the building of "the social" as a loving and compassionate matrix—or, adversely, if malevolence is the dominant perception, for the anti-social world of paranoid fear and exclusion. Here, we see the origins of heaven and hell within the nascent human mind.

Psychoanalytically informed observations in depth psychology include studies of mothers and babies, symbolic play, developmental crises through childhood and adolescence, and complex adult mental disorders. They reveal how early embedded experiences of love–hate, and perceptions of good–evil, shape personality and human relationships, and societal civilization. Ancient Greek and Hebrew scribes knew well these human mental vicissitudes, triumphs and tragedies, kindnesses and cruelties. And Shakespeare provided a diversity of such narratives long before the casework of Freud and Jung, who seemed to value mythology more than the Bard's plays to support their core theories. Jung's arraignment of Yahweh and criticism of a flawed Trinity, and Freud's model of a ubiquitous triangular Oedipal conflict and the vulnerable threefold structure of human psyche, were set in modern psychology, not theology. But, as root cause analyses of suffering, their theses largely have models in ancient narrative attempts to chronicle and explain existential human drama in mythical archetypal enactments.

Psychology is the Fall from Theology,[8] from the innocence of positive belief in God and from the contents of imagination. With the conscious awareness of consciousness, *thought* becomes the Absolute, suggests Giegerich. I see his point. The human absolute has now become what we think and believe. But in our defensiveness, dogmatic ideology is paradoxically aggressive, the cause of age-old clashes of civilization. Love is really the Divine Absolute in terms of the wholeness of thought, word and action. It is clear that in the beginning our Creator had loving Thought—to make humans in "their" image—before becoming Word and then Action through incarnation of spirit. In terms of the human experience, we see how thought can become disordered and deranged, and in need of reconfiguration.[9] Modern psychotherapeutic healing interventions are very much focussed on thinking about thinking, and mind-mindedness, which means love for oneself as well as for others, all made in the image of God. Jesus's two great commandments (Matthew 22:37–40) sit right here. Therapy is held up as a corrective emotional experience, where thinking about oneself and others can change— radically, if necessary—and mental projections can be reclaimed for the shadow selves to be reintegrated.[10]

So, far from being the curse of Original Sin, the acquired knowledge of good and evil is an original blessing: the eyes and ears of the human being are opened to understand the naked truth of existence (in a

---

[8]   Wolfgang Giegerich, "The Patriarchal Neglect of the Feminine Principle: A Psychological Fallacy in Jungian Theory", *Harvest* 45:1 (1999), p. 15.

[9]   I use a term from computer technology as analogy where the thinking elements of our consciousness need to be rearranged after corruption—a system reset becomes necessary. Several re-boots may be required.

[10]   The opposite pole, arising out of mistrust and cynicism, produces a negative radicalization, as seen in the mind of the terrorist, terrified of the wrathful condemnation of God and banishment to outer darkness, who has to placate the dreadful father by destroying the other as infidel.

Garden-of-Eden sense); if we keep certain body parts private, we may bask in benevolent unconditional love and non-judgmental positive regard and eternal acceptance. But the caveat was added: *as long as you don't cross Father, the Law-giver.*

Therefore, it seems that irreparable damage to trust was done. So, where was *Mother, the Advocate* who did not come to mediate and plead for forgiveness, who failed to rescue and restore her children as gods? The scribes wrote her out of the story—presumably totally mistrustful of the Feminine as exposed in the Eve-Serpent crime. Archetypal wily beguilement, as the most feared destructive power of the female to displace the male, meant monotheistic religion had to be a Patriarchy, to keep it safe and sound. Thus, the potential original maternal blessing was enviously reduced to a paternal curse against the curious human mind and blights our whole species for the "cardinal sin" of perfectly natural disobedience—a risk necessary to get onto the learning curve.

This is how mythical and symbolic thinking prevails until such time as there is emotional and psychological insight and understanding within the maturing mind. Then, there can be awareness, reflection, realization, thinking and processing, and changes in attitudes and behaviours. There has to be capacity and will to be so, and to do so, as ongoing mental and spiritual discipline. Some may choose self-sanctified withdrawal from the world but most of us need the help of one another. Studies in depth psychology show this to be the developmental process from an initially bewildered dependent Ego towards a whole sense of interdependent Self.[11] The individual from infancy through adulthood can progress with

---

[11]   I capitalize these terms for psychic structures that Freud and Jung used, as they are important in linking psychology of the human with theology of the deity. Ego is the "I Am" of being, and Self is the "We Are" of becoming. The ego "I-ness" of the individual, which strives to be an ego-ideal acceptable to the super-ego, the perfected God-image, has to die to the little self to be reborn as the greater Self which is the interdependent social being of human community. This seems to me to be the fully humanizing process our Creator shares with us in establishing the "kingdom" of Heaven on Earth—One Sovereign Nation—A Resurrection People.

good fortune and reach maturity within a lifetime, but collectively as a species it seems to take for ever—until Kingdom Come!

Through our darkness dawns our salvation

Are we, therefore, cursed by our human shadow (whether or not it is the image of God's shadow) continuously in our everyday lives, let alone until final salvation? This is, of course, the so-called received wisdom of the male biblical scribes and the church fathers, despite the Good News brought by Jesus. But sin does not have to be a crime. It is a "falling short" as the original biblical words in Greek, *hamartia*, and Hebrew, *hata*, have their meanings: "to miss the mark", and "to go astray". Paul used this meaning in saying, "All have sinned and fall short of the glory of God" (Romans 3:23). But God, in *Being* as Spirit, is complete, with no falling short, and is the only "Sinless One". In this respect, I think Jung was wrong about Yahweh's criminal side. God, in *Becoming* as Matter, in the fullness of time as complete humanity, shares responsibly in our falling short and guides us from darkness to light. This is the essence of healing and deliverance in church ministry and in the restoration of the soul in psychotherapy.

In the Gnostic Gospel of Thomas, Jesus said, "If you bring out what is within you, what you bring out will save you; if you do not bring out what is within you, what you do not bring out will destroy you."[12] This was exactly what Freud was talking about as "unresolved conflicts repressed in the unconscious mind", or Jung on "split off complexes that have autonomy in the shadow". Freud would not have seen the above scriptural quote[13] as it had not been discovered in his lifetime; although he would have known Jesus's examples of mental projection in his exposures of hypocrisy, accusation, blame, condemnation and criticizing another without first examining one's own character.

---

[12]   There are different translations of the second sentence, but this one makes the most sense of what Jesus meant by the consequence of not bringing into the light what is harboured in the shadow of the mind.

[13]   *Nag Hammadi Library*, ed. J. Robinson (San Francisco: Harper & Row, 1977).

My talk on Jesus and his human shadow side arose from considering, often with priests, the difficulty in fully understanding or accepting the nature and position of the second person of the Holy Trinity. It also followed on from Jung's continuous struggle with the Trinity and where Evil and the Feminine belonged in the divine drama, since he held that there should be a completed quaternity in the Godhead. One conundrum boiled down to, "Was Jesus fully divine as the perfect sinless Son of God who became an incarnate human for our sakes, or was he the fully human Son of Man who became as the sinless God himself elevated to the Godhead in the way that his human mother, Mary, was later 'taken up'?"[14] I wondered if it might be more accurate to name Jesus as Son of Woman[15] as well as Son of God. I will come back to this point later.

It also left a question, "Was Jesus the one and only Son of God, or was there another Son as Lucifer or Satan?" This was clearly Jung's position, for which he cited evidence.[16] And I found myself thinking that the Satan figure, let loose on Job and thereby on the whole of humanity, and encountered by Jesus with his confrontations in the wilderness, was able to be bound in the shadow side of Jesus the Man; he was the Evil within the shadow side that had to be lovingly integrated into the wholeness of Humankind and the fullness of God, in whose image we are made.

I had been struck by Jesus's own probable understanding of himself as not being "without sin" but, instead, knowing the sinful potential of his own human nature, which he could overcome and master in his complete dedicated submission to the Will of God being lived out on Earth as it is in Heaven. Jesus knew all about lust in the heart being as adulterous as that acted out in everyday human life (Matthew 5:28). In his address

---

[14] Why did it take so long? Despite a belief over centuries, the Catholic Church only announced this as infallible truth in 1950. Mary was anointed Queen of Heaven from the conception of Jesus (Luke 1:26–38).

[15] Jesus ventured gradually to reveal his purpose, in reference to himself as Son of Man, according to the name given for the Messiah in the prophetic book of Daniel.

[16] Jung took Satan to be the eldest son of God, relying on Job 1:6–2:1, and on the dualistic doctrine of Pseudo-Clement of Rome, as expounded in C. G. Jung, *Aion* (1950), CW 9ii (London: Routledge & Kegan Paul, 1959).

to the woman taken in adultery, after there was none "without sin" left to cast the first stone, neither did he condemn her, but he simply said go and sin no more (John 8:11). So, he did not see himself as better than, or above, the adulterer. He is one with the rest of us, and he shows the way of becoming pure in thought and word and deed, to be true to the Creator God who is the only "Sinless One".[17] Jesus is The Way of At-one-ment.

Jesus knew all about character, not just by observing others but also through a complete awareness and understanding of himself. His personal discipline is so clear, and could be summarized in a saying that may have its origin in ancient wisdom:[18]

> Watch your thoughts, they become your words
> Watch your words, they become your actions
> Watch your actions, they become your habits
> Watch your habits, they become your character
> Watch your character, it will become your destiny.

Members of Holy Rood House community take care with thoughts, words, and actions in everyday living together. The habits of being alongside, listening, with inclusivity and non-judgmental acceptance, are spiritual disciplines that define our character. We are a Community of Practice— meaning that we are all practitioners individually and collectively within a continuous experience of knowing and learning together. It is a relational culture with a clear identity, interactive in sharing stories, conversations, ideas, information and skills with passion and commitment to human flourishing. We are all apprentices, our curriculum is lived experience, and our destiny is the coming home to God.

Above all, we value and treasure the presence and guidance of the Holy Spirit, and the gifts our guests bring in person, which we can share together in love and care, learning and growing and flourishing. The word "care" in the name of our charity is the core of what we are about. We all

---

[17] Jesus said, "Why do you call me good? There is no one good except God alone" (Mark 10:18).

[18] Often quoted, but consistently attributed to Lao-Tzu, founder of Daoism in the sixth century BCE.

know what it means: cherishing, protecting, supporting—of ourselves, one another, all creatures great and small, and our environment. It begins at home,[19] where we are, and it is a statement of love and care for the cosmos.

A teaching curriculum for wisdom from the Garrison Institute in the USA is called CARE—"Cultivating Awareness and Resilience in Education". It made me think of the core value of education—which originally means a "leading from" or "drawing out" (Latin *educere*)—and how we need to be the constant minders of the awareness of God as Creator in everything and everywhere, and of the resilience that rests in the faith and trust in God's promise. That is all there within—and we are charged to draw it out and follow the lead it gives. Jesus taught exactly this and urged us to really know God. And that is why we have a Centre for the Study of Theology and Health.

A statement of the World Health Organization 12 years ago, "There is No Health Without Mental Health", emphasizes the key word "health", which we have in our charity's name. We have been promoting and nurturing health and wellbeing for 30 years! We continue, and we would add, "There is no health without Spiritual Health."

The guest house

I have rather laboured the point about human suffering, individually and collectively, being tracked back to early adverse experiences, sometimes also prenatal and trans-generational; they leave their wounds on mind and body, but our natural defences enable us to keep going; we may survive more than thrive. The unthinkable, and the traumata that cannot be processed or contained, are often reduced in acute toxicity by repression into the unconscious shadow side, where they usually take a chronic inflammatory toll on mental and physical health. As already

---

[19]   *Oikos,* Greek for "house", gives us *oikoumene* for the "whole of humanity", and that is the true meaning of *ecumenical*—not simply the coming together of Christian denominations. It also gives us the word *ecology*, which is a passion in the health and healing "Ecotherapy" at Holy Rood House.

discussed, some of the ego-alien content of the developing mind gets separated out, often in fragments, and makes a way into others, or into interpersonal relations, by projection.

Many of our guests at Holy Rood House bring their broken selves, broken relationships, chronic damage from trauma or frequent serial abuse, some experienced in early life and some perpetuated within families and institutions. The shame and fear of powerfully destructive effects, such as rage and hate, grievance and revenge, and the guilty self-punitive thinking, are burdens that feel too bad to carry. But it often seems that they have had no choice, particularly when we discover they are carrying others' projections. These damaged and damaging effects are responses to betrayal, and defences against the excruciating longing for love. Some people feel permanently unforgiven but have no evidence of any crime they have committed. They may have been innocent victims in someone else's drama. Sometimes a genogram can map out possible sources that can be brought into the light—prayer or mass for a departed soul may start the healing from ancestor downwards.

The receptive, containing milieu encourages understanding, which is the beginning of forgiveness, and the welcoming and loving of those difficult parts. I recall a poem that Elizabeth liked, which I would read out occasionally:

The Guest House—by Rumi

This being human is a guest house.
Every morning a new arrival.
A joy, a depression, a meanness,
some momentary awareness comes
as an unexpected visitor.
Welcome and entertain them all!
Even if they're a crowd of sorrows,
who violently sweep your house
empty of its furniture, still,
treat each guest honourably.
He may be clearing you out
for some new delight.

The dark thought, the shame, the malice,
meet them at the door laughing
and invite them in.
Be grateful for whoever comes,
because each has been sent
as a guide from beyond.
Always check your inner state
with the lord of your heart.
Copper doesn't know it's copper,
until it's changing into gold.
Your loving doesn't know majesty,
until it knows its helplessness.[20]

Where is the divine feminine?

I start from a human woman. I had a simple realization a long time ago that all of us, male and female, spend the first 40 weeks of our lives inside woman. She is the containing creator, providing blood, sacred blood, to bathe the babe's implanted placenta,[21] bringing the oxygen and nutrients necessary for the genetic programming to form the new person. The rapid multiplication and differentiation of our cells, and formation of organs and internal connecting networks, is phenomenal. Woman supplies a major part of the genes that are active in shaping us when we look just at the sex-specific chromosomes.

As we know, the sex chromosomes of a female are XX, and those of a male are XY. The X of the father comes from his own mother and is

---

[20] Jelaluddin Rumi (1207–73), Persian mystic and poet. Translation by Coleman Barks in *Rumi: The Book of Love* (New York: HarperCollins, 2003), p. 179.

[21] The *placenta* (Latin: "flattened cake") is the most vital organ during pregnancy, co-created by foetal and maternal tissues, with the thinnest membrane between blood circulations allowing the intimate selective transfer of nutrients and waste products. Many societies revere it as sacred, like a sibling with a soul needing special burial rites. Icelandic *fylgia* for placenta means "guardian angel".

passed on to his daughter to be XX but not to his son, who receives the X from his mother. The X chromosome in males and females is three times as large and has about 900 genes, compared with about 55 genes for the Y chromosome.

It is the male sperm gamete X or Y that determines the sex of the zygote, suggestive of a decisive masculine principle. The ripe ovum is ready to receive either, in keeping with a containing feminine principle. We do not know if the ovum has any choice.[22] We do know that Y sperm swim faster than X sperm, so more males are conceived, but the Y chromosome later, after replication in every cell, may meet incompatibilities with the mother's X chromosome and suffer gene deletions. We know that there are more male spontaneous abortions than female—and the genders balance out in the end. This first adversarial encounter might be the origin[23] of the male defensive drive to subjugate woman, and perhaps the othering of any difference that threatens the fragile Y.

In the female, only one X remains active, and the other is inactivated—randomly it seems, so it could be the maternal or paternal grandparental X that presides. In the male, the maternal grandparental X presides. I say "presides" because there is the evidence of size, power and influence that X has over what develops (or mal-develops in the case of specific X-linked disorders).

I have taken this biological trip to emphasize that the female human is bestowed genetically with special power and authority, with her body consecrated to be a starter-temple for the coming god-child.

The divine feminine[24] had been in men's consciousness from the beginning, not just in this biological sense but also in the awesomeness of the power of the mother from whose body they are thrust and on whom they depend for a considerable time before individuation.

---

22   Fortunately, young mother Mary, on behalf of her ready ovum, said "Yes".

23   This may seem a far-fetched idea—but quantum science shows that subatomic particles, not just cells, have consciousness and memory and communication.

24   Other contributors to this book write with far more historical and experiential knowledge than I on the divine feminine, of which there have been countless manifestations through the ages. My approach is confined here to a personal subjective understanding where I can also find some objective correlates.

Historically, from ancient times, men had to elevate woman to heaven as Mary, or to hell as Eve, to remove her as a competitor and a threat to male dominance. The Deuteronomists had to write her out of scripture, suggesting for Jung that Yahweh had excluded Feminine Wisdom from the Divine Psyche (to great cost). This could never be so. But Jung did credit Yahweh as correcting the error by sending Jesus to restore the feminine to humanity.[25]

Several years ago, I found myself having some visionary experience with X and Y. I saw Y as the crucified Jesus on the cross. I saw X as Jesus completely open to welcome and embrace the whole world. It reminded me of the Leonardo da Vinci drawing of the *Vitruvian Man* with superimposed X and Y positions of the body inscribed in perfect proportions within both a square and a circle. It linked with Jung's fascination about quaternity and mandala symbolism. Anyway, for me now, X "marks the spot": Jesus is Son of Woman, and the Divine Feminine is within.

Masculine and feminine principles may be outmoded stereotyped concepts in the twenty-first century—and we see the confusion of the interchangeability of personality qualities today at the root of so much gender dysphoria and the trans movement. At best, there is a fluidity which may be a hopeful indicator that, in the heaven whence we are bound to return as fully humanized souls, "there is neither male nor female". This is what Jung meant by the "Transcendent Function" of the human psyche.

---

[25]   I think Jung was right, but for the wrong reason. Jung held that Yahweh had eventually been shamed by his actions against Job, who had shown himself to be morally above Yahweh, who was then obliged to repair the damage by sending his only begotten son to put things right. It seems more likely to me that God had to repair the ongoing damage caused by the scribes and elders, and timed the intervention of Jesus to bring a profound punctuation mark to the Hebrew narrative.

Onwards and upwards

Stanley Baxter's frequent exhortation, "Onwards and Upwards, Brother!", is an apt rubric for my conclusion. He could have added "Sister", of course, but I think he was addressing himself as exemplar for anyone ready to catch on to that knowing optimism, inspiration and courage that was the hallmark of the active and inclusive community church he and Elizabeth were co-creating with God. Stanley's call has a distinctively male tone, but I like to think of *Upwards* being the structural masculine, a spiral energy, always creating, building, and striving for improvement and perfection, inseparably married with *Onwards* as the nurturing feminine, the continuous steady connectedness and completeness, the circular energy for essential grounding—for Earthing the Spirit, so to speak.

The eternal feminine is creating through endlessly birthing, and the eternal masculine is creating by repeatedly seeding. Together as God, they co-create, as the explosive dynamic energy starting from the orgasmic Big Bang; and in the visible transformation of their invisible force, as incarnation, we humans pro-create on their behalf—Spirit becomes Matter made in their image.

In the eight years since Stanley's passing, the seed entering the ground to be continually reborn, Elizabeth has been that very steady onward connectedness, nurturing the community through shared loss and change, and affirming the same continuously upward trajectory—that steep and rugged pathway we all tread rejoicingly. As many younger staff members would join with the community, and learn and develop, and then move on, the parental matrix remained constant. And the grounding that Elizabeth ensured for the community was translated from spirit to matter in that great fundraising project to achieve ownership of the literal ground of our being, fulfilling the ecological promise of whole health in our estate. Guests and staff and companions and members, and all creatures great and small, and every plant and blade of grass can know they belong and are loved completely and unconditionally. This is the secure base. This is the place where the redeemer rests that weary head. The Redeemer in all of us who is just waiting to come home: "*The Place to*

Turn to", as Holy Rood House is known. It is no coincidence that HRH[26] stands for "Her/His Royal Highness". This is the reality—God is always happening in a loving compassionate community.

The panentheistic nature of community is comfortable with the gnosis of Divine Spirit as both being and becoming everywhere, an infinite particle and wave choreography in an eternal dance with and within everything. I often find I can link modern scientific findings, particularly the various energy fields, to ancient mystical wisdom and spirituality and that quantum[27] physics proves what has always been known, indeed as *a priori* knowledge, but I do not have space to expand on this here. We continue, onwards and upwards, in our mystical journey of human–divine relatedness.

---

26   Like Jung, I can enjoy symbolic play with words, letters, numbers. Here, I am reiterating the elevation of Mary and Jesus as the real human royal highnesses, and the promise that we, too, would be so alongside them. We are fully human when we know our royal highness and common lowness in complementary relationship within—handmaid queen and servant king. The true saint is one who knows and embraces the sinner within.

27   *Quantus* (Latin: "how great"). This eternal science is all about relationship. "How Great Thou Art!"

1 5

Spiritual darkness and spiritual accompaniment

Andrew De Smet

This essay started life as a day for a group of spiritual accompaniers in the Diocese of York.[1] The day included some experiential exercises and group work. As this whole area makes more sense if connected with our own experiences, I have kept the exercises as part of this essay. Consequently, this is more a practitioner's than an academic piece, although the two are not mutually exclusive! I will use the terms spiritual accompaniment, spiritual direction and soul friending as speaking about broadly the same thing.

Spiritual accompaniment is one of the pillars of ministry at Holy Rood House. For some years, I have facilitated a supervision group for spiritual accompaniers and chaplains there. Many people come to Holy Rood in a state of spiritual darkness, some of them in a state of mental distress, so being able to accompany those in a dark place spiritually is an important part of ministry at Holy Rood House. The spiritual accompaniment group is important for anyone offering spiritual accompaniment.

Exercise: Have some pastels or other drawing or painting materials and paper to hand. Think about a time of spiritual darkness or spiritual boredom you have experienced. What was it like? What were the emotions? What was prayer like? What, if anything, triggered it in the

---

[1]   An expanded version of talks given at a day for spiritual directors in the Anglican Diocese of York at Wydale Hall in November 2023.

first place? Draw something that expresses what it was like, a scene or colours and shapes. When you have spent some time on your drawing/painting you might like to jot down on top of what you have drawn/painted some words that describe the experience. Or, if art fills you with a sense of dread, go straight to jotting down some words that describe the experience.

Spiritual greyness

Scripture tends to feature the more extreme experiences of spiritual darkness, but one place we can look for something less dark is Ecclesiastes 1:2: "Vanity of vanities! All is vanity." What is the point? The writer sees this refrain of "vanity" in hard work, in pleasure, even in seeking wisdom. There is a sense of dialogue in the book: perhaps with someone else; perhaps an inner dialogue within the writer's head.[2] Alongside the futility of existence, there is another view, however. In Ecclesiastes 3, the writer sees meaning and happiness are to be found in the rhythms of life in moderation, and in seeking wisdom, and in detachment. The idea of being able to let go of excessive attachment is to be found in the monastic tradition, for example in the Rule of St Benedict Chapters 4, 33 and 34.[3] This letting go is very much part of the Christian contemplative tradition and also Buddhist teaching. The late Anthony de Mello, in his book *Awareness*, drew on both Christian and Buddhist practice of detachment and of not making our happiness dependent on stuff, possessions, success, being well thought of, or even spiritual experience. Also important is attending to our own inner dialogues.[4]

In John of the Cross's typology, spiritual greyness may correspond to the passive night of the senses when, after the initial enthusiasm of conversion, renewal or rediscovery of faith, things go off the boil: people

---

[2]   *The Bible: Revised Standard Version with the Apocrypha*, 4th edition (Oxford: Oxford University Press, 2010).

[3]   Timothy Fry (ed.), *The Rule of St Benedict in English* (Collegeville, MN: The Liturgical Press, 1981).

[4]   Anthony de Mello, *Awareness* (London: Collins Fount Paperbacks, 1990).

may struggle with boredom, loss of a sense of God's closeness or a sense of their stuckness, and/or an awareness of their sinfulness and imperfections. There can also be a falling away or "laxity".[5] In spiritual boredom/*acedia*/ *accidie*, prayer can be boring and/or very distracted. John of the Cross makes a distinction between dryness and lukewarmness.[6]

Ignatius Loyola wrote of spiritual states of "consolation" and "desolation".[7] Spiritual consolation is when we are aligned with God. This may be when we are "on fire with the love of God" or when we are aware of and saddened by our shortcomings, or when we are making sacrifice but are very aware that it is of God. Spiritual desolation is when we lose that alignment with God. There will be a loss of faith, hope and love. Our faith can go cold. Spiritual activity seems barren. There can be a sense of inner turmoil or darkness. There may well be a sense of selfishness. This fits in either with what I have described as spiritual greyness or spiritual darkness. Like John of the Cross, Ignatius says spiritual desolation can be about us becoming tepid in our faith. He adds that it can be a time of testing allowed by God, or it can be a time of recognizing our lack and spiritual poverty so that we may grow in our openness to divine grace. Spiritual desolation is often seen as a time of spiritual growth,[8] although, in practice, this may only be evident in retrospect.

In spiritual accompaniment, various things can be helpful: to normalize ("this is what can happen at this stage of the journey"), to encourage perseverance, to keep talking, to attend to the inner dialogue, rather as in Ecclesiastes. John of the Cross says, "Be content to live with a loving and peaceful attentiveness to God, and to live without the concern, without the effort, and without the desire to taste or feel [God]".[9] This is the detachment described by Anthony de Mello.

---

[5]   Marc Foley (ed.), *John of the Cross: The Ascent to Joy: Selected Spiritual Writings* (New York: New City Press, 2002), p. 25.

[6]   Foley, *John of the Cross*, p. 81.

[7]   David L. Fleming, *The Spiritual Exercises of St Ignatius: A Literal Translation and a Contemporary Reading* (St Louis, MS: The Institute of Jesuit Sources, 1978), p. 206ff.

[8]   Fleming, *Spiritual Exercises*, pp. 206ff.

[9]   Foley, *John of the Cross*, p. 26.

As noted above, it is also worth noticing the inner dialogue, which is often populated by differing and contradictory voices. It helps to recognize this as both/and rather than either/or and attend to them. "When is it different?" is always a good question. In times of greyness or darkness there are often glimpses of light. Attending to these, keeping the spiritual rhythms going even at a basic level, for example basic patterns of prayer, keeping faith on the agenda, are all beneficial.

So, what might help more specifically with the practices of prayer? I am indebted for some of what follows to the late Sr Cecilia Goodman and her CD *Distractions as Creative Prayer*.[10] Conscious distractions that make us lose focus can include:

1. Issues around finding it difficult to settle. These can be wandering thoughts, replaying conversations, remembering stuff to be done. "Bluebottle on the window" stuff. Some of these can help: 1) Prepare for prayer by making a conscious change of gear, having a special place, stilling yourself bodily, recollecting the presence of God. 2) The Ignatian approach recommends doing an examen prayer of recollection, asking for a particular grace from the time of prayer and a short review of the prayer time at the end of prayer. 3) In the contemplative tradition noticing, naming and setting aside the distractions and returning to the focus of the time of prayer is encouraged.

2. Drowsiness or looking at the clock a lot and avoiding getting started. These raise the question: do we really want to pray or pray in this way at all? Things have a season. Some seasons are long, some short; so maybe a different way of praying would help—a new season.

3. Daydreams. These are often an escape, and it is worth exploring the themes and content, as one might with dreams.

---

[10] Cecilia Goodman, *Distractions as Creative Prayer*, CD produced by St Bede's Pastoral Centre, York. <https://www.stbedes.org.uk/>, accessed 3 April 2024. It is planned to make these talks available as downloads from the website.

Discerning whether the distractions themselves are something that need prayerful attention. Cecilia Goodman talked about the "mosquito level" of more insistent buzzing, such as replaying of conversations, resentments, hurts or relationships. Notice them and name them. If they seem significant, pray about them either then or later and take them to spiritual direction.

In Cecilia's talk this then leads into subconscious reasons for our distractions. Here I shall just highlight and expand a little on two of them; and I will examine the others when we consider spiritual darkness.

One is unacknowledged anger with God. For example, in bereavement, "Why did you take her?" Prayer is avoided or feels distant or unreal as there is a lack of honesty with God. The psalms of lament provide a good model of honesty with God. They include anger, anxiety, doubts and despair. Examples of such psalms are Psalm 22, Psalm 74, Psalm 79, Psalm 137. Psalm 137 reaches a point of rage:

> O daughter Babylon, you devastator!
> Happy shall they be who pay you back
> what you have done to us!
> Happy shall they be who take your little ones
> and dash them against the rock!

We probably won't agree with the sentiment, even if it is sung beautifully by a cathedral choir, but being able to voice anger can be part of the journey towards letting it go or acting on it in a more constructive way.

Another is poor self-image/self-loathing/feeling unlovable, so God again can feel distant, disinterested, uncaring. In accompaniment, uncovering these can be liberating. As much as the content of spiritual accompaniment, the process of being accepted and attended to by a spiritual accompanier can be part of the process of growth and healing.

Ignatius Loyola's Spiritual Exercises were written for spiritual directors guiding people through either a 30-day retreat or the same process in daily life. He offers several suggestions for those in a place of spiritual desolation:

Not to make major decisions at such times, and not to go back on earlier decisions, but not to sit back, and to stick with or even intensify prayer. So, keep spiritual practices going. (Although from today's perspective we might want to reflect on what practices are helpful and appropriate at such times).[11]

Ignatius suggested the spiritual director fosters patience and encourages the person to recall times of spiritual consolation in the past as a way of giving hope in the present:

To talk openly through things with a spiritual director or confessor.
To be aware we will be attached at our weak points.[12]

Spiritual boredom can often be about church. A recurring complaint about churches is the lack of silence in worship and a lack of depth in teaching about the life of the spirit. From my experience of counselling and spiritual accompaniment with clergy, I suspect this links to institutional anxiety, and a compensating culture of overwork which frequently squeezes out clergy's exploration of silence, prayer and spirituality in favour of more "results"-focussed activity. Holy Rood House and other centres provide places of being rather than doing and, thereby, the possibility of seeing things from a new perspective. In its offering of feminist ideas, and an inclusive ethos in its spirituality and worship, Holy Rood House provides an oasis for those alienated by more "mainstream" worship, which often carries patriarchal assumptions and exclusive language or attitudes to sexuality which can alienate many.

In the West, we live in an age that is corrosive to faith, and religion is often regarded as irrelevant or even infantile; and this "spirit of the age" can seep into people's belief and practice of faith. So again, it can be useful to reflect on this in spiritual accompaniment, to allow questions to be explored, doubts examined, ambivalence held, as occurs in Ecclesiastes. The spiritual accompanier and communities such as Holy Rood House

---

[11]   Goodman, *Distractions as Creative Prayer.*
[12]   Fleming, "First week rules", *Spiritual Exercises*, pp. 209ff.

provide a safe space. Also, on occasions, simply by being a person or community of faith holds out a possibility of having a faith with integrity.

Exercise: Pause and think: What kinds of things make you or those you accompany feel bored or alienated from Church? What has helped you or those you accompany out of spiritual greyness or boredom?

Spiritual darkness

There is not a clear distinction between spiritual greyness or boredom/ *acedia* and spiritual darkness; grey can easily darken into black or black lighten to grey! We can look on *acedia*, spiritual darkness and spiritual crisis as overlapping circles.

Exercise: Where is there spiritual darkness or crisis in the Bible? What can we learn from the Bible about this?

Exercise: What are the triggers into spiritual darkness for you and those you have accompanied?

Triggers into spiritual darkness are varied. These categories overlap:

- Life factors include illness (chronic, sudden or terminal), suffering, bereavement/loss, relationship breakdown, overload, stress, burnout, bullying, abuse, the state of the world, climate anxiety, poverty, discrimination. Sometimes there is no trigger; it just happens.
- Psychological factors, often triggered by life events, include depression, anxiety, shame, guilt, trauma (past or present); complicated or stuck grief; psychosis or other mental illness; self-loathing; internalized homo- or transphobia. These latter factors come, of course, from experiences of homophobia or transphobia and their presence in society.
- Spiritual factors include moving to a new stage of faith, "Dark night of the soul", loss of faith, disillusionment with church,

unacknowledged anger with God, unhelpful images of God. Often these too link to past experiences.

The experience of spiritual darkness has much in common with the spiritual greyness described earlier, but with a profound sense of absence and disorientation. Expanding on life and psychological factors takes us into the interface of spirituality and psychology. John of the Cross wrote rather abstractly about dark nights, but his life situation was that he was thrown into jail by his fellow brothers for trying to reform the religious order he was part of. Small wonder he was tipped into spiritual darkness. Change in church can provoke strong reactions! So too can things that are happening in the world. Climate change, wars, the state of politics, can all induce a sense of despair and powerlessness. Climate anxiety is increasingly prevalent, and we will return to this below.

One challenge in being alongside someone in spiritual darkness is discerning whether it is spiritual darkness and/or depression and whether there is anxiety and/or grief. I see these as overlapping circles.

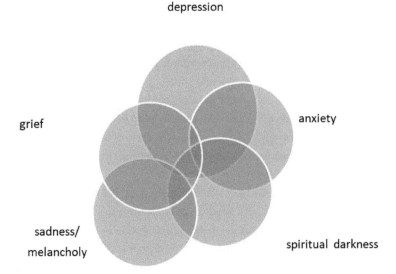

depression

grief

anxiety

sadness/
melancholy

spiritual darkness

Spiritual darkness alone affects a person's sense of God, prayer, purpose and spiritual life, but other areas of life may well carry on more or less as normal. Mother Teresa spent long periods in spiritual darkness but continued to do remarkable work. Depression and anxiety disorders are more global in their effects, stopping a person functioning and blanketing all areas of life. Periods of sadness or melancholy are, however, a normal part of human experience. The problem is when they become deeper and longer and tip into depression. Something similar is true of anxiety. We all get anxious about things, but when anxiety becomes overwhelming and/or habitual it is a problem. Likewise, grief related to bereavement or other losses is a normal response but can slide into depression. So, as the diagram illustrates, it is possible to be in one or more of these states at one time.

Good listening and discernment in spiritual accompaniment are vital when being alongside someone in spiritual darkness. If someone moves into depression or severe anxiety, then referral for counselling/ psychotherapy and/or medical help may well be needed. At Holy Rood House, Elizabeth Baxter has gathered a team of chaplains, spiritual accompaniers/directors and counsellors/psychotherapists, some of whom bridge those categories; so Holy Rood House staff and volunteers are well suited to discern and respond to these overlaps between spirituality and mental health, and attend to the spiritual dimensions of mental distress.

Having a sense of spirituality can be an important part of a person's recovering mental wellbeing and health. It can help in several ways: at an existential level through finding a sense of meaning and purpose in life, and a sense of the transcendent; at the level of spiritual practices such as prayer, meditation or contemplation, mindfulness or the Ignatian examen prayer.[13] Communal prayers and worship all help give a sense of connectedness both to God and to an accepting inclusive community. Research has shown the value of mindfulness and meditation in reducing depression and anxiety.[14] Contemplation is a Christian form of meditation using similar techniques but with the goal of opening us to God's presence, so will have similar physiological and psychological

---

[13] <https://www.ignatianspirituality.com/ignatian-prayer/the-examen/>, accessed 3 April 2024.

[14] Mark Williams, John Teasdale, Zindel Segal and Jon Kabat-Zinn (eds), *The Mindful Way through Depression* (London: Guildford Press, 2007).

effects. There is good evidence that being in and attending to the natural world both enhances mood[15] and connects and grounds us spiritually. The garden at Holy Rood House is an important therapeutic and spiritual resource. Mindfulness and forms of body prayer can help reconnect us with our bodily experience, as a mind/body/spirit unity.

As with spiritual darkness, when someone is going through a time of mental distress, good listening is at the heart of good spiritual accompaniment. As implied above, attending to issues of meaning and purpose and maybe introducing techniques of meditation, contemplation and mindfulness can help both in spiritual darkness and in times of depression and anxiety. The accompanier can also hold up a mirror and reflect back to the person being accompanied, suggesting that they are showing symptoms of burnout, depression or anxiety. Because these conditions often develop gradually and almost imperceptibly, this noticing and reflecting back can be valuable. It is useful to explore whether spiritual accompaniment should continue alongside counselling/ psychotherapy. If the therapy is with a secular therapist, there is a risk that the spiritual or belief dimension might be ignored or avoided. With proper collaboration, the two processes can run in parallel.

Grief is a normal and natural but painful response to loss, be that death, divorce, loss of job, retirement, dying, illness or loss of capacity. Therapy is usually only needed if the process is overwhelming or complicated, or gets stuck. Good listening by someone aware of the grief process is usually sufficient, allowing the person to express the shock, loss, pining, any anger or guilt they may feel at any particular point. Normalizing the experiences, for example the waves of emotion and the unexpected length of the process, is helpful. This is at the overlap of spiritual accompanying and pastoral care and chaplaincy.

If someone is feeling trapped in a situation or a spiritual state of darkness, it can help to brainstorm with them all available choices: good and bad. Ignatian discernment techniques, noticing desolation and

---

[15]   <https://www.ncbi.nlm.nih.gov/pmc/articles/PMC8125471/>, accessed 3 April 2024.

consolation[16] and the glimpses of light, "both/and" rather than "either/or", can help clarify choices and possibilities.

Trauma, abuse and bullying often produce a deep sense of shame. Again, referral may be appropriate. Trust and safety will often be issues. Spiritual questions can be present, such as "Where was God?", "Can God and/or the church be trusted?" Low self-worth and shame can lead to God seeming distant, perhaps condemning; or prayer can be rather distant and polite. Exploring images of God and how they have been influenced by the past may be fruitful.

Exercise: Have some drawing materials ready. Fold a piece of paper in four and unfold. Still yourself. Spend some time thinking back to when you were five, 15 and 25 years old, and now. What were your images for God at these points? What pictures come to mind? It is quite possible to have contradictory images at any point. For example, God as the finger-pointing old man in the sky, alongside a more compassionate image. Draw the images using a quarter of the page for each age. When you have finished, stay with the images and, as you look at each image, maybe jot a few words that come to mind onto the page.

For someone with a damaged sense of self and/or a deep sense of shame, connecting with the love of God is both hard and necessary; particularly that "eighteen-inch journey" from head to heart. St Ignatius Loyola begins his *Spiritual Exercises* with the "Principle and Foundation", which is very much in this territory of connecting with the love of God and responding to that, before anything else.[17]

Guilt is an emotion of feeling unacceptable after wrongdoing, and shame is a more generalized emotion of being unacceptable at the level of being. Much traditional Western Christianity starts with the dynamic of:

Sin → Guilt → Repentance → Forgiveness

---

[16]   A good introduction to this area is Margaret Silf, *Landmarks: An Ignatian Journey* (London: Darton, Longman & Todd, 1999).

[17]   Fleming, *Spiritual Exercises*, pp. 22ff.

Practices around naming and exploring the consequences of the "sin", maybe making amends in some way and, for some, the sacrament of confession as an assurance of forgiveness can be very powerful.

For many people, however, the dynamic is:

Trauma or very conditional limited love → Self-loathing and Shame → Acceptance

Both in spiritual accompaniment and in community, the experience of acceptance by others and by God is healing.

More on the spiritual state of darkness

Exercise: As earlier, recall a time when you lost any sense of God. How did you feel? What did you want? What helped? What hindered? How (if you have) did you start to emerge?

From *acedia*/spiritual boredom and greyness, spiritual darkness is going to another level. Some linked takes on this are the works of James Fowler[18] and Elizabeth Liebert[19] on stages of faith. It is beyond the scope of this essay to explore these, but a key point is that the time when you are moving from one stage to another can be a time of real pain, disorientation and questioning. What made sense and gave meaning no longer does so; and what is new has not emerged or is not clear yet. Some examples of this are:

1. Someone moving from a very literal faith, losing their confidence in and struggling with the very black-and-white teaching of their church and view of the Bible, but maybe still liking the style

---

[18] James Fowler, *Stages of Faith: The Psychology of Human Development and the Quest for Meaning* (San Francisco: Harper & Row, 1981).

[19] Elizabeth Liebert, *Changing Life Patterns: Adult Development in Spiritual Direction* (St Louis, MS: Chalice Press, 2000).

of worship and fellowship of that place. So, they experience confusion and maybe guilt or frustration.

2. Someone who had been a conscientious and faithful church member for years struggling with church, developing a new thirst for spiritual things and greater self-awareness, but is questioning what prayer is.

3. Someone who finds ways they have prayed drying up and feels drawn into silent prayer; but is not clear what this new way is and wants help in this.

"Mid-life crisis" is a term popularized by Carl Jung, the first half of life often having been around striving for career, recognition, family or whatever. Then a sense of stuckness or questioning of values and an awareness of mortality can lead to a change in direction. Richard Rohr explores this in his book *Falling Upwards*.[20]

John of the Cross describes the dark nights, and the best explanation of the Dark Night of the Soul I have come across is the late Cecilia Goodman's CD *Crisis of Faith: Danger or Opportunity?*[21] She makes links to lay Christians' spirituality, rather than it being somewhat abstract and solely about monks and nuns who spend hours a day in prayer. There are links but not direct correspondences to the stages of faith outlined by Liebert and Fowler. Rather like different personality typing methods, they are looking at the same thing but from different angles.

When we are relatively new to faith, or our faith has been reawakened, there are often moments of awareness/encounter/religious experience. Different people will describe it differently, and often we will find patterns of prayer can differ to suit these differences. They can be based on the daily offices, *lectio divina*, shared bible study, prayer groups, intercession, body prayer, free prayer or prayer groups. Once established, these will

---

20 Richard Rohr, *Falling Upwards: A Spirituality for the Two Halves of Life* (London: SPCK, 2013).

21 Cecilia Goodman, *Crisis of Faith: Danger or Opportunity?* CD produced by St Bede's Pastoral Centre, York, <https://www.stbedes.org.uk/>, accessed 3 April 2024. It is planned to make these talks available as downloads from the website.

often remain part of our prayer life throughout our journey. Relating to this context, John of the Cross warns of "spiritual avarice",[22] of wanting more special experiences or spiritual highs.

He goes on to write of the "dark night of the senses" which links to the spiritual greyness and *acedia* described earlier. St Teresa of Avila uses an analogy to illustrate this: that we are like panes of glass that look clear on a cloudy day, but when the sun comes out it reveals the dirt and dust on the glass.[23] This phase is a movement deeper into God. We become more aware of and pained by our shortcomings and seek to change. We may become frustrated by lack of time and space for the things of God. People may experience both longing and reluctance—a vacillation. In practice, we get on with life and keep a prayer life going, but there is the ache of longing. There may be what John and Teresa describe as the "Prayer of Quiet". For some, this is a movement into contemplative prayer; for others, it is those moments of presence sensed during other ways of praying.

John explores the transformation of intellect, memory and will through the virtues of faith, hope and love. The idea is that in growth in these we grow into God. The knowledge of God is not so much an intellectual knowledge but a felt sense that "brings certitude" but "does not produce clarity". The "night of the spirit" can be a paradoxical experience. We can be pushed into it by a life crisis. We are closer to God but may well feel further away. We can end up operating at two levels: at one level, a feeling of confusion and loss, while at a deeper level, a longing and an intuitive knowledge. Previous ways of praying and church worship can seem dead. What we previously knew about prayer is, in Cecilia's words, "turned on its head", and we move into a more passive place. This can be a real crisis of faith. With this can come a sense of shame: we are failing in our faith; we have lost connection; we can no longer see the signposts. Dangers, at this point, can be to walk away from faith, or to settle for second best—what is safe, and we are in control of; or to slip into mental illness or addiction. Repressed or unconscious parts of self can emerge.

---

[22]   Foley, *John of the Cross*, p. 75.

[23]   Quoted by Cecilia Goodman in *Crisis of Faith: Danger or Opportunity?*

John of the Cross says that, in the earlier stages of the journey, God enters into our world in a way we can understand, for example, as warmth, peace and so on. Later, God invites us into Godself, which is an unknown landscape.

Part of this new landscape is within the darkness that John of the Cross and Teresa of Avila call "infused contemplation": prayer purely as a gift of God rather than coming from our own efforts. This is the paradox of "losing everything to gain everything"; again, deep-down longing is part of that prayer. To put it very simply, the opportunity is at a very deep level to "let go and let God", which can ultimately lead to the "Prayer of Union": a profound sense of being in a place of quiet, safety, divine love and oneness, and perceiving God in all things. Here is the freedom to become who we really are in God's eyes. The dark night of the soul can last for years; 20 years in Teresa of Avila's case. St Teresa of Calcutta similarly struggled for many years; and much of Henri Nouwen's writing comes from that place.

Stages of spiritual growth, whether they are Counter-Reformation like those of John of the Cross, Teresa of Avila or Ignatius Loyola, or modern, such as those of James Fowler and Elizabeth Liebert, can be criticized. They risk making some people's experience into a theory of everything. Not everyone has these experiences of darkness or follows these sequences. There is also a cultural element. How much is culturally specific to Western Christianity? How much translates to different cultures and eras? Cecilia Goodman and others have made that translation for a new era. Ignatian spirituality enjoys wide popularity in our time, so clearly these Counter-Reformation spiritualities can speak into our time and experience, but questions about the possibility of translation into less individualistic cultures remain.

Another area of critique is the hierarchical value judgments in models of spiritual growth. Some stages are considered more "advanced" than others, leading to a risk of devaluing some forms of spiritual experience. These models in overlapping ways do affirm importantly, however, that spiritual darkness is not solely a negative experience, but a means of growth and development, where God is in some way present.

Returning to the place of spiritual accompaniment in times of spiritual darkness and reinforcing what has already been said:

1. It is very important to have someone alongside when you are in a place of darkness, doubt or spiritual disorientation—someone you can honestly share these experiences with. As ever, good listening is key, as is having some understanding of the process.
2. If they notice it is tipping into depression, it is important for the spiritual accompanier to encourage the person to seek help.
3. Faithfulness is central in seeing the process through, carrying on with some of the rhythms of prayer and worship. A spiritual accompanier from the community of faith can be a source of stability.

In addition:

1. Keep in touch with the longing; notice the sparks of light in the darkness. "When is it different?" can be a good question; maybe explore more contemplative ways of praying. The Christian tradition stresses the importance of attending to desire/longing/being drawn. This goes back through the many spiritual commentaries on the Song of Songs, through Patristic times and the Middle Ages, back at least to St Augustine of Hippo, who famously wrote: "Our hearts are restless until they find their rest in you."[24] Inner language can be important here. For some, the inner critic language of oughts, shoulds, musts, have to or expected to can take over; so, it is desirable to drill down to a deepest God-given desire, and a positive sense of being drawn. This being drawn can be to the hard or sacrificial choices as well as "nice" choices; but it is getting to a deeper more positive motivation, in therapeutic language, to core self rather than "conditions of worth" or "introjects".
2. Looking at choices can be empowering in times of stuckness and darkness. We can feel trapped and powerless. So, perhaps brainstorming choices, including bad ones and "off the wall" ones, as well as the good ones, then doing the sifting, will be helpful.

---

24 *St Augustine Confessions*, ed. and tr. R. S. Pine-Coffin (London: Penguin, 1961), Book 1.1, p. 21.

3. We are in a time of climate anxiety, global injustice, increasing poverty in this country and wars abroad. As has been said, people can feel a sense of despair and powerlessness. It is important to acknowledge this in spiritual accompaniment. In responding to the sense of powerlessness, one way forward is the old Christian Aid slogan "Think Global, Act Local", prompting us to combine awareness of the issues with realistic possibilities for local action.

Exercise: loosely based on the woman at the well (John 4:1–26): Still yourself. Imagine you are in a dry place. Set the scene: the sights, the sounds, the smells, the sensations. You see a well and approach it. Jesus is there. You draw him some water. You drink together. Then he draws a container up, saying: "I am the living water." What is the living water Jesus gives you now? What are your deep-down desires and longings? Is there anything you need to ask Jesus for? Stay with the meditation. Perhaps use the pastels to draw the well and draw or write what came to mind; or use the space in whatever way you desire.

For the spiritual accompanier, being alongside people who are in dark places, spiritually or mentally, is demanding and can trigger our own stuff. Accompanying someone who is "stuck" needs patience and restraint of our own desire to give answers and move things on. So, it is important to have regular insightful supervision and spiritual accompaniment for ourselves. It is also useful to have some understanding of the terrain. Even though the journey is different for each of us, there is, as we have seen, some commonality of experience and process.

Spirituality and mental health

David Ibrahim and Christopher C. H. Cook

Holy Rood House includes spiritual health as a core concern in its ecology of health, a concern shared with a variety of other organizations including the former Centre for Spirituality, Theology and Health at Durham University and the Spirituality and Psychiatry Special Interest Group at the Royal College of Psychiatrists. Engaging with spiritual health in professional practice in today's health service requires both an engagement with the research evidence base and an ability to argue the case in a pluralistic and secular context. In the following essay, we explore some of the arguments in support of the importance of spirituality in relation to mental health.

Introduction

Spirituality is increasingly recognized as an important component of holistic care for those who face mental health challenges. Research has shown that spirituality and/or religion (S/R) are generally associated with lower prevalence of mental disorders (with strongest evidence for depression, suicide and substance misuse) and, when addressed in treatment, better outcomes.[1] However, these headline findings conceal

---

[1]   H. G. Koenig, T. VanderWeele and J. R. Peteet (eds), *Handbook of Religion and Health* (Oxford: Oxford University Press, 2024), pp. 45–233, <https://doi.org/10.1093/oso/9780190088859.001.0001>, accessed 3 April 2024.

many questions as to the complex nature of the relationship between mental health and spirituality.

In this essay, we summarize multiple aspects of the intersection between spirituality and mental health. We will consider definitions of spirituality, mental health and religion. We will also highlight differences between positive and negative influences of spirituality on mental health and use examples of different kinds of mental psychopathology. We will briefly consider the recent challenges of the Covid-19 pandemic and its impact on mental health.

The medical model of mental healthcare can sometimes overly emphasize the biological aspects of mental disorders. However, properly understood, it takes a biopsychosocial approach which balances the biological with the cultural, social, and psychological aspects of mental illnesses and their treatments. Alongside this, as already mentioned, it is important to give attention to spiritual and religious aspects of mental health and wellbeing, and to do this well requires a patient-centred approach.[2] A series of surveys has, however, shown that there is a religiosity gap[3], whereby mental health professionals tend to be less religious than the general population. This situation easily leads to neglect of S/R considerations in patient care and, worse, sometimes results in the pathologizing of S/R beliefs, experiences and behaviour. Unfortunately, the negative aspects of religion and religious institutions have often overshadowed (in the minds of some mental health professionals) the benefits that come with spiritual values and religiosity.

In recent decades, research has highlighted multiple benefits of spirituality and religion. Given the current pace of life, socioeconomic challenges and a huge burden of loneliness and search for meaning, there is a need for deeper insight into the bio-psycho-social model,[4] to address

---

[2]   Person-Centred Training and Curriculum (PCTC) Scoping Group (2018). *Person-centred care: implications for training in psychiatry CR215.*

[3]   C. C. H. Cook, "The Faith of the Psychiatrist", *Mental Health, Religion & Culture* 14:1 (2011), pp. 9–17. <https://doi.org/10.1080/13674671003622673>, accessed 3 April 2024.

[4]   C. C. Kuhn, "A Spiritual Inventory of the Medically Ill Patient", *Psychiatric Medicine* 6:2 (1988), pp. 87–100.

spiritual concerns. Amongst other advances in the inclusion of spirituality into clinical care, the Royal College of Psychiatrists (RCPsych) has adopted a position statement on spirituality and mental health which provides recommendations for psychiatrists on good practice regarding inclusion of the spiritual aspects of the mental health history, as well as on treatment, training, and collaboration with chaplaincy and spiritual care colleagues.[5] The position statement points out that "spirituality and religion are concerned with the core beliefs, values, and experiences of human beings. Faith communities, and spiritual or religious practices, have the potential to influence the course of mental illness and attitudes towards people with mental illness, for good or ill. A consideration of their relevance to the origins, understanding and treatment of psychiatric disorders is therefore an important part of clinical and academic psychiatry."

Recent years have been especially challenging. They have included a global pandemic, a cost-of-living crisis, wars in Europe and the Middle East, and instability in multiple areas around the world. If we have learned anything during such exceptional times, it is that we tend to lean on our deepest and most core beliefs during tough times. Our mental resilience and mental health are strongly tested. A clear example of this is the prediction by the Centre for Mental Health in October 2020 that "up to 10 million people (almost 20 per cent of the population of the UK) will either need new or additional mental health support as a direct consequence of the pandemic crisis".[6] Taking into consideration the religiosity gap mentioned earlier, it was noted by Adrian James, then President of the RCPsych, that half of mental health service users hold spiritual or religious beliefs that they consider helpful in dealing with their mental illness.[7]

---

[5] C. Cook, "Recommendationsf or Psychiatrists on Spirituality and Religion", in *Position Statement PS03/2013* (Royal College of Psychiatrists, 2013), p. 5.

[6] G. Durcan, N. O'Shea and L. Allwood, *Covid-19 and the Nation's Mental Health: Forecasting Needs and Risks in the UK* (Centre for Mental Health, 2020). <https://www.centreformentalhealth.org.uk/publications/COVID-19-and-nations-mental-health-october-2020/>, accessed 3 April 2024.

[7] C. Cook and A. Powell (eds), "Foreword to the Second Edition", in *Spirituality and Psychiatry* (Cambridge: Cambridge University Press, 2022), pp.

Definitions

It is crucial to have a clear definition of the terms and terminology used in discussions around spirituality and mental health.

What is spirituality?

Spirituality as a concept has had multiple definitions across different cultures and different times. The word itself in English originates from Latin, relating to the human spirit in the Christian context, which developed to differentiate between what is spiritual and what is material. To highlight the contrast between an older, more classic and a newer, more comprehensive definition, we need only to look at the difference between the definition in the *Cambridge Advanced Learner's Dictionary & Thesaurus* (2013)[8]: "Spirituality (noun) the quality that involves deep feelings and beliefs of a religious nature, rather than the physical parts of life", and a definition designed to be inclusive, and cited in the RCPsych position statement:

> Spirituality is a distinctive, potentially creative and universal dimension of human experience arising both within the inner subjective awareness of individuals and within communities, social groups and traditions. It may be experienced as relationship with that which is intimately "inner", immanent and personal, within the self and others, and/or as relationship with that which is wholly "other", transcendent and beyond the self. It is experienced as being of fundamental or ultimate importance and is thus concerned with matters of meaning and purpose in life, truth and values.[9]

---

xvii–xviii. <https://doi.org/10.1017/9781911623311.001>, accessed 3 April 2024.

[8]   C. McIntosh (ed.), *Cambridge Advanced Learner's Dictionary*, fourth edition (Cambridge: Cambridge University Press, 2013).

[9]   C. C. H. Cook, "Addiction and Spirituality", *Addiction* 99:5 (2004), pp. 539–51. <https://doi.org/10.1111/j.1360-0443.2004.00715.x>, accessed 3 April 2024.

Spirituality has thus moved away from its religious context and taken on a wider and more encompassing perspective.

What is religion, and how does it differ from spirituality?

Religion, like spirituality, has varying definitions. The definition found in the *Cambridge Dictionary* focusses on religion being "the belief in and worship of a god or gods, or any such system of belief and worship". Yet religion is not only, or even mainly, about dogma. It is about symbols and meaning, following, belonging, identity and social cohesion.[10] Religion is concerned, in the minds of many, with socially and traditionally shared beliefs and experience.

The main differences between spirituality and religion, at least in many people's minds, is that spirituality tends to be understood as more individual and more inclusive, and it doesn't have to adhere to certain rules or belief in deities. However, both terms are difficult to define and, in clinical practice, it is more important to understand what they mean to an individual patient than to refer to the academic debate.

Mental health

What does a mentally healthy individual look like? The World Health Organization (WHO) defines mental health as:

> a state of mental well-being that enables people to cope with the stresses of life, realize their abilities, learn well and work well, and contribute to their community. It is an integral part of health and well-being that underpins our individual and collective abilities to make decisions, build relationships and shape the world we live in. Mental health is a basic human right. And it is crucial to personal, community and socio-economic development. Mental health is more than the absence of mental disorders. It exists on a complex continuum, which is experienced differently from one

---

10   C. Cook and A. Powell (eds), *Spirituality and Psychiatry*, second edition (Cambridge: Cambridge University Press, 2022). <https://doi.org/10.1017/9781911623311>, accessed 3 April 2024.

person to the next, with varying degrees of difficulty and distress and potentially very different social and clinical outcomes.[11]

From this definition, we can understand that mental health is not about always being happy; it is more a journey of resilience, growth and contribution to the community. Although the WHO definition does not explicitly mention spirituality, it addresses some important spiritual themes.

Positive and negative influences of spirituality and religion on mental health

Having considered these definitions, we can now attend to the main focus of this essay. Is S/R beneficial to mental health? The following clinical vignettes derive from the clinical experience of one of us (DI) in his practise of psychiatry both in the UK and in Egypt. Details have been anonymized.

Lina, age 18, grew up as part of a religious community, and was struggling with depression and regulating her emotions after experiencing sexual abuse as a child. Her experience of sharing this with her family was difficult, and they initially blamed her for meeting with an unknown person and putting herself in a dangerous situation. Lina at this point decided to share this with the priest in confession. The priest was highly empathetic and supportive. He explained to her that it was not her fault and encouraged her to seek support from mental health services. The priest also encouraged her to engage with a big church community which provided activities, friends and a safe space for growth and exploration. She described this S/R experience as positive and vital to her mental stability and resilience and how this helped her accept herself. Her religious beliefs of self-acceptance, self-care and inherent value were useful to her also when she decided to embark on her therapy journey.

Mario, age 24, who grew up in a religious family in upper Egypt, came to the clinic struggling with low mood and inability to sleep. He

---

[11] World Health Organization, *Mental Health: Key Facts* (17 June 2022). <https://www.who.int/news-room/fact-sheets/detail/mental-health -strengthening-our-response>.

was guarded at the beginning of therapy and appeared to hold a lot of shame and sense of guilt. When he started to open up, he identified as trans female, which was the main cause of his symptoms according to him. At this point, she asked to be referred to using she/her pronouns and to be called Flora, which was her preferred name. During therapy, Flora explained that she grew up in a family that adopted a culture of shame and guilt which contributed to her feeling ashamed of her "sin" of being trans and not seeking therapy. She had a negative experience going to a priest who confirmed her negative ideas about herself. She identified S/R as having a negative influence on her mental health.

These examples illustrate that S/R, and its effect on mental health, is heavily dependent on factors such as the culture, the individual personal experience, and even how S/R was approached in that person's life. It is really important for mental health professionals to be curious about and mindful of their patients' spiritual and religious views. It is also very important for religious and spiritual leaders to be aware of the influence of their congregation's spiritual ideas and beliefs on their mental wellbeing.

Confounding factors in assessing spirituality's effect on mental health

While spirituality is a helpful concept to facilitate clinical conversations with patients, it has proven problematic for research. This arises because the kinds of questions that might be asked about spirituality in research tend to elicit answers which are highly dependent upon psychological wellbeing. The independent variables (spirituality) and dependent variables (mental wellbeing) are thus highly confounded. Because of this, it has been proposed that religiosity is a more useful variable for research purposes than spirituality.[12] However, for most religious people spirituality and religion are closely interrelated. In the following consideration of the positive and negative influences of spirituality, we will therefore refer to S/R.

---

[12]   H. G. Koenig, "Concerns about Measuring 'Spirituality' in Research", *Journal of Nervous & Mental Disease* 196:5 (2008), pp. 349–55, <https://doi.org/10.1097/NMD.0b013e31816ff796>, accessed 3 April 2024.

Positive influences of S/R

Increasingly, research has explored the profound impact of spirituality on mental health, shedding light on its positive influence. S/R encompasses a broader sense of connection, purpose and transcendence, offering a holistic framework for understanding and coping with life's challenges, all of which seems to have a beneficial impact on mental health and wellbeing. Below are some examples of this.

Reduced rates of mental illness: This was shown in the early study in Emile Durkheim's book *Le Suicide*, published originally in 1897, which observed lower suicide rates in Catholic regions than in Protestant regions; he attributed this to the nature of cohesive practice in Catholicism at the time.[13] Many religions prohibit suicide, and this prohibition and moral rejection is associated with lower likelihood of suicidal behaviour.[14] Similar factors may account for the lower rates of substance misuse amongst those who are more religious.[15]

Different studies showed inverse relationships between S/R and depression (61 per cent of studies), suicide (75 per cent), anxiety (49 per cent), and alcohol use (86 per cent). These numbers are even higher if considering only the higher quality studies.[16] This clearly suggests a positive influence of S/R on mental health, although correlations alone do not prove a causative link.

---

[13]   Emile Durkheim, *Suicide: A Study in Sociology*, ed. G. Simpson, reissue edition (New York: Free Press, 1997).

[14]   D. Lizardi, K. Dervic, M. F. Grunebaum, A. K. Burke, J. J. Mann and M. A. Oquendo, "The Role of Moral Objections to Suicide in the Assessment of Suicidal Patients", *Journal of Psychiatric Research* 42:10 (2008), pp. 815–21. <https://doi.org/10.1016/j.jpsychires.2007.09.007>, accessed 3 April 2024.

[15]   K. R. Morton, J. W. Lee and L. R. Martin, "Pathways from Religion to Health: Mediation by Psychosocial and Lifestyle Mechanisms", *Psychology of Religion and Spirituality* 9:1 (2017), pp. 106–17. <https://doi.org/10.1037/rel0000091>, accessed 3 April 2024.

[16]   H. G. Koenig, "Religion, Spirituality, and Health: a Review and Update", *Advances in Mind-Body Medicine* 29:3 (2015), pp. 19–26.

Increased social support: Religion provides a community where a person is able to bond, feel safe and benefit from the social capital of that community, a factor that nowadays appears to be increasingly important with the rise of loneliness and its associated negative effects. Rote, Hill and Ellison (2013), for example, demonstrated that religious attendance contributed to a reduction in loneliness through social integration and a wider network of social support.[17]

Resilience: A longitudinal study that focussed mainly on resilience and its role in recovery showed that growing up in a family that held religious beliefs—in turn providing some stability and meaning—was one of the factors that enabled those who experienced adverse childhood experiences, such as poverty or abuse, to develop into competent, confident and caring adults.[18]

Happiness: A study by Pew Centre in the USA revealed that 36 per cent of actively religious adults in the United States identified as very happy, while only 25 per cent of both inactive and unaffiliated Americans expressed the same level of happiness. In 25 other surveyed countries, actively religious individuals reported significantly higher levels of happiness than unaffiliated people in 12 countries, and they were happier than inactively religious adults in nine countries. Although this study reflects on the fact that it is difficult to establish a direct causative link, it attributes higher levels of happiness to different virtues of religion, such as forgiveness, compassion and helping others.[19]

These examples demonstrate some of the benefits of S/R in relation to mental health; and are consistent with the general notion that spiritual and religious views are crucial influences on mental wellbeing, albeit in different ways in different people.

---

[17] S. Rote, T. D. Hill and C. G. Ellison, "Religious Attendance and Loneliness in Later Life", *The Gerontologist* 53:1 (2013), pp. 39–50. <https://doi.org/10.1093/geront/gns063>, accessed 3 April 2024.

[18] E. E. Werner, "Risk, Resilience, and Recovery: Perspectives from the Kauai Longitudinal Study", *Development and Psychopathology* 5:4 (1993), pp. 503–15. <https://doi.org/10.1017/S095457940000612X>, accessed 3 April 2024.

[19] Pew Research Center (2019), *Religion's Relationship to Happiness, Civic Engagement and Health Around the World.*

Negative influences of S/R

Although, as illustrated above, spirituality generally seems to be positively associated with mental health, there is also a negative side, where S/R may have negative effects on a person's mental wellbeing in various ways.

False spirituality: Battista, Scotton and Chinen described the negative side of spirituality as "false spirituality"[20] and divided this into two aspects: defensive and offensive spirituality. Defensive spirituality is about hiding certain aspects of oneself. This may be expressed differently in different religions. For example, it might include rejecting anger or considering it as alien or as a sin, or rejecting sexuality or other aspects of humanity like fear or anxious feelings and thoughts and attributing them to lack of faith. This only prolongs suffering, isolation and anxiety and creates a burden on the person's mental wellbeing. It also constitutes a barrier to the person seeking mental health support. Offensive spirituality, on the other hand, is the narcissistic use of spirituality to provide a false sense of superiority, potentially leading to control and abuse. Unfortunately, examples of abusive S/R tend to attract more media attention than positive influences, especially in secularized Western communities.

Spiritual bypassing is a term coined by John Welwood, who was a psychotherapist and a Buddhist teacher.[21] Spiritual bypassing is a tendency to use spiritual explanations to sidestep or avoid facing unresolved emotional issues, psychological wounds and unfinished developmental tasks. These concepts are based in the defence mechanisms of avoidance and repression.

Harmful spiritual groups: Another possible negative influence of S/R is the danger of adverse group influences and loss of individuality. This

---

[20] J. R. Battista, B. W. Scotton and A. B. Chinen, "Offensive Spirituality and Spiritual Defenses", in *Textbook of Transpersonal Psychiatry and Psychology* (New York: Basic Books/Hachette Book Group, 1996), pp. 250–60.

[21] T. Fossell, "HUMAN NATURE, BUDDHA NATURE: On Spiritual Bypassing, Relationship, and the Dharma. An interview with John Welwood by Tina Fossell", <https://johnwelwood.com/articles/TRIC_interview_uncut.pdf>, accessed 3 April 2024.

has been found in harmful spiritual groups of various kinds, including cults, sects and some new religious movements and charismatic groups.[22]

Shame and guilt: In addition to suppressing individuality, harmful spiritual groups often have a culture of engendering shame and guilt. High religiosity has been proven to intensify the relationship between shame and psychological distress.[23]

Evidence such as this reveals that S/R, albeit having many beneficial aspects for mental health, also carries a risk of being harmful in a variety of ways.

Intersections between religion and mental health in practice

Incorporating spiritual care in psychiatry

It is important for mental health professionals to ask patients about S/R in clinical practice, but this has to be done with sensitivity and care.[24] A full discussion of this is beyond the scope of the present essay, but one creative example was developed by the service users and staff of Tees, Esk and Wear Valleys NHS Foundation Trust, and it summarizes what spirituality represents to them and how it positively affects them in a visual form, as a flower. The flower can be used with the service user to explore their spiritual or religious needs, to help them feel comfortable and properly supported.

---

22   N. Crowley and G. Jenkinson, "Pathological Spirituality", in C. Cook and A. Powell (eds), *Spirituality and Psychiatry* (Cambridge: Cambridge University Press, 2022).

23   F. M. El-Jamil, "Shame, Guilt, and Mental Health: A Study on the Impact of Cultural and Religious Orientation", *Dissertation Abstracts International: Section B: The Sciences and Engineering*, 64(3-B)(1487) (2013).

24   L. Ross, L. Grimwade and S. Eagger, "Spiritual Assessment", in C. Cook and A. Powell (eds), *Spirituality and Psychiatry* (Cambridge: Cambridge University Press, 2022), pp. 23–41.

The Spirituality Flower—Tees, Esk & Wear Valleys NHS Foundation Trust (copyright, used here with permission)[25]

Spiritually integrated treatments

S/R have now been incorporated into multiple treatments for mental disorders in a variety of ways. Below are some examples of techniques that have origins in spiritual or religious practices that have now been used and trialled in psychological therapies:

---

[25] *Spirituality: Health and Wellbeing Information about Spirituality for Service Users, Carers and Staff* (n.d.), Tees, Esk and Wear Valleys NHS Foundation Trust, <https://www.tewv.nhs.uk/about-your-care/health-wellbeing/spirituality/>, accessed 3 April 2024.

Mindfulness, now well studied in research and practice, is believed to be an especially useful protective, preventive and therapeutic tool in multiple conditions, e.g. in prevention of relapse in people with depression.[26] Although mindfulness is often seen as rooted in Buddhism, similar practices are found in other religious traditions, such as Christianity.[27]

Compassion Focussed Therapy: Several spiritual practices emphasize the significance of nurturing compassion over prioritizing self-centred motives.[28,29,30] A psychotherapeutic modality named Compassion Focussed Therapy was created by Paul Gilbert. It focusses on how we approach ourselves with compassion, acknowledging our own weaknesses and having more acceptance towards our self. These concepts are rooted in various spiritual beliefs and have proven to provide a lot of therapeutic benefits in support of mental resilience and wellbeing.

12 Step facilitation: S/R has had a particularly big impact in the field of addiction psychiatry, largely through the work of Alcoholics Anonymous (AA) and Narcotics Anonymous (NA), whose 12 Step programmes have shown success in rehabilitation of patients suffering from different addictions. Professional interventions designed to facilitate engagement with 12 Step programmes have been shown to be effective in

---

[26] National Institute for Health and Care Excellence (NICE, 2022). Depression in adults: treatment and management (NG222). In *National Institute for Health and Care Excellence.*

[27] J. J. Knabb, "Centering Prayer as an Alternative to Mindfulness-Based Cognitive Therapy for Depression Relapse Prevention", *Journal of Religion and Health* 51:3 (2012), pp. 908–24. <https://doi.org/10.1007/s10943–010–9404–1>, accessed 3 April 2024.

[28] P. Gilbert, *The Compassionate Mind: A New Approach to Life Challenges* (London: Constable & Robinson, 2009).

[29] T. Plante, *The Psychology of Compassion and Cruelty: Understanding the Emotional, Spiritual, and Religious Influences*, first edition (London: Bloomsbury Publishing, 2015).

[30] R. Matthieu, *Altruism: The Power of Compassion to Change Yourself and the World* (New York: Back Bay Books, 2016).

a large study comparing different interventions (Project MATCH).[31] The 12 Step Programme offers a spiritual approach to recovery. The 12 steps of recovery describe the experiences of the founders of AA[32]:

1. We admitted we were powerless over alcohol—that our lives had become unmanageable.
2. We came to believe that a Power greater than ourselves could restore us to sanity.
3. We made a decision to turn our will and our lives over to the care of God as we understood Him.
4. We made a searching and fearless moral inventory of ourselves.
5. We admitted to God, to ourselves and to another human being the exact nature of our wrongs.
6. We were entirely ready to have God remove all these defects of character.
7. We humbly asked Him to remove our shortcomings.
8. We made a list of all persons we had harmed and became willing to make amends to them all.
9. We made direct amends to such people wherever possible, except when to do so would injure them or others.
10. We continued to take a personal inventory and when we were wrong promptly admitted it.
11. We sought through prayer and meditation to improve our conscious contact with God as we understood Him, praying only for knowledge of His will for us and the power to carry that out.
12. Having had a spiritual awakening as the result of these Steps, we tried to carry this message to alcoholics, and to practise these principles in all our affairs.

---

[31] "Matching Alcoholism Treatments to Client Heterogeneity: Project MATCH Three-Year Drinking Outcomes", *Alcoholism: Clinical and Experimental Research* 22:6 (1988), pp. 1300–11. <https://doi.org/10.1111/j.1530–0277.1998.tb03912.x>, accessed 3 April 2024.

[32] Alcoholics Anonymous World Services, *Twelve Steps and Twelve Traditions* (New York: Alcoholics Anonymous World Services, 1983).

Use of the word "God" (Steps 3, 5, 6, 11) is taken to refer to a "Higher Power" (Step 2), understood in a variety of different possible ways, depending upon what that person believes in.[33] AA and NA (and the other, related, 12 Step organizations) are thus open to agnostics and atheists, as well as to members of any of the world's major faith traditions. The 12 steps depend upon belief in a spiritual Higher Power, and the concept of letting go/surrendering. This is a common theme amongst different religions. As an example, the name of the religion Islam comes from Arabic الإسلام, literally meaning "submission" (to the will of God), from the root of *aslama*: "he resigned, he surrendered, he submitted".[34] In Christianity and Judaism, similar themes are to be found concerning the importance of surrendering to God.

Addressing mental health in faith communities

The work reviewed above has demonstrated potential benefits of religious leaders and mental health professionals working collaboratively to support the mental health of their service users and congregations, thereby affirming the practice at Holy Rood House. It is beneficial also for spiritual communities to support each other when a member suffers from mental health difficulty or challenge; again, as is best practice at Holy Rood House.

Although spirituality is a protective factor, that does not mean that in religious communities one will not encounter people struggling with their mental health within those communities. According to the US Institute for Health Metrics and Evaluation (IHME), in 2019, one in every eight people around the world (that is, 970 million) were living with a mental disorder, with anxiety and depressive disorders being

---

[33] S. Sussman, M. Reynaud, H.-J. Aubin and A. M. Leventhal, "Drug Addiction, Love, and the Higher Power", *Evaluation & the Health Professions* 34:3 (2011), pp. 362–70. <https://doi.org/10.1177/0163278711401002>, accessed 3 April 2024.

[34] *Online Etymology Dictionary.* <https://www.etymonline.com/search?q=islam>, accessed 3 April 2024.

the most common.[35] In 2020, the number of people living with anxiety and depressive disorders rose significantly because of the Covid-19 pandemic. Initial estimates show 26 per cent and 28 per cent increases respectively for anxiety and major depressive disorders in just one year. While effective prevention and treatment options exist, most people with mental disorders do not have access to effective care. Many people with mental ailments also experience stigma, discrimination and violations of their human rights.[36]

As implied by the IHME and WHO statistics, it really matters that people who belong to spiritual or religious groups are aware of basic mental health concepts, because it is more likely than not that they will encounter a person within their group who struggles with their mental health. Members of faith communities also need to learn how to provide safe spaces for those members of their community who struggle with their mental health. A good way to do this is by helping the person not feel alone, encouraging them to speak up and to reach out for help. This can also help to destigmatize mental illness.

It is important to note that a person who holds deep religious or spiritual beliefs and is affected by psychosis may have their psychotic symptoms (whether delusions or hallucinations) centred around religious themes. Mental health chaplains can be extremely helpful in managing this interface between psychopathology and spirituality in a sensitive and constructive way, but it is often a source of tension. Better education of clergy and other faith leaders about mental illness, and better education of mental health professionals about S/R, is also needed to ensure that spirituality and religiosity can be utilized as positive coping resources.

The following case history highlights the importance of collaborative working of an S/R community with a mental health professional.

---

[35]   United States: Institute for Health Metrics and Evaluation (IHME), *Global Burden of Disease Study 2019 (GBD 2019)* (2020). <https://vizhub.healthdata.org/gbd-results/>, accessed 3 April 2024.

[36]   World Health Organization, "Mental Health and COVID-19: Early Evidence of the Pandemic's Impact: Scientific Brief", in *Mental Health and COVID-19: Scientific brief*, World Health Organization, 2022.

Orla was a 56-year-old woman whose family came from Ireland, although she was born in the Midlands in England. She had experienced childhood trauma (sexual abuse and some neglect), which led to her believing herself to be "not good enough, dirty, defiled and unlovable".

Her spirituality was explored gently, with curiosity and respect, and it was found that her family belief system was that to have an evil thought was as bad as or almost equivalent to actually carrying out an evil act. This belief caused a lot of anxiety-provoking thoughts and a sense of shame. Often, this would make Orla feel guilty and it was a contributing factor in her obsessive compulsive disorder (OCD). She lived in fear of intrusive, unpleasant thoughts, which for her were mainly about religion. Those thoughts were atrocious to her, but she did not have any way of controlling them on her own. For example, she would think: "Mary is a slut", "Jesus is the devil". Orla used to try to "neutralize" the thoughts by begging for forgiveness in her prayers, thousands of times daily, pleading for forgiveness for being "dirty and disgusting and evil". The intrusive thoughts proved to her how vile she truly was. The prayer turned into a compulsive act that she had to do to reduce her anxiety.

Orla engaged in therapy, but it proved to be very difficult to change her fundamental beliefs about these intrusive thoughts, no matter what the dose of SSRI (Selective Serotonin Reuptake Inhibitors, a type of antidepressant medication used to treat OCD) or number of sessions of Cognitive Behavioural Therapy (CBT). Due to the immense distress her condition caused her, she engaged in several acts of self-harm, apparently aimed at ending her life. Despite this being (in her eyes) a mortal sin, Orla would say that "it can be no worse than what I am already". It was ascertained that most of the same beliefs were held by Orla's family.

At this point, the help of a known and trusted Catholic priest was enlisted. He emphasized Orla's inherent preciousness and goodness, and how OCD thoughts were not the same as an intentional rejection by the Divine. Orla was genuinely stunned. She disbelieved him the first time, so he was invited back. After sessions with both the priest and the therapist, Orla seemed to be reassured. This allowed CBT to be started, because she felt safe enough; and eventually she recovered from her depression and OCD. Although the wounds of her childhood trauma remain, she can live with them, and use her experiences to genuinely help others. Her faith is now stronger, and more supportive to her wellbeing.

This case history provides a wonderful example of the benefits of cooperation between spiritual leaders and mental health professionals. It is apparent that gentle exploration by the therapist played a vital role in identifying the core beliefs and problem in the patient's life. This in turn emphasizes the importance of openness, gentle curiosity and exploration by mental health professionals of their patients' spirituality and faith. In addition, the understanding of the priest and his readiness to support and be present was crucial to helping her get better. Orla might also have benefitted from religiously integrated cognitive behavioural therapy (RCBT). RCBT is based on the same theories as CBT, but explicitly uses the client's own religious beliefs, practices and values to help them challenge their unhelpful cognitions and behaviours.

Conclusion

This exploration has demonstrated that it is important not to view S/R as either entirely beneficial or entirely harmful to mental health, but rather to always adopt a respectful and curious approach, considering both the positive and negative factors in each case. This applies as much to mental health professionals as to chaplains and spiritual leaders. It is also important to remember that not only is there an influence of spirituality on mental health, but also the other way around. A person's depression is likely to colour their spiritual approach to the divine, to the world and to the people around them. Someone's anxiety might only let them see the future through a lens of the worst possible outcome. Having a supportive spiritual community, which does not judge and exclude, yet accepts, understands and explores, may be a lifeline to a person in need.

Embodied theology in an age of Zoom

Jan Berry

For many years, I have been a passionate advocate of embodied theology, in my teaching, my research and my creating of liturgy. When I discovered Holy Rood House, I found a place that resonated not only with my feminist theological convictions, but also with the embodied theology that derived from them. The work of Elizabeth Baxter and the liturgy and healing ministry of Holy Rood House resisted dualisms of body and spirit in favour of a holistic theology which views the human body as holy and sacred, a site for the revelation of the divine.

When the Covid pandemic struck, and lockdown forced churches, educational establishments, retreat houses and conference centres to close their doors, many resorted to Zoom or other online technologies to continue their work in some form. Holy Rood House kept in touch with guests and supporters through phone calls, emails and cards, as well as offering online retreats through Zoom.[1] Zoom had many benefits, in allowing some forms of worship and human interaction to continue when physical presence was not possible; and some groups have continued to use online platforms for meetings, teaching and even worship, finding that the convenience of being able to meet across distance, with the saving of time and economic resources, makes it a more preferred means of communication than visible meeting. But for myself, and for Holy Rood House, we have to ask whether, in spite of all its advantages, Zoom negates our emphasis on the importance of the body and physicality. In this essay I seek to explore some of the issues that the prevalence of

---

[1]   Helen Warwick, *Holding Real Hope through Crises*, Holy Rood House, 2021.

online platforms raises for an embodied theology. There are, of course, various ways of using the internet and social media, but it was Zoom that seemed to enter our consciousness, adding phrases such as "you're on mute" and "zooming" to our vocabulary; so I am using it here as a kind of shorthand for the many and varied ways in which we connect with one another in virtual reality.

Embodied theology

Embodied theology has its roots in feminist theologies. From its earliest days, feminist theology has critiqued the dualisms of much traditional theology, the roots of which began in forms of Greek philosophy. The dualism of male/female in Christian theology has often been associated with other dualisms—for example, reason/emotion, culture/nature, and of course soul or spirit/body. Feminist theology (or, as some would prefer to call it, thealogy), by contrast, has opted to put women's bodily experiences at the centre, and to claim bodily experience, sexuality and the senses, and the material world as equally sacred and sites of divine revelation:

> The central claim of thealogy is that women image the divine in the embodied reality of their daily lives including the bodily changes and processes that patriarchal religion has found so difficult to deal with—menstruation, birth, sexual activity, menopause, ageing and death.[2]

Other forms of theology have developed their own critiques of dualisms and developed their own expressions of embodied theology. So, for example, in the context of people with disabilities, theologians such as John Hull and Nancy Eiesland have developed critiques of imagery which uses terms such as blindness, sickness, deafness or paralysis as metaphors for sin or resistance to God's purposes. In her classic book *The Disabled*

---

[2] Lisa Isherwood and Elizabeth Stuart, *Introducing Body Theology* (Sheffield: Sheffield Academic Press, 1998), p. 79.

God, Nancy Eiesland challenges us, for example, to see a disabled person in a wheelchair as an image of God.[3] If, as the opening of the book of Genesis asserts, humanity is made in the image and likeness of God, then our imagery of God must reflect and express the full range of human experience, embracing gender diversity, sexuality, race and colour, and all forms of (dis)ability.

An embodied theology is an inclusive theology, embracing the full range of human experience. But it goes beyond that, to affirm that all of the material world is created by God and therefore sacred.

An embodied theology finds expression in liturgy and ritual which makes full use of our senses, rejoicing in the creativity of art and embracing bodily movement. It will recognize the importance of touch and intimacy in relationship, although an awareness of how some have been abused means that a sensitivity to inappropriate touch is vital. Alma Fritchley writes of the impact of the loss of such embodied ritual in a care home setting during the pandemic:

> With the coming of this disease and the "pausing" of our usual way of being both in the secular world and also in the life of the church, the rituals that have helped us through such transitions and crisis in life are no longer there to undergird our humanity. There has been added grief for those whose loved one has died in a Care Home setting. The ritual of visiting has been stopped. Even the *ritual* of saying goodbye has been altered—imagine waving goodbye to a dying loved one through a locked window.[4]

Such ritual will often (although not always) be communal, shared with others. It will honour and respect the natural and created world around us, affirming it as God-made and God-given, with humanity an integral part of the dance which connects us with earth and its seasons.

---

[3] Nancy L. Eiesland, *The Disabled God: Toward a Liberatory Theology of Disability* (Nashville, TN: Abingdon Press, 1993).

[4] Alma Fritchley, *Are People's Relationship to God or Ways of Understanding Faith Affected by the Death of a Loved One in a Care Home Setting?* Unpublished MA dissertation, Luther King House, 2021.

Although much of traditional Christian theology has been dualistic, embodied theology has its roots firmly in Christian doctrine. It is built on the foundation of a theology of creation—not in any denial of evolution, but in the sense that there is a dynamic, divine energy and process at work in the world. It affirms the traditional doctrine of *imago Dei*—of humanity made in the image of God. It finds expression in the Incarnation—the eternal, timeless Word of God becomes human flesh, made known in the particularity of place and time. And our human bodies are temples, sacred dwelling-places, of divine Spirit.

> But in truth Christian theology has always been an embodied theology rooted in creation, incarnation and resurrection, and sacrament.[5]

Zoom and disembodiment

Our first reaction to Zoom may well be that, for all its benefits in enabling remote communication, it negates and undoes all the work that feminists and others have done to develop theologies of the body which claim the human body and the material world as sacred and holy. The intimate interrelationship of face-to-face human contact and the possibility of touch are replaced by talking heads on screens:

> Subtleties were missed, emotional triggers lost in the electronic ether, and I could not simply pass a handkerchief over to someone when grief overwhelmed.[6]

Rather than enjoying the sense of taste, touch and smell we use only sight and sound, reduced to 40 per cent of our senses. Adam Thomas, a man who describes himself as very much at home in the online world, and aware of its possible benefits for Christian discipleship, writes:

---

[5]   Isherwood and Stuart, *Introducing Body Theology*, p. 11.

[6]   Fritchley, *Are People's Relationship to God or Ways of Understanding Faith Affected by the Death of a Loved One in a Care Home Setting?*

> Therefore, during the time I spend in the virtual world, the Tech
> never stimulates three out of my five senses. When my avatar eats
> an apple pie, I can't taste the tartness or smell the aroma of baked
> crust and cinnamon. When I video chat with a friend in need of
> consoling, I can't wrap her in an embrace.[7]

Many church congregations, unable to meet during lockdown, developed
services of worship on Zoom. But in a paper entitled "How can we gather
now?" Bryan Cones, from one such congregation, argues that for all their
value, services on Zoom or other online platforms lacked all elements of
movement or ritual and became symbolically impoverished:

> Still, it is hard to call our Zoom service ritual. The absence of
> bodies rules out their movement together, along with any touch
> associated with the sign of peace, blessing or communion.
> Overall, our time together remains a service of the word.[8]

If we argue, as embodied theology does, that the Incarnation is central to
Christian theology, surely online religion runs the risk of losing all sense
of the mystery and truth of the Word become flesh.

Embodiment in a virtual world

On further reflection, however, I began to wonder whether there are
not elements of embodiment that remain when we meet online. Using a
computer, tablet or mobile phone still involves the use of our bodies—we
sit, use our hands, position ourselves so that we can be seen on screen. We
are very aware of bodily comfort or discomfort—sometimes preferring
the comfort of a warm settee or even a bed to a cold hard pew in a
draughty church! Zoom became the source of many amusing anecdotes

---

7   Adam Thomas, *Digital Disciple: Real Christianity in a Virtual World*
     (Nashville, TN: Abingdon Press, 2011), p. 76.
8   Bryan Cones, "How do we Gather Now?", *Christian Century* 26 August 2020,
     pp. 22–4.

relating to embodiment—for example, of cats photo-bombing meetings, or the embarrassment of someone forgetting to turn off their microphone whilst visiting the toilet!

More seriously, on Zoom we become aware of people's facial expressions and bodily movements at a close range that would not be possible in real life, without it becoming an inappropriate invasion of another's physical space. We can also become unhelpfully aware of our own expressions and mannerisms—when doing one-to-one sessions on Zoom, I always turn the setting to "speaker", so that I am much more conscious of the other's expression than my own. For many, Zoom transcends bodily and physical limitations, so that people who are vulnerable, or living with disabilities, are able to share and engage much more fully. One of my friends, who suffers from increasing hearing loss, has found that Bluetooth technology allows her to connect Zoom with her hearing aids, and so participate much more effectively and enjoyably in group settings. Dyer argues that we have set up false dichotomies, between real or virtual, embodied or disembodied, that are no longer helpful; both the real life and the online world contain elements of both.[9] So, now I want to go on to explore ways in which it may be possible to catch glimpses of the Body of Christ, of the mystery of Incarnation, in an online world.

Connection and relationality

One area in which Zoom was undoubtedly significant was in enabling people to maintain relationships and connections during lockdown when physical presence was no longer possible. Family members who could no longer meet in person gathered on Zoom—and some, who lived at a distance, possibly saw more, rather than less, of each other. In care homes, where visitors were forbidden for longer periods due to the vulnerability of residents, connection via Zoom or Facetime became a

---

9   John Dyer, "Exploring Mediated *ekklesia*: How we Talk about Church in the Digital Age", in Heidi A. Campbell and John Dyer (eds), *Ecclesiology for a Digital Church* (London: SCM Press, 2022), pp. 3–16.

lifeline in reducing isolation for some—although for others, particularly those suffering from dementia, the attempted use of technology caused further confusion and distress.

In local neighbourhoods, Facebook groups sprang up as people gathered to help one another, and to run errands, fetch shopping and provide much-needed help for those who were particularly isolated or vulnerable. In many ways, Zoom and other online resources or platforms enabled people to transcend the barriers of time and space that separated them. One of my friends met regularly for an international "cocktail hour", and another of my friends took the opportunity to enrich her experience of Christian worship by attending services across the world. Zoom enabled an opening up of relationships and connectivity that otherwise would not be possible. Paul Fiddes, a Baptist theologian, argues that an important tenet of Baptist ecclesiology is covenanting together, and that in a time of lockdown and physical isolation, online worship and gathering was an essential way of maintaining faithfulness to that covenant.[10]

However, Thomas, whilst recognizing these advantages, also points out the dangers of what he calls "remote intimacy"—assuming that we know someone far better than we do; and points out that the use of avatars online has the potential for disguising age and gender.[11] Although deliberate deception may seem unlikely in the context of Christian meeting, it is not impossible, and Antonio Spadaro offers this cautionary note:

> The Internet connects people. Online, however, everyone can create his or her own fictitious and simulated identity, begging the question how much faith can we put in online identities and relationships?[12]

---

[10] Paul Fiddes, "Zoom Ecclesiology: The Church Gathered and Scattered". <https://www.baptist.org.uk/Articles/592958/Zoom_Ecclesiology_the. aspx>, accessed 3 April 2024.

[11] Thomas, *Digital Disciple.*

[12] Antonio Spadaro, *Cybertheology: Thinking Christianity in the Age of the Internet*, tr. Maria Way (New York: Fordham University Press, 2014), p. 29.

We could argue that meeting people we already know and love through Zoom is much easier and safer than encountering strangers for the first time online. Nevertheless, significant relationships have been formed and developed online before, or even without, any "real life" meeting taking place. But if the Body of Christ is a reality, then those we have never met are a part of it too—and perhaps connecting with one another online can enable us to expand and enlarge our understanding of that Body.

A sense of place

One aspect of embodied theology is that our bodily existence is located in a particular time and place—human (or animal) bodies do not exist in a vacuum, but in a specific context. One of the advantages often claimed for internet connection is that it can transcend place, allowing people to meet and encounter one another across towns, cities and countries, avoiding the need for travel, which is costly not only to the individual, but also to the planet. But in doing so, there is a sense in which online encounter makes place abstract: the location could be anywhere—there is a sense of place becoming invisible. Thomas argues that this can be seen as an advantage, allowing our focus to be on people rather than place:

> And the Net's imperviousness to distance allows people from all across the world to meet in virtual space. Once again, *place* holds little significance and the focus shifts back to the people gathered.[13]

But whilst it may be beneficial to focus on people rather than place, it is important to remember that individuals exist in a context which is geographical and physical—they are not disembodied entities floating in cyberspace but are earthed in a particular place and location.

It is true that place can become anonymous and invisible. It is possible for people to use or create their own backgrounds online, zooming in for a meeting from a tropical paradise, or appearing against a corporate

---

13   Thomas, *Digital Disciple*, p. 33.

background emphasizing their professional status. But it can work the other way round too. Many people appear at meetings, at church, at the office or school, surrounded by their home backgrounds: books, pictures, ornaments, pets (in my partner's case, her guinea pigs are now known throughout the Methodist circuit!). People are embedded, or embodied, in their own specific contexts, with the mess and the clutter, or the knick-knacks and ornaments that convey something of their taste and personality. Rather than being lost, context is expanded, and we see people embodied in their chosen setting, rather than artificially located in a blank or anonymous space. This applies not only to home contexts. Through social media and online connection, we visit and engage with contexts and cultures that we would never otherwise encounter. We may not literally be embodied in another country or even continent, but the virtual experience of it gives us at least a brief glimpse of alternative realities.

Cones argues that, in relation to worship and liturgy, this anonymizing of place can have a levelling effect, negating the boundaries and divisions of status which we often erect:

> Yet the absence of the building and its hierarchical sorting of people—pews for some, chairs for leaders, all in greater or lesser proximity to the table—also serves to level the assembly: on Zoom, everyone gets the same box.[14]

But whilst appearing inclusive, this may mask real divisions of class, status or gender which continue to exist, just rendered less visible. So online gatherings are two-edged: on the one hand they may anonymize place and location, rendering geographical context invisible. But they can also root or embody people in their home contexts, and expand our sense of place to embrace distant horizons.

---

[14]   Cones, "How do we Gather Now?", p. 23.

The virtual Body of Christ?

Probably the most controversial questions remain in relation to the celebration of the Eucharist. Can we celebrate the Eucharist online? For many Catholics, and I suspect for some Anglicans too, the answer is a definitive "No"; and if you try, it is not really a Eucharist! The Catholic theologian Spadaro (admittedly writing before the question was sharply focussed by the pandemic) writes:

> The Catholic Church always insists that it is impossible and anthropologically erroneous to consider virtual reality to be *able* to substitute for the real, tangible and concrete experience of the Christian community. The same applies, virtually and historically, to liturgical celebrations and sacraments . . . There are no sacraments on the Internet.[15]

In the Anglican tradition, it was agreed during the pandemic that the priest could preside and take the elements on behalf of those watching online, but they could not participate in the bread and wine; and it could not be considered a shared sacrament unless people were physically present in the same place. However, there were different interpretations, and Richard Burridge, for example, argued for "a zone of intention". He used the analogy of presiding at a large festival, and argued that this could be analogous to online celebrations:

> . . . since these various communion vessels appear much closer to me than the twenty yards or more of eucharistic assistants around an altar in a large cathedral or festival, I have no difficulty when presiding in intending to consecrate all I can see in my "zone of intention" in accordance with the intentions and desire of each person present.[16]

---

[15] Spadaro, *Cybertheology*, pp. 74–5.

[16] Richard A. Burridge, *Holy Communion in Contagious Times: Celebrating the Eucharist in the Everyday and Online Worlds* (Eugene, OR: Wipf & Stock, 2022), p. 170.

At the start of the pandemic, Methodism in this country did not allow the celebration of online communion, but the Methodist Conference of 2021 recognized that this was a very real deprivation for some worshippers, and so authorized the celebration of communion online, provided that it was celebrated "live" and not as a recording, ruling that

> presbyters and other persons authorized to preside at the sacrament of the Lord's Supper be permitted to lead celebrations of Holy Communion in which some or all of the worshippers gather together through electronic means.[17]

Generally, Baptist and United Reformed congregations had fewer issues with this; and many adopted the pragmatic approach of encouraging members of their online congregations to have bread and wine at the ready, and to consume the elements in their own homes at an appropriate moment after a prayer of thanksgiving. Paul Fiddes argues that God's presence is equally real and valid online, although mediated in a different way, and so there is no reason why the sacraments cannot also be valid online.[18] Since the universe is created by God and is, therefore, sacramental, all material objects can be sacramental.

Conclusion

Throughout lockdown and social distancing, Zoom and other online platforms brought undoubted benefits to Christian worship and community. In some ways, this seems to be at the cost of an embodied theology, denying human embodiment, face-to-face relationship and

---

[17] The Methodist Church, Conference Reports 2021, 39 *Holy Communion and Online Worship*. <https://www.methodist.org.uk/for-churches/governance/faith-and-order/holy-communion-and-online-worship/>, accessed 3 April 2024.

[18] Paul Fiddes, "Sacraments in a Virtual World?", in Philip Thompson and Anthony Cross (eds), *Baptist Sacramentalism*, volume 3 (Eugene, OR: Cascade Publications, 2020).

the creative realities of symbol and symbolic action. But on further examination, the questions raised by online worship and gathering are more complex. Although challenges and questions remain, it can be argued that the use of Zoom and online technology push us to re-examine, challenge or expand our understanding of embodied theology, and along with it, the reality of Incarnation.

Called to go deeper in pastoral care

Paul Avis

"As the Father has sent me, so I send you" (John 20:21). Where did the Father send the Son on his unique saving mission? The Father sent the Son into the world and into the deepest parts of the world, the darkest and most dangerous places that human sinfulness could devise. Jesus fully engaged the murky depths of human experience and the human psyche. Christ now sends his church in the same way and to the same place. "So I send you."[1]

Conforming to Christ

This text is telling us that the mission and ministry of the church must conform to the mission and ministry of Jesus Christ. The church's ministry is nothing less than a continuation and an extension of his work (John 14:12). The ministry exercised by the church is the ministry of Jesus Christ in and through his body the church. The priesthood of the church is an expression of the priesthood of Christ. The church is animated by the priesthood of Christ and all baptized believers participate in his one priesthood (1 Peter 2:4–10).

When Jesus called the fishermen and tax collectors, saying, "Follow me", he was calling them to conform their lives, their minds and hearts to him, to his character and ministry. At the start of *The Imitation of Christ*, Thomas à Kempis (1380–1471) quotes John 8:12: "Whoever

---

[1]   An early version of this paper was published in *Chrism* 56:1 (2019), pp. 28–32.

follows me shall not walk in darkness," and adds: "In these words Christ counsels us to follow his life and way if we desire true enlightenment and freedom from all blindness of heart." He continues: "Whoever desires to understand and take delight in the words of Christ must strive to conform [their] whole life to him."[2] Similarly, St Paul longs to be conformed to Christ, to share his sufferings and be made partaker of his resurrection (Philippians 3:10–11).

To follow Jesus Christ, the Good Shepherd, in ministry takes us in his name to the sickbed and the deathbed, to those who are marginalized and oppressed, traumatized, lonely and despairing, and to the lost sheep who have strayed from the fold (Luke 15:1–7). I suspect that we all know more people who have stopped going to church than still go to church. I think we also know where the Good Shepherd's heart would be in that situation. To follow Jesus Christ in ministry also takes us to situations of injustice and oppression where we are bound to confront evil in his name. "For the dark places of the earth are full of the habitations of cruelty. O let not the oppressed return ashamed: let the poor and needy praise thy name" (Psalm 74:20–1, KJB).

In the Psalms it is said that "deep calleth unto deep" (Psalm 42:7, KJB). Often, however, it is the shallow in ministry that appeals to the superficial in our culture, a formulaic approach reaching out to a stereotyped modern person. We are called to go deeper in pastoral engagement, to access more profound resources from Scripture, theology and the human sciences, and to tap into the moral, intellectual and spiritual depths of those with whom we engage pastorally. To do all that safely and with good outcomes for all concerned takes prayer, study, experience, humility and wisdom.

---

2   Thomas à Kempis, *The Imitation of Christ*, tr. Leo Sherley-Price, Penguin Classics (Harmondsworth: Penguin, 1952), p. 27.

Physical, mental and spiritual wholeness

The ministry of Jesus of Nazareth described in the Gospels is orientated to the salvation and healing of the whole person. His compassion, care and power embrace the physical, mental and spiritual dimensions of human need.[3] The Gospels reveal the profound insight into the complex needs and motives of individuals that Jesus possessed. He searched the heart, sometimes posing a challenge ("Go and call your husband", to the Samaritan woman at Jacob's well: John 4:16) or a question ("Friend, why have you come?" to Judas in Gethsemane: Matthew 26:50).

The ministry of Jesus of Nazareth shows us that the care of the soul is inseparable from the care of the body. The physicality of Jesus's ministry in the Gospels is striking. Jesus cares compassionately for the ailing, aching and stricken bodies of those who come to him for help. He feeds the hungry multitudes and sees that Jairus's daughter, whom he has brought back from the sleep of death, needs something to eat (Luke 8:55). In both word and deed, he shows that the Kingdom of God is near (Matthew 4:23; Luke 7:18–23; 11:20). The Collect for St Luke's Day (18 October) in the *Book of Common Prayer* (1662) states that God "called Luke the physician, whose praise is in the Gospel, to be an evangelist and physician of the soul". Within the severe limitations of first-century medical knowledge, Doctor Luke spanned the physical and spiritual dimensions of healing. He patched up the Apostle Paul's wretched physical health and kept him on the road during his journeys and tended him in prison, while at the same time gathering material for his Gospel and its sequel, the Acts of the Apostles.

Like Luke, ministers know that sometimes a person in their care needs to seek medical (or perhaps psychiatric) attention before they can be further helped spiritually. The proper care of the body is not only a matter of surgical procedures and administering medication, but also includes a wholesome diet, exercise and fresh air, human company and satisfying occupations. But healing may also require the cathartic

---

[3]   For an exposition of the healing ministry of Christ in the Gospels see Robin Gill, *Health Care and Christian Ethics* (Cambridge: Cambridge University Press, 2006).

physical expression of emotional states and psychological tensions, especially through creative activity, however amateur or even clumsy it may be, in drama, dance and visual art. Physical, as well as spiritual and intellectual, self-expression is needed.

Christian ministry leads us along the path of the healing of body, mind and spirit, a healing that we find only in the God who makes us whole. All human wellbeing—not only spiritual, but physical and mental too—comes to us from the hand of God our Creator–Redeemer–Perfecter and is received as a gift and a trust. The ministry of Jesus Christ shows that God does not want anyone to suffer in body, mind or spirit, and that God seeks ways to heal and restore all such, normally through the instrumentality of human wisdom, knowledge and skill, which itself comes from God and is inspired by the Holy Spirit.[4]

If we are to do justice to the salvation of the whole person, it makes sense to allow the insights and skills of those disciplines that can provide understanding of the whole person to enrich our approach. Such disciplines as psychotherapy and trained counselling, together with skill in physical therapies, are examples of disciplines that can deepen our understanding of the ministry of the word, of the sacraments and of pastoral care. These two pathways towards healing, Christian ministry of word and sacrament and therapies of talking and doing, are concerned with "the cure (or care) of souls". "Cure of the soul" is a proper translation of the Greek origins of the term "psychotherapy". But the care of the soul requires the care of the body also and will not work without it. We must look at human beings in the round.

This essay now explores some connections and parallels between the priestly, pastoral ministry of the church and the work of therapists: depth psychologists, psychotherapists, trained counsellors and physical therapists. A mandate for that approach can be found in the fact that the biblical words for salvation, in both the Old Testament and the New, are also the biblical words for healing. "Heal me, O Lord, and I shall be healed; save me and I shall be saved" (Jeremiah 17:14). In both the Hebrew Old Testament and the Greek New Testament, the

---

[4] Key biblical material on this theme is found in Ecclesiasticus (Sirach) 38:1–15.

vocabulary of salvation and the vocabulary of healing are interchangeable or synonymous. The same words can mean "healing" and "salvation"; they are often convertible terms and refer to acts of divine help and deliverance.[5] These biblical semantics suggest that the mission and ministry of the church should lead to the saving or healing of the whole person within their social, economic and political environment.

The priestly and therapeutic dimensions, the ministry of word and sacrament on the one hand, and the skills of psychotherapy and counselling on the other, are complementary pathways towards wholeness, because both are concerned with "the cure (or care) of souls". Unless we are professionally trained in psychotherapeutic skills (as some clergy and lay ministers are) we should not attempt to play the therapist. But I offer these reflections as a priest and theologian who believes that the church's priestly-pastoral ministry needs to become informed and enriched by the insights and enlightenment that depth psychology, in its various forms, can bring. My approach has been stimulated by engagement with the work and personnel of Holy Rood House over many years, and by the pioneering example of my sister Elizabeth Baxter. Under her leadership, together with her late husband, Stanley, Holy Rood House has been a beacon of holistic body–mind–spirit therapy and a haven of healing for many.

Exploring the depths of the human psyche

We do not need to accept all the details of the theories of Sigmund Freud (1856–1939) or Carl Gustav Jung (1875–1961) and their respective followers and successors—who disagree with each other on many points anyway—in order to recognize the massive significance of their pioneering work. We also need to recognize that psychotherapy is not the only viable method of treating mental troubles; Cognitive Behaviour Therapy (CBT) seems to help many people. But person-centred therapy, focussed on "the talking cure", where non-judgmental attention and

---

5   See Paul Avis, *A Church Drawing Near: Spirituality and Mission in a Post-Christian Culture* (London and New York: T&T Clark, 2003), Chapter 2.

regard are central, is perhaps the nearest equivalent to priestly-pastoral ministry in the church.[6] Over the past century or so, various schools of depth psychology or psychotherapy have mapped out for us, at least in outline, a dimension of the human psyche of which previous generations were only vaguely aware. It is true that, throughout history, humankind has given artistic expression to the promptings of the unconscious in (for example) cave painting, social ceremonies and religious rites, music making and dancing. Our forebears were in touch with the depth dimension, but probably they feared it more than they understood it. It is now universally accepted that ordinary human life in community is imbued with psychological dynamics that operate at an unfathomable pre-conscious level. There is much more going on in the human psyche (soul), human behaviour and all forms of interpersonal contact than meets the eye. What presents itself to our conscious minds is merely the tip of the iceberg. If theology and pastoral practice were to ignore this depth dimension, it would decree its own irrelevance and futility.

Beginning with Freud's work *The Interpretation of Dreams*, the psychotherapeutic revolution of the twentieth century made us aware of the power and importance of symbols that emerge from the unconscious, and which may have integrating, healing power. While Freud tended to see such symbols as warning signals or symptoms of problems to be solved and conditions to be cured, Jung saw them as often pointing to healing and wholeness.[7] Obviously, the Bible itself is full of dreams,

---

[6] The expression "the talking cure" was coined by Josef Breuer's patient Bertha Pappenheim (referred to as "Anna O.") and was discussed by Freud in *Five Lectures on Psycho-Analysis* (1909), which are included in Sigmund Freud, *Two Short Accounts of Psycho-Analysis*, tr. and ed. James Strachey (Harmondsworth: Penguin, 1962), p. 35.

[7] Sigmund Freud, *The Interpretation of Dreams*, tr. and ed. J. Strachey; *The Pelican Freud Library*, Volume 4, ed. Angela Richards (Harmondsworth: Penguin, 1976 [1900]); C. G. Jung, *Symbols of Transformation: Collected Works of C. G. Jung*, Volume 5 (Princeton, NJ: Princeton University Press; London: Routledge & Kegan Paul, 1967); Sigmund Freud, *Dreams*, tr. R. F. C. Hull (London: Ark, 1985). There is an exploration of the relation of both Freud and Jung to Christianity in Paul Avis, *Faith in the Fires of Criticism:*

visions and mysteries from beginning to end; so it is a big mistake to try to take it all literally. As William Blake put it, "The Whole Bible is fill'd with Imagination and Visions."[8] These visionary revelations are one of the ways in which the Word of God to humankind has been made known, giving instruction, guidance and warning. Why should we assume that these imaginative media are confined to biblical history? Dreams and waking visions may still help us to understand ourselves and God's will for us today. They are basically natural, universal phenomena that lend themselves to purposes beyond the natural. In deep sleep, the unconscious mind is sorting through the experiences of the past day and relating them to what we have been through in our past lives, our previous experiences. Sometimes that process dredges up unresolved issues and tensions, which often express themselves in dreams as the unconscious embodies them in symbolic scenarios. However, we do not need to be dreaming in order to be affected by the unconscious; it impinges on our lives in many other ways. Here are three everyday examples.

Intimations of the unconscious

(a) We have probably all had the experience of being puzzled by something that happens—usually an interaction with another person. There may be a sense of not relating to each other properly, of some emotional friction or mismatch of perceptions. Something just does not click. We may find that the penny drops much later when it dawns on us that what we thought at the time was happening was not actually the case. We see the encounter in a different light and at last it makes sense. In Iris Murdoch's *Bruno's Dream*, a dying man recalls that his estranged wife, to whom he had been consistently unfaithful, had asked him to come to her on her deathbed. At the time, he had refused to go to her, assuming that

---

Christianity in Modern Thought (London: Darton, Longman & Todd, 1995; reprinted Eugene, OR: Wipf & Stock, 2006, Chapters 5 and 6.

[8]   Cited in Peter Ackroyd, *Blake* (London: Sinclair Stevenson, 1995), p. 27.

she wanted to castigate him for his transgressions. Only now, when it is too late for both of them, does he realize that she wanted to forgive him.[9]

(b) Sometimes we have an irrationally strong reaction to another person, positive or negative; there can be an overpowering feeling of attraction or repulsion. This is our unconscious reacting for reasons that escape us but actually make sense deep down in terms of our formation and make up. What else can explain the universal, overwhelming and irrational experience of falling in love—"truly, madly, deeply"? What strange emotional chemistry is at work here? A familiar transaction in psychotherapy is the projection of the image and impact of a past significant other (usually a parent, teacher or pastor) onto the therapist. Another is the transference of our own strong emotions to the therapist, so that we imagine that they feel what we feel (and the corresponding phenomenon of counter-transference). These two psychological transactions help to explain the common phenomenon of the patient/client falling in love with the therapist and being absolutely convinced that their feelings are reciprocated. Such interactions are not confined to the therapist's couch. The phenomenon of a parishioner becoming infatuated with the vicar or curate (of either sex) is endemic in ministry, and the mechanisms are the same. Many a priestly/pastoral ministry has been shipwrecked, temporarily or permanently, in this way. It inevitably happens sometimes when we give our undivided attention to those seeking our help. Such affirmation is experienced as bestowing personal value on them, which is the most precious gift that any of us can receive. The merits of Carl Rogers's "client-centred therapy", in which "unconditional positive regard" is the key attitude, have been debated among psychotherapists, but it seems to me that the basic approach is a vital starting point in pastoral engagements.[10] How many training institutions prepare the clergy for such hazards as becoming the object of infatuation? Projection and transference belong to the stock-in-trade of the therapeutic relationship; they are its raw materials, and it would not work without them. The fact that we experience the same emotional

---

[9]   Iris Murdoch, *Bruno's Dream* (Harmondsworth: Penguin, 1970).

[10] Carl Rogers, *Client-Centered Therapy*, third edition (Boston, MA: Houghton-Mifflin, 1956).

transactions in Christian ministry suggests that priestly and psychotherapeutic approaches have some key aspects in common.

(c) Then there is what we call "the Freudian slip", when we mean to
say one thing and a slightly different word, proposed by the unconscious,
comes out, sometimes embarrassingly so, revealing what we are really
thinking and feeling, but unknowingly. The guard that we place on our
deepest emotions has momentarily slipped.[11]

These three scenarios are common examples of the unconscious mind
at work. Though we would love to be able to inspect its workings, the
unconscious is not directly accessible. According to Jung, unconscious
archetypes express themselves in symbols that well up into consciousness
and demand attention. For Freud, on the other hand, unresolved tensions
in the unconscious manifest themselves through physical symptoms and
maladies. Both theories are true to human experience. I will now touch
briefly on three widely recognized major symbols of the unconscious.

Symbols of the unconscious

(a) The ocean is a primary symbol of the unconscious, speaking to us of
the depth, energy and creative power of an element that is nature's source
of life. The Psalmist cries to God: "Deep calls to deep . . . all your waves
and your billows have gone over me" (Psalm 42:7). In its heights and
depths, the sea can speak to us of the transcendence and the immanence
of God. At times of emotional and psychological turbulence, to look
out on a roaring sea can have a calming effect. And in a normal state of
mind, to contemplate a placid sea, with wavelets rippling gently on to
the sand, can bring an even deeper peace; we internalize its tranquillity.
The unconscious is interacting with the ocean which, according to Jung,
is its primary symbol. "The sea", he wrote, "is the symbol of the collective
unconscious because it hides unsuspected depths under a reflecting

---

[11]   Sigmund Freud, *Psychopathology of Everyday Life*, ed. and tr. A. A. Brill
       (Harmondsworth: Penguin, 1938 [1914]).

surface." Ocean and unconscious reflect each other; there is a rapport between them.[12]

(b) The common dream of going into a strange house and entering room after room, opening doors into mysterious spaces, can stand for fresh possibilities in our lives, new opportunities that beckon and demand to be explored (in a different mood this dream can speak of a sense of disorientation and homelessness). Jung records that, as a young-middle-aged man, he had a recurring dream of descending from one floor to another in a strange house, until he came to steps into a dark cellar and beyond that an even deeper layer. Jung knew that, from then on, he had to go deeper and explore what his unconscious was trying to tell him.[13]

(c) The heavenly bodies—the sun, the distant stars, the moon and the planets—also resonate with the unconscious. The stars are remote in both space and time, inaccessible, unvarying, pure and bright in a clear night sky. They speak of a realm of perfection beyond our grasp and that is how the ancients understood them. But, as they twinkle, they seem to be reaching out to us, trying to communicate, flashing indecipherable messages. Siegfried Sassoon, a poet who survived the trenches of the First World War, wrote in his poem *Human Bondage*: "I know a night of stars within me;/Through eyes of dream I have perceived/Blest apparitions who would win me/Home to what innocence believed."[14]

In Vincent van Gogh's *The Starry Night*, the stars are huge, glowing, swirling orbs, filling the sky above a sleeping village.[15] The church spire is elongated, pointing and stretching up into the night sky, almost touching the stars—a kind of lightning conductor channelling the energy of the

---

[12]   See Edmund Newell, *The Sacramental Sea* (London: Darton, Longman & Todd, 2019). The quotation from Jung is on p. 120.

[13]   C. G. Jung, *Memories, Dreams, Reflections*, ed. Aniela Jaffé, tr. R. and C. Winston (London: Flamingo, 1983), pp. 182–4.

[14]   Siegfried Sassoon, *Collected Poems 1908–1956* (London: Faber and Faber, 1984), p. 300.

[15]   Available at <https://en.wikipedia.org/wiki/The_Starry_Night#/media/ File:Van_Gogh_-_Starry_Night_-_Google_Art_Project.jpg>, accessed 3 April 2024.

stars into the unconscious. Something deep within us responds to the inarticulate messages of the stars.

Even more remarkable is the depiction of the stars in Australian Aboriginal dot art (paintings made up of numerous coloured dots of paint). One exceptional such painting depicts the earth far below, seen from space or from heaven. In this painting there is a profusion of large white dots that partly obscure the face of the earth. What could these be? They are stars, as seen from beyond those stars, from the far side of them. We are gazing, from deep space, at the back of the stars. The Aboriginal artist, possibly envisaging the sky as a fixed firmament (as in the Bible), has assimilated the stars into the psyche, internalizing them, so that they have become integral to their perception. This speaks of the integration of the resources of the unconscious into one's life with healing effect.

But I mentioned the moon also as resonating with the unconscious. Some mentally disabled or mentally disturbed people are strongly affected by the full moon; they can become excited, and their behaviour can become troublesome for no rational reason. The full moon is also seen as beneficent, as shining a blessing on us. This full-orbed source of reflected light, with a magnetic pull, impacts the unconscious. The moon affects not only the tides, but also the human psyche. Rather like a mandala, the perfect sphere of the full moon, shining bright, speaks to us of the possibility of a wholeness welling up from the unconscious.

Depth psychology teaches us that the unconscious always gets its way. If it is ignored, it will get its way in the form of revenge. You cannot elude or outwit the unconscious. So, we need to turn its energies to our benefit, where it can bring a psychotherapeutic enlightenment of priestly, pastoral ministry. Whether we are clergy and pastors or therapists and counsellors, we need to be alert to the workings of unconscious processes both in ourselves and in those to whom we minister. Many practical difficulties and intractable problems in ministerial life—those dysfunctional pastoral encounters that clergy and other ministers experience from time to time—may stem from a lack of awareness in this area. We need to be open to the deep psychological and emotional currents of ministry.

Insights for enlightened practice

It is good to read widely in the works of the classical psychoanalysts, depth psychologists and their successors. But they were not writing for Christian ministry. The writings of Wesley Carr (1941–2017) may still help clergy and pastors, indeed all in a therapeutic (healing) role, to be aware of the unconscious, even irrational, processes that are taking place in themselves and in those to whom they minister—such psychosocial dynamics as transference and counter-transference, projection, symbolic representation, dependence and vicarious action. These are often the source of those unexplained emotions that we sometimes feel in pastoral encounters—such as anxiety, guilt, anger or excitement—that I mentioned earlier. These psychosocial dynamics, which work in the concealed, devious and cunning way that is typical of the unconscious, cannot be handled simply by means of acquired skills and techniques—though such professional attributes are obviously vital—but they also call for qualities of moral character, marked by the classical and Christian virtues, and also by the gift of imagination, in tune with metaphor, symbol and myth, which are the native modes of discourse in this particular realm.[16] Without such self-knowledge—an understanding of our own motivations, impulses and reactions—we may find ourselves blindly working out our own psycho-pathological drives and needs on the members of the congregation and parish, behaving like the proverbial bull in a china shop and leaving a trail of damage.

Such psycho-dynamic processes give rise to an unavoidable degree of ambiguity in any pastoral situation: it could be understood in more than one way and could go in more than one direction. Pastoral encounters are not under our control, but are negotiated in an open-ended way, one-to-one or one-to-a-few, even though we are mindful of professional boundaries and other disciplines and protocols. Along with ambiguity in the situation, these unavoidable psycho-dynamic processes also generate psychological ambivalence within us as ministers, simultaneously pulling us in different directions emotionally and exploiting our own

---

[16] Paul Avis, *God and the Creative Imagination: Metaphor, Symbol and Myth in Religion and Theology* (London: Routledge, 1999).

vulnerability. Ambiguity, experienced as insecurity, is the inescapable milieu in which we seek to do our priestly-pastoral and therapeutic work. We need to be able to negotiate it safely for all concerned.

Role and responsiveness

I have mentioned two separate but interacting professional pathways towards wholeness: the ministerial and the therapeutic. Both of these roles involve the whole person of the practitioner in order that they may lead to the healing of whole persons. Neither role is merely functional, performing technical tasks to a formula. Both roles are: (a) vocational, involving a life-long calling and professional training; (b) intentional, having a deliberate direction and purpose that belongs to their discipline; and (c) ontological, belonging to our very being; affecting us to the depths. Within a vocation such as Christian ministry we inhabit various specific roles, which we fulfil successively over time. As ministers, we are not so much doing a job as fulfilling a given role within a specific *locus* or context, within which we carry out certain commissioned tasks. Our tasks are specified, laid down in our mandate, awarded by higher authority. Therapists too are not merely doing a job but fulfilling a role, within a vocation, that involves the whole person and life and demands virtue and self-discipline to carry out specified tasks.

"Role" is the key to how both therapists and clergy are perceived by others. Clergy, especially bishops, are not seen as real people by those who observe them from a distance. Clergy are hardly taken to be ordinary human beings! By virtue of their role, clergy are containers of projections, the recipients of certain contents of the unconscious, both positive and negative, on the part of parishioners. Until they have become known in a personal way, over time and at close quarters, and a rapport of trust and friendship has been created, clergy and bishops are mere cardboard cut-outs. The same is true of all who minister to the deep emotional and spiritual needs of individuals. So, therapists are more like mirrors, sounding boards or echo-chambers than they are real individuals to their clients.

Whether as priests or as therapists (never trying to be both at once), we do our work in a context of expectation, receptivity and response. So the path of ministerial sanity is to set out to respond to people's expectations (they hope to receive something from you that will help them), while not buying into all their assumptions (about what miracles you are capable of, or what sacrifice you are likely to require from them). This discipline involves a critical reserve, holding oneself in check and controlling our own emotional impulses. A slightly extreme but common example is when, as a priest, deacon or lay minister, you officiate at a funeral. You cannot afford to let yourself go with the emotional flow; you can't have tears rolling down your cheeks or let your voice crack with emotion, however tragic the death may have been. You inwardly pay a price by staying within the role in order to preserve your usefulness in ministering to others who look to you with trust as someone who can handle the situation with its turbulent emotions. You can work them through privately afterwards if necessary. So self-regulation means setting up a disposition of availability, receptivity and responsiveness, rather than ebullient assertion or clumsy intrusion. This emotionally and morally neutral stance is a posture of waiting, observing and gently inviting. It holds back the ego and keeps it at bay. That attentive attitude—centred and focussed on the person or persons who have opened themselves to our ministry—allows us to monitor and interpret the signals that we are receiving, and then to respond tentatively, but incrementally, from step to step as a pathway opens up.

So, whether as clergy or as therapists, we come to know through our professional experience that, in the perception of others, we are objectified, reified: we *stand for* something. What we stand for lies beyond ourselves. We acknowledge it as a power that is not our possession and is greater than ourselves, but one that is also a potential source of help and healing. We also know that the powerful source beyond, which is also at work within the psyche of those to whom we relate, has the capacity to make or break us; we are merely its channels. So "Handle with care!" We need to be aware that at all times both therapists and clergy are being requisitioned and used to suit the emotional or political agenda of others. The difference between the person (who I am in myself) and the *persona* (how I appear in role to others) needs to be reckoned with.

Inner enlightenment comes when we can truly say two things: "I am the recipient of dependence, but I am also myself dependent"; and "They need me, but I need them more than they need me". When we reach that point of self-knowledge, we are fit for ministry. Ministry, like therapy, takes place in a series of interpersonal transactions. It is not an ego-trip, not "all about me" and my personal affirmation and self-esteem. I am being made—constituted in my role—by the pastoral–priestly relationship in which I have been placed and I am dependent on it to that extent. So, there can be no binary division between healer and healed, for we all need to be made whole. We receive as much as—or more than—we give in a ministry situation. In different circumstances, the roles could be reversed. Just as St Paul called himself the greatest sinner, so we know that there is no one with greater needs than ourselves. "Mirror, mirror, on the wall, who is the neediest of them all?"

Boundaries, polarities and identity

Clergy, like therapists, operate across boundaries, standing on both sides. Priests are liminal people, straddling thresholds, and so are all pastoral ministers.[17] The boundaries that we criss-cross all the time are the familiar polarities: sacred and secular; private and public; personal and social. We reach out across the threshold, take the other person by the hand, and gently lead them back over the threshold with us, into the fold. These polarities are not ultimate. We accept them as working assumptions, demarcating spheres of experience, but we should never concede that they are set-in-stone divisions of reality. For example, the term "secular" cannot mean "living in a God-free space", as much

---

[17]   On the concept of liminality, see A. Van Gennep, *The Rites of Passage* (London: Routledge & Kegan Paul, 1960); Victor W. Turner, *The Ritual Process* (London: Routledge & Kegan Paul; Chicago, IL: The Aldine Press, 1969); and Roger Grainger, *The Message of the Rite: The Significance of Christian Rites of Passage* (Cambridge: Lutterworth Press, 1988). See also the application of these concepts to priestly-pastoral ministry in Avis, *A Church Drawing Near*, Chapter 6: "Transformations of Being".

contemporary Western culture readily assumes, because for Christian faith there is no place and no person where God is not actively present and no situation that is beyond the reach of the Holy Spirit. By the same token, Christians can never concede that faith is a purely private matter, even though modern society generally tries to treat it as such in order to keep it out of the way. Christian faith is public faith or it is nothing, because it is concerned with the whole of God's creation, material and spiritual. Similarly, there can be no hard and fast division between the personal and the social, because it is interpersonal relations that make us the people that we are. We are always persons in relation who have no existence without a community.[18]

The church manages these boundaries, traversing them all the time, especially in its liturgical ministry. The church's liturgical ministry refers to the performance of public ceremony or ritual, in the form of services, sacraments, other pastoral offices and commemorations, which invite participation. These liturgical rites are spiritually effective for the healing of the whole person because they embody powerful symbols that resonate with the unconscious: water, bread and wine, light, powerful words, things of beauty, music and human persons. The symbols have received their authority from a collective and objective source, the faith and practice of the Christian church. They do not draw their power from the individual minister's subjective piety or theological leanings, so not from what takes our fancy as we plan a service! The church intends these liturgical events to meet the deep needs of those who participate in them to varying degrees of depth or intensity, holding out to them a framework of transcendent meaning and a source of spiritual succour. Clergy and lay ministers, like therapists and counsellors, are the human instruments and agents that help to facilitate the crossing of the threshold, the transition into a place of new life, for people coming to faith and commitment, finding the path to healing and wholeness. Those who minister are guides, companions, facilitators and even channels, on the common journey of Christian discipleship.

---

[18] For starters: John Macmurray, *Persons in Relation*, two vols (London: Faber and Faber, 1961). Alistair I. McFadyen, *The Call to Personhood* (Cambridge: Cambridge University Press, 1990).

As Christian ministers, we learn to distinguish (as do therapists and counsellors) between the overt or presenting issue raised by the person who comes to us for advice or support, which may seem comparatively trivial or irrelevant, and the underlying problem that we are being tacitly invited to recognize and to discern. Sometimes the real issue is not hard to discern; but in some cases it eludes us because it is too coded. The penny drops very much later, as we think and pray about a pastoral situation. But that may be too late to be of any help, thanks to our own obtuseness, over-confidence, formulaic approach or ignorance of the terrain.

But Christian ministry is not solely defined by the church, the clergy or the worshipping community. A ministry encounter is not in our gift or at our disposal to shape as we prefer; it is also defined by those who stand outside the church or on the edge of it. The experience of Christian ministry is unstable, because it is a dynamic and negotiated experience and the minister, therefore, receives a dynamic and negotiated identity through it. Like many forms of therapy, ministry is an ongoing transaction between two parties. Clergy are "set apart" by their ordination and role. Today clergy are fewer and some of them prefer to pass invisibly through the parish, having discarded the dog-collar, so that they are not identifiable and therefore not known and cannot help. (When I told a North-of-England taxi-driver recently, in answer to his enquiry, that I was visiting an institution that trained vicars, his reply was, "Are there any these days?") The church's public representatives are now a rare sight. But clergy are not set apart in the sense of secluded, so that practically no one outside of the regular congregation knows that they are there. They are set apart by the Holy Spirit and the church for interaction, engagement and sacrificial self-giving. Part of the sacrifice they make is being willing to be publicly identifiable, readily recognized and available, with all the weight that such visibility and openness places upon us.

Conclusion

We might say that the ministerial vocation is to place the experiences and challenges of everyday life within the framework of transcendent meaning provided by the scriptural and ecclesial narrative of salvation history. Salvation history is the history of how saving grace has been and still is mediated through Israel and its prophets, Jesus Christ, the apostles and the church. This framework, which is not of human invention, can endow our always incomplete and sometimes chaotic experience of life with transcendent meaning, value and significance, making it a life lived before God and with God, a graced life. As ministers, we seek to help others to place their lives within that salvific framework, not only by preaching, teaching and writing, and not only by the public celebration of the sacraments of the gospel, but also by *being*—by being certain persons in certain contexts at certain times in a visible, identifiable way. The priestly life is a sign to the world. But so also is the life of every baptized Christian disciple who is willing to be known as such.

Just as therapists need to stand back, to be opaque to some extent, a sounding board, a blank canvas, in order for the therapeutic interaction to do its work, so too clergy and lay ministers, as interpreters in the realm of revealed meaning, need to maintain a degree of detachment even in the thick of involvement. Without that discipline of objectivity and restraint, our discernment of the situation would fail, and the pastoral relationship would be compromised. We interpret God's Word to human needs, in preaching and teaching, in pastoral counsel, in the celebration of the sacraments and the "pastoral" offices, and by standing up for justice, freedom and inclusion for all. Thus, we may become an ecclesial sign by virtue of our calling and office. In such ways, we can assist people to find within themselves, where the Holy Spirit works and speaks deep down, the emotional, moral and intellectual resources that point to the meaning of their life with God through Jesus Christ. Then we can step back.

www.ingramcontent.com/pod-product-compliance
Ingram Content Group UK Ltd.
Pitfield, Milton Keynes, MK11 3LW, UK
UKHW022311030125
453077UK00009B/137